Southern Literary Studies

Louis D. Rubin, Jr., Editor

Robert Penn Warren's *Brother to Dragons*

Robert Penn Warren's

Brother to Dragons: A Discussion

Edited by James A. Grimshaw, Jr.

Louisiana State University Press
Baton Rouge and London

Copyright © 1983 by Louisiana State University Press
All rights reserved
Manufactured in the United States of America

Designer: Rod Parker
Typeface: Linotron Palatino
Typesetter: G&S Typesetters, Inc.
Printer and binder: Thomson-Shore, Inc.

Library of Congress Cataloging in Publication Data

Main entry under title:
Robert Penn Warren's Brother to dragons.

(Southern literary studies)
Bibliography: p.
1. Warren, Robert Penn, 1905–   .   Brother to
dragons.   I. Grimshaw, James A.   II. Series.
PS3545.A748B737   1983   811'.52   82-16207
ISBN 0-8071-1065-5

Grateful acknowledgment is made to Random House, Inc., for permission to quote
from the copyrighted material of Robert Penn Warren: *Brother to Dragons: A Tale in Verse
and Voices*, copyright 1953 by Robert Penn Warren; and *Brother to Dragons: A Tale in Verse
and Voices, A New Version*, copyright 1953, 1979 by Robert Penn Warren.

To Jesse and Audrey Gatlin

Contents

Reviews

Interpretations: 1979 Edition

Appendices

Robert Penn Warren's *Brother to Dragons*

Introduction

James A. Grimshaw, Jr.

Brother to Dragons is to Robert Penn Warren's poetry what *All the King's Men* is to his fiction: a pivotal point, a highwater mark, a seminal introduction to his other works. As a pivotal point, it heralded Warren's return to poetry. Before the publication of excerpts of *Brother to Dragons* in the *Kenyon Review* (winter, 1953), *Poetry* (June, 1953), and the *Partisan Review* (July–August, 1953), Warren's last published poem was "The Ballad of Billie Potts," in the *Partisan Review* (winter, 1944)—nine long, but not otherwise unproductive years. He had, after all, produced four novels, twelve essays, two dramas (unpublished), and yet another textbook with Cleanth Brooks. *Brother to Dragons* was in progress during that time, but Warren was having difficulty finding a form—not only for his long verse drama, but also for his shorter poetry. In a 1969 interview, Warren confesses: "I must have started fifty short poems. Not one panned out. . . . they died on me. . . . I began to see that I had, in a way, too abstract a view of what constituted the germ of a poem *for me*."[1] With that reassessment and with his interest in drama, *Brother to Dragons* did take form, the form of a dramatic dialogue.[2] Warren described "the way it was written" for the *New York Times Book Review* editor this way:

> About ten years ago, I got the notion of doing something with the story of Thomas Jefferson's family in Kentucky. The story is a shocker.

1. Richard B. Sale, "An Interview in New Haven with Robert Penn Warren," *Studies in the Novel*, II (1970), 341.
2. Readers may recall that *All the King's Men* started as a drama, "Proud Flesh," in 1937; was made into an Academy-Award-winning screenplay by Robert Rossen in 1949; premiered as "Willie Stark: His Rise and Fall" November 25, 1958; and was subsequently published as *All the King's Men: A Play* in *Sewanee Review*, LXVIII (1960), 177–239 and in book form by Random House, April 25, 1960. William M. Schutte ably traces its development in "The Dramatic Versions of the Willie Stark Story," in *"All the King's Men": A Symposium* (Pittsburgh: Carnegie Institute of Technology, 1957), 75–90.

At first, I wasn't sure what caught my fancy. Then I knew: It was that this was Jefferson's family. The philosopher of our liberties and the architect of our country and the prophet of human perfectibility had this in the family blood. Bit by bit, the thing began to take thematic shape. But the form didn't get settled.

First I thought of a novel. But this wouldn't do—the historical material doesn't have the structure of a novel, it doesn't fulfill itself circumstantially, it spreads out and doesn't pull in at the end. A novel, too, couldn't bear the burden of comment probably necessary to interpret the material.

Next I started a collaboration for a play in which Jefferson would serve as a commentator, a chorus, brooding over the affair. But again, the plot problem appeared. And also we discovered that the role of Jefferson would be disproportionate for a play. So we abandoned that.

Then, at last, I struck on the notion of using the form of a dramatic dialogue—not a play but a dialogue of all the characters, including Jefferson, at some unspecified place and time—really "no place" and "no time." This would allow me, I hoped, to get out of the box of mere chronology, and of incidental circumstantiality. In this form I might be able to keep alive the issues among the various participants—all the actors of the old horror—and keep a dramatic relation between them and Jefferson. But I wanted to give the thing a wider perspective than even Jefferson, or the ghost of Jefferson, would provide. I wanted a sense of the modern man's relation to the business. So I slipped in another character—the "poet"—R. P. W., as a kind of interlocutor. But more and more Jefferson became the real protagonist, the person who had to come to terms with something.

I needed provocation for Jefferson's redemption from mere shock and mere repudiation of his old dream. So I developed Lucy, his sister, and I introduced Meriwether Lewis, who had stood, in fact, in a sort of filial relation to Jefferson, and was the cousin of the tragic Lilburn and Isham. I shan't explain this further now, except to say that Meriwether's story of the opening of the West to the Pacific, and of his death by suicide (if it was suicide) form a parallel, and a contrast to the story of his cousins, Lilburn and Isham—who also went "West." In other words, these are all among our "Founding Fathers."

One problem that I found more and more fascinating, and more distressing, as composition proceeded, was that of keeping episodes as sharp as possible in a symbolic as well as a narrative sense. In all fiction, of course, even the most realistic fiction, there is such a problem—though "symbolic" is probably not a good word here. But in a poem, I'm sure, the problem gets more acute, as you can't depend on mere narrative interest and logic, and must pare away the merely circumstantial interest—but keep enough for conviction.

Another problem in this particular poem was that of language, or languages, suitable for the various characters. This couldn't be literally done, of course. A matter of slant and flavor. And I'm still too close to the thing to know how this came out. Last, there was the big problem, enclosing all other problems—that of keeping interest and readability at the level of action and debate and at the same time keeping that inwardness that is the central fact of poetry.[3]

Within that statement and within the verse drama itself, readers find the thematic thrusts which permeate the entire Warren canon: man's relationship to his past, his need to accept the past as a basis for his future, the nature of evil and its bearing on man, man's acquisition of knowledge (especially self-knowledge), and the role of love in helping man come to terms with the human condition. However one catalogs those themes, they result in the same world view. Whether Willie Stark's screaming, " 'Gimme that meat ax!' " or Lilburn's clutching the axe in the meat house, man is conceived in sin, finds redemption in knowledge, and learns another name for knowledge is love. Because of the singleness of vision, Warren's imagery of the Garden— the tree of knowledge, the tree of life, snakes, water, the West, and the web—recurs throughout his work. In *Brother to Dragons*, John (George) is butchered on a cross section of tulipwood, R. P. W. sees the black snake as he approaches the ruins, the broken water pitcher serves as catalyst for the sin, Isham runs to the West, and Lilburn's act ripples the web which touches Jefferson,

> "Author
> Of the Declaration of
> American Independence
> Of
> The Statute of Virginia
> For Religious Freedom, And
> Father of The University
> Of Virginia"

---

3.   Robert Penn Warren, "The Way It Was Written," *New York Times Book Review*, August 23, 1953, pp. 6, 25. Copyright © 1953 by the New York Times Company. Reprinted by permission.

Warren's consistency in theme and imagery thus reinforces his contention that "if poetry is the little myth we make, history is the big myth we live, and in our living, constantly remake."[4] His poetic reassessment which found form in this verse drama is reaffirmed in his subsequent poetry and fiction.

Although *Brother to Dragons* has not received as much formal recognition as *All the King's Men* has, it marks a turning point in Warren's career as artist. Critics have harshly condemned Warren's fiction since 1946 as second to *All the King's Men* and have praised his poetry since 1953 as consistently improving in maturity of voice and structure. Part of that maturation may be measured in his three versions of *Brother to Dragons:* 1953, 1976 (two-act play), and 1979.

Those three versions are different renderings of the same story: "the progressive decay of the notion of self."[5] However, his telling of the story in verse, as poem, "is a dynamic affirmation of, as well as the image of, the concept of the self."[6] It is, perhaps, one answer to the persona's request in *Audubon: A Vision:*

> Tell me a story.
>
> In this century, and moment, of mania,
> Tell me a story.
>
> Make it a story of great distances, and starlight.
>
> The name of the story will be Time,
> But you must not pronounce its name.
> Tell me a story of deep delight.[7]

That typically Warren paradox of notion and concept is the subject of his 1974 Jefferson Lectures in which he regards poetry as "diagnostic" and as "therapeutic." The diagnosis centers on "Jefferson's conversion from a restrictive idealism to a more integral view of life," as Frederick P. W. McDowell suggests (see p. 53 herein).[8] But Warren discovered that one can see more clearly the malady if he does not

4. Robert Penn Warren, *Brother to Dragons: A Tale in Verse and Voices, A New Version* (New York: Random House, 1979), xiii.
5. Robert Penn Warren, *Democracy and Poetry* (Cambridge, Mass.: Harvard University Press, 1975), 42.
6. *Ibid.*, 68.
7. Robert Penn Warren, *Audubon: A Vision* (New York: Random House, 1969), 32.
8. References to essays included in this volume will be parenthetically cited. The orig-

look directly at the image. Thus, he does not look directly at Jefferson in history; he looks at modern man's (R. P. W.'s) view of Jefferson in history and thereby bridges the important gap between past and present. Warren's concern remains, as Cleanth Brooks has observed, with "the relation of actor to the act—of the thing done to the interpretations which are placed upon it, the 'meanings' that it bears."[9] In the 1953 edition, R. P. W. responds to Laetitia: ". . . every act is Janus-faced and double, / And every act to become an act must resolve / The essential polarity of possibility" (55). The resolution is the therapy:

> In that hell-broth of paradox and internecine
> Complex of motive and murderous intensity
> We call the soul, and from that
> Anguish of complication any act,
> Any act at all, the bad, the good, affords,
> Or seems to afford, the dear redemption of simplicity:
> The dear redemption in the mere fact of achieved definition,
> Be what that may. (56)

What that may be is, like Job, a "brother to dragons, and a companion to owls" (Job 30:29)—although as Lewis P. Simpson points out, Warren "does not present a resolution of the meaning of self in America" (see p. 249 herein). For Dr. Charles Lewis, the self is the shellfish, "its poor palpitation, boxed in dark" (13), isolated in and by place; but paradoxically for R. P. W. "it is only by / That isolation that we know how to name / The human bond and thus define the self" (205–206). For Lucy, however, it is not such a paradox; for her, the human bond is a bond of love. She urges Jefferson to

> . . . take his [Meriwether's] hand, and recognize, at last,
> That his face is only a mirror of your possibilities,
> And recognize that you
> Have a deeper need of him than he of you,
> For whatever health we have is not by denial,
> But in confronting the terror of our condition.
> All else is a lie. (191–192)

---

inal publication of each essay is documented in the source note accompanying the essay.
9.   Cleanth Brooks, *Modern Poetry and the Tradition* (Chapel Hill, N.C.: University of North Carolina Press, 1939), 85. Cf. Yeats: "How can we know the dancer from the dance?"

The fact that self-knowledge is a kind of self-redemption—a lesson that Lucy gives Jefferson—repudiates the vanity of the earlier Jefferson and relates directly to gnosticism:

> Man's instrument of redemption is knowledge, for knowledge is power. At the end of the road to redemption is either a world transformed, a world without conflict, pain, suffering; or a change in the nature of man; or both. The old world, the old Adam must be *destroyed* if the new world, the new man is to arise.[10]

The historical Jefferson, Lewis Simpson observes, may have been aware of the larger implications of his act:

> In a deep way, the Declaration came from the hand of an actor-relator who understood that his own personal being and the being of each and every person in a "candid" and expanding world of letters . . . was becoming committed to a self-evident, self-reflective, and self-fulfilling interpretation of history. . . . It also announces a civilizational crisis, the crux of which is a repudiation of society as a model of history in deference to the promise that the person—the existential self—is at once the creature of history and its autonomous source and end.[11]

The poetical Jefferson remarks that after the Declaration was signed, he "woke to the new self, and new doom" . . . "And doom is always domestic" (9–10). The domestic doom is not just familial betrayal, as Richard G. Law's admirable essay describes, but is self-betrayal. "All truth is bought with blood, and the blood is ours" (10), Jefferson states somewhat sardonically. After his long summation of the events in this tale in verse and voices, R. P. W. concludes:

> And the death of the self is the beginning of selfhood.
> All else is surrogate of hope and destitution of spirit. (215)

When Warren returned to *Brother to Dragons* twenty-three years later in 1976, he selected as form the drama which, he notes in his "Foreword," "was developed from a number of different productions" (see p. 297 herein). Although we may never be quite certain the extent to which those productions influenced Warren's dramatization of his poem, Warren reiterates his concern with "the symbolic implication

10. Gregor Sebba, "Order and Disorders of the Soul: Eric Voegelin's Philosophy of History," *Southern Review*, n.s. III (1967), 302.
11. Lewis P. Simpson, *The Brazen Face of History: Studies in the Literary Consciousness in America* (Baton Rouge: Louisiana State University Press, 1980), 98.

of the event for the Jeffersonian notion of the perfectibility of man and of the good American notion of our inevitable righteousness in action and purity in motive." Most of the changes, though, are superficial: the murdered slave is John instead of George, Laetitia's unnamed brother becomes Billy Rutter, and R. P. W. is simply Writer, a history teacher. Revelation of the concern becomes a matter of emphasis. Act I deals with the Writer's first visit to Rocky Hill and culminates in John's death; Act II concerns the Writer's second visit and climaxes with Lilburn's death.

One of the most significant changes is the lessened role of the Writer, who serves more as an interlocutor without personal involvement. He does, however, maintain his function as bridge between modern man and eighteenth-century man, thus preserving the two levels of action (present and past). Too, contrasts pervade the stage: light and dark, motion and stillness, realism and fantasy, noise and quiet—as Warren explains in the production notes. Those contrasts are accented by the Frontier People and the Slaves, each group of whom assumes the role of a chorus:

> *First Frontier Woman*: Deeper and deeper in that darkling thicket—
> *Second Frontier Woman*: Of his [Lilburn's] dark dream—
> *Fourth Frontiersman*: Ah, deeper, deeper, has the dark no center—
> *First Frontier Woman and Third Frontiersman*: Where hope is happy
>   and the dark hangs down
> Like benediction and you smell the grass? (104)

The action focuses on the two deaths. John's death is the product of an unrighteous act, an impure motive; Lilburn's death, the attempt at expiation, a redemptive motive. The first act closes with Jefferson's repudiating Lilburn: "I had no son. I had only—my country. / My country!" (112). But in the opening dialogue of the second act, Jefferson says to Writer: ". . . all's one in the common collusion" (114);[12] he has lost his strength to uphold the "lie" of man's perfectibility. John's death, then, symbolizes the human bonds of community; Lilburn's death, the atonement and man's acceptance of the burden of innocence as well as guilt for, as Jefferson remarks, "all blood's the same" (113). As in the earlier edition, love redeems; Lucy says to Jefferson:

---

12.   Cf. the Easterner's remark in Stephen Crane's "The Blue Hotel": "Every sin is the result of a collaboration." In *Stephen Crane: Stories and Tales*, ed. Robert Wooster Stallman (New York: Vintage Books, 1958), 316.

> . . . if once you have loved,
> That love is yet valid, and is all
> You can bring with you into the inhabited silence. (133–34)

Those alterations notwithstanding, the two-act play remains remarkably faithful to the 1953 edition in thematic intent and is indeed harbinger of the 1979 revised edition, which provides another excitingly provocative rendition of a psychological journey into the human heart of darkness.

In 1979 the publication of *Brother to Dragons, A New Version* marked a quarter of a century in its evolution. And, indeed, it is "a new version," a point well made in William Harmon's Drydenesque dialogue, "Three Italians Visit Monticello" (see p. 263). Other authors represented in this collection carefully demonstrate the differences between the 1953 and the 1979 editions: Victor H. Strandberg, Richard N. Chrisman, and Margaret Mills Harper, for example. And in the 1979 "Foreword," Warren himself comments:

> Now there are a number of cuts made from the original version, and some additions. Meriwether is given a more significant role. There is, in large measure, a significant change of rhythm. A number of dramatic effects are sharpened. Though the basic action and theme remain the same, there is, I trust, an important difference in the total "feel." For the reworking was not merely a slow and patchwork job. It meant, before the end, a protracted and concentrated reliving of the whole process. (xiv)

Warren's concern, nonetheless, consistently remains unchanged: "But poetry . . . is committed to the obligation of trying to say something, however obliquely, about the human condition. Therefore, a poem dealing with history is no more at liberty to violate what the writer takes to be the spirit of his history than it is at liberty to violate what he takes to be the nature of the human heart" (xiii). What the poet takes to be the nature of the human heart, though, changes, perhaps mellows, over the years. In 1953 Jefferson recounts his Philadelphia experience thus: His triple boast was made "if in pride, then a pride past pride, / In [his] identity with the definition of man" (6). But in 1979 a more humble Jefferson admits that "in senility / And moments of indulgent fiction [he] might try / To defend [his] old definition of man" (5). That change follows the opening exchange, which Lewis Simpson points out may be one of the most significant revisions; and it helps establish the "important difference in the total 'feel'" of the new version.

Through tighter structure and verse, Warren places passion in bold relief against rationality. In the beginning Jefferson tried to bring himself to say, "Knowledge is only incidental, hope is all—" (5). Remembering that "One name for [love] is knowledge" (*Audubon*, 30), we are not surprised when Jefferson later rejects the "old-fashioned" notion of love:

> I've long since come to the considered conclusion
> That love, all kinds, is but a mask
> To hide the brute face of fact,
> And that fact is the un-uprootable ferocity of self. Even
> The face of love beneath your face at the first
> Definitive delight—even that—
> Is but a mirror
> For your own ferocity—a mirror blurred with breath,
> And slicked and slimed with love—
> And even then, through the interstices and gouts
> Of the hypocritical moisture, cold eyes spy out
> From the mirror's cold heart, and thus,
> Self spies on self
> In that unsummerable arctic of the human lot. (33)

In the end, however, he learns from Meriwether:

> For nothing we had,
> Nothing we were,
> Is lost. All is redeemed,
> In knowledge. (120)[13]

Knowledge, and therefore love, is the redemptive force for the human lot. It is the blending of the eighteenth-century head-heart dichotomy which R. P. W. articulates: "We know that much, but what is knowledge / Without the intrinsic mediation of the heart?" (130).

R. P. W. thus leaves Rocky Hill with what he has come for, with a sense of past humanness and future hope. He has heard "a story of deep delight": "the full flesh bulges / With the deep delight of being flesh, for flesh / Is its own blessing, and nobility" (128). In assuming modern man's responsibility for innocence, he can say to himself: I was prepared

13. In the 1953 edition, Jefferson speaks these words (195).

To go into the world of action and liability.
I had long lived in the world of action and liability.
But now I passed the gate into a world

Sweeter than hope in that confirmation of late light. (132)

All three versions of *Brother to Dragons*—individually or collectively—provide immense reading pleasure. Warren takes a shocking, but intriguing, incident from history and superimposes the eighteenth-century concept of knowledge, the nineteenth-century concern with passions of the heart, and the twentieth-century combination of the two. Thus, as he has throughout his canon, he uses the Hegelian dialectic in grappling with considerations of the human condition, considerations which offer no finite conclusions. Nor would he necessarily want finite, simple answers:

Sometime we must probe more deeply the problem of complicity.

Is civilization possible without it?

This is a question which Warren asks in a later poem, "Dream, Dump-Heap, and Civilization."[14]

The twenty-four essays and reviews plus the three appendices included herein address in greater detail the broader implications of Warren's themes and techniques. Most of the authors wisely avoid absolute answers in interpreting Warren's long poem. They do, however, provide provocative analyses which suggest that there are indeed more than thirteen ways of looking at a blackbird. And their collective thoughts stand as testimony and tribute to the artistry of Robert Penn Warren.

---

14. Robert Penn Warren, *Being Here: Poetry 1977–1980* (New York: Random House, 1980), 46.

Interpretations: 1953 Edition

Experience Redeemed in Knowledge

Cleanth Brooks

The poetry, the fiction, and even the critical essays of Robert Penn Warren form a highly unified and consistent body of work. But it would be impossible to reduce it, without distorting simplifications, to some thesis about human life. The work is not tailored to fit a thesis. In the best sense, it is inductive: it explores the human situation and tests against the fullness of human experience our various abstract statements about it. But Warren has his characteristic themes. He is constantly concerned with the meaning of the past and the need for one to accept the past if he is to live meaningfully in the present. In this concern there are resemblances to Faulkner, though Warren's treatment is his own. Again, there are resemblances to W. B. Yeats in Warren's almost obsessive concern to grasp the truth so that "all is redeemed / In knowledge." Again, as with Yeats, there is a tough-minded insistence upon the facts, including the realistic and ugly facts—a fierce refusal to shield one's eyes from what is there.

This commitment to the truth, and the deep sense that the truth is rarely simple, account for Warren's sharp scrutiny of the claims of rationality. He never glorifies irrationality: he is not the poet of the dark subliminal urges or the novelist with a mystique to exploit. But he does subject the claims of twentieth-century man to the sternest testing, and he is suspicious of the doctrine of progress and of the blandishments of utopianism.

Faulkner's effective, though perhaps unwitting and unconscious, belief in original sin constitutes a bulwark against this heresy. Yeats's vigilant and unflagging resistance to what he calls "Whiggery" constitutes a similar safeguard. One could argue that, in general, the artist's commitment to the concrete situation and his need to focus upon the

13

dramatic exigencies of the human predicament make it easier for him to reject this form of abstraction. Dedication to his art, then, would not necessarily bring the artist to Christianity. It would be foolish to claim *that*. But dedication to his art may well protect the artist from some of the deceptions endemic to our time. On the positive side, dedication to his art will probably help him at least to *see* the problems of the human spirit to which Christianity—and any other serious philosophy—addresses itself.

The work in which Robert Penn Warren challenges most direclty some of the liberal secular ideas of our time is his long poem *Brother to Dragons*, published in 1953. It is about Thomas Jefferson, or rather about Jefferson's nephews, Lilburn and Isham Lewis, the sons of Jefferson's sister, Lucy Jefferson Lewis. The Lewises removed from Virginia to western Kentucky. There, after the death of their mother and after their father, Dr. Charles Lewis, had returned to Virginia, the two young men, Lilburn and Isham, murdered one of their slaves. On the night of December 15, 1811, the night when the New Madrid earthquake shook the Mississippi Valley, Lilburn, having called the other slaves together into the meathouse to witness what he was going to do, butchered on the meatblock a slave named George. George's offense had been to break a water pitcher on his way back from the spring to which he had been sent to fetch fresh water.

After some months, hints of the crime leaked out. Lilburn and Isham were indicted for murder, but before they could be arrested and put in jail, Lilburn was dead. Apparently the brothers had planned to stand, each on one side of their mother's grave, and shoot each other. When the sheriff's posse came up, Lilburn had been shot and was dying. Isham was captured, but while awaiting trial, broke jail and disappeared—to turn up, of all places, at the battle of New Orleans in 1815, one of the two Americans killed in that engagement. This, at least, was the story that the Kentucky riflemen brought back with them from New Orleans. In any case, the indictment naming Isham bears under the date March 20, 1815, the docket: "Ordered that this suit abate by the death of the defendant."

It is a fantastic story, a terrible and blood-chilling story. It is, however, a true story, with the documents on record.[1] Thomas Jefferson

---

1. *Editor's Note*: See Boynton Merrill, Jr., *Jefferson's Nephews: A Frontier Tragedy* (Princeton, N.J.: Princeton University Press, 1976), from which chapter 25, "The Murder," is appended to this collection, p. 283.

must have been aware of the depths of wanton cruelty to which his nephews had sunk, but nowhere among the Jefferson Papers is there any reference to it. It is hard to imagine what the great Virginian who thought so much of man's possibilities, who penned the Declaration of Independence with its confident claims for man, who knew and was sympathetic to the French eighteenth-century rationalists—it is difficult and exciting to try to imagine what Jefferson's reaction must have been. This is the task that Warren takes upon himself. To my mind his effort of imaginative reconstruction results in a great and moving poem. That has been also the opinion of some of the most discerning critical minds here and in Great Britain. But not of all, I should add. For a great many Americans, Jefferson comes close to being a sacred figure, and to dare to portray a Jefferson troubled and in doubt, a Jefferson embittered and cynical, even though only temporarily, was to lay profane hands upon the idol. In fairness to Warren's conception of Jefferson, I should say that *Brother to Dragons* is not written in any spirit of debunking. It is a great Jefferson who emerges at the end of Warren's poem, a Jefferson who has, in giving up his more callow hopes in man, actually strengthened his basic belief in man's potentialities. At the end of the poem Jefferson is a chastened though not a disillusioned man.

A book-length poem does not adequately reveal itself in brief quotations. If I confine myself to quotations of reasonable length, I can hope to do no more than suggest something of the flavor of the poem. The impassioned dialectic and the stages of the drama through which the action works to its final resolution must be taken on faith unless one has read the poem. Yet I do want to quote two or three excerpts. Here is the way in which Warren imagines Jefferson's hopes for man as he sat down to write the Declaration of Independence:

> We knew we were only men
> Caught in our errors and interests. But I, a man,
> Suddenly saw in every face, face after face,
> The bleared, the puffed, the lank, the lean, all,
> On all saw the brightness blaze, and I knew my own days,
> Times, hopes, books, horsemanship, the praise of peers,
> Delight, desire, and even my love, but straw
> Fit for the flame, and in that fierce combustion I—
> Why, I was dead, I was nothing, nothing but joy,
> And my heart cried out, "Oh, this is Man!"

And thus my minotaur. There at the blind
Blank labyrinthine turn of my personal time,
I met the beast. . . .
          . . . But no beast then: the towering
Definition, angelic, arrogant, abstract,
Greaved in glory, thewed with light, the bright
Brow tall as dawn. I could not see the eyes.

So seized the pen, and in the upper room,
With the excited consciousness that I was somehow
Purged, rectified, and annealed, and my past annulled
And fate confirmed, wrote. And the bell struck
Far off in darkness, and the watch called out.
Time came, we signed the document, went home.
Slept, and I woke to the new self, and new doom.
I had not seen the eyes of that bright apparition.
I had been blind with light. That was my doom.
I did not know its eyes were blind. (8–10)

I would like to quote also the poet's own commentary on man
seen against the background of nature—man who is not "adjusted"
to nature and can never be adjusted—who must live in an agony of
will,[2] and who finally in his need projects upon nature itself the struggle with circumstance that engages his own heart. The scene is winter, as it descends upon the Lewis brothers after their mother's death
and burial:

And the year drove on. Winter. And from the Dakotas
The wind veers, gathers itself in ice-glitter
And star-gleam of dark, and finds the long sweep of the valley.
A thousand miles and the fabulous river is ice in the starlight.
The ice is a foot thick, and beneath, the water slides black like a
     dream,
And in the interior of that unpulsing blackness and thrilled zero
The big channel-cat sleeps with eye lidless, and the brute face
Is the face of the last torturer, and the white belly
Brushes the delicious and icy blackness of mud.
But there is no sensation. How can there be
Sensation when there is perfect adjustment? The blood
Of the creature is but the temperature of the sustaining flow:

2. *Editor's note*: Cf. Jack Burden's reflection on his two friends, Willie Stark and Adam
Stanton: "They were doomed, but they lived in the agony of will." Robert Penn Warren, *All the King's Men* (New York: Harcourt, Brace, 1946), 462.

> The catfish is in the Mississippi and
> The Mississippi is in the catfish and
> Under the ice both are at one with God.
> Would that we were! (94)

By the end of the poem Jefferson can accept the past with its violence and evil; he is willing to acknowledge the fact of his kinship with his black-browed butcher of a nephew, and he exults that

> . . . nothing we had,
> Nothing we were,
> Is lost.
> All is redeemed,
> In knowledge. (195)

Jefferson tells his sister that "without the fact of the past we cannot dream the future," and he remembers that he had once written to Adams, his old political rival and friend,

> To Adams, my old enemy and friend, that gnarled greatness, long
>   ago.
> I wrote to him, and said
> That the dream of the future is better than the dream of the past.
> Now I should hope to find the courage to say
> That the dream of the future is not
> Better than the fact of the past, no matter how terrible.
> For without the fact of the past we cannot dream the future. (193)

Robert Penn Warren's Promised Land

Sister M. Bernetta Quinn, O.S.F.

Since his Vanderbilt days, Robert Penn Warren's poetry has charted a movement toward that country to which everyone gives a name of his choosing, Warren's being the Promised Land. Unfettered by adherence to schools of verse (Black Mountain, Objectivist, new-Romantic), Warren has left behind conceits and witty ironies, "little magazine" academic pieces in the Augustan vein, ever deepening and simplifying until the present when "His years like landscape lie,"[1] as he once wrote of his grandfather. Whether looking backward or forward he now can view an interior terrain which need yield to no other in American writing in its power to create the sense of place, and never "of this place only."

All his professional life, until recently, Warren the novelist and critic has overshadowed Warren the poet. During the forties, playing the second role, he composed the essay "A Poem of Pure Imagination: An Experiment in Reading" on *The Ancient Mariner,*[2] a landmark deserving to rank with that of Lowes on "Kubla Khan" or Brooks on "Ode on a Grecian Urn." The distinctions he there makes between symbol and allegory help in appreciating his own work. Following Coleridge, he attributes symbol to the imagination, allegory to the understanding (Warren's edition of *The Rime of the Ancient Mariner,* 74). His differentiation rests on the same kind of idealism whereby Coleridge defines the primary imagination as "the perception which produces our ordinary world of the senses" (68), with the secondary

"Robert Penn Warren's Promised Land" by Sister M. Bernetta Quinn, O.S.F. From *Southern Review,* n.s., VIII (Spring, 1972), 329–58. Copyright © 1972 by the Louisiana State University, Baton Rouge, La. Reprinted by permission of the author.

1. Quotations from Warren's verses are from *Selected Poems: New and Old, 1923–1966* (New York: Random House, 1966) unless otherwise indicated.
2. *Editor's note:* Samuel Taylor Coleridge, *The Rime of the Ancient Mariner* (New York: Reynal & Hitchcock, 1946), 59–148; Warren's essay was reprinted in *Selected Essays* (New York: Random House, 1958), 198–305 with fewer notes.

imagination adding what makes life worthwhile. Further dividing the primary, Warren contrasts symbols of necessity, running through all cultures (for example, the wind in *The Ancient Mariner*) with symbols of congruence, resulting from an artist's manipulation of an image within a special context, like Byzantium in Yeats. Of Warren's symbols of congruence, the most prominent is the cedar tree, named over thirty times and always with resonances of mortality far beyond those of its cousins the yew and the cypress. Sun and moon, storm, gull, and river are among his symbols of necessity, but none has the importance of the West, or Promised Land.

Landscapes of Nature, dream, and memory abound in Warren's writing. In the accents of W. H. Auden he speaks of "the wide landscape of probability," a Mexican setting in a poem the title of which evokes an oil or water color: "Small Soldiers with Drum in Large Landscape." Elsewhere, he becomes a small child, day by day staring out of a classroom window studying the "accustomed landscape" of "School Lesson Based on Word of Tragic Death of Entire Gillum Family." Like Randall Jarrell, he finds the word useful for life itself: "the landscape of his [Warren's father's] early experience" in *Brother to Dragons*.[3] Characteristically he identifies inner and outer scenes, as in that moving line "And a gray light prevailed and both landscape and heart were subdued" ("What Was the Promise That Smiled from the Maples at Evening?"). The major motif of his recognition that a bond of spirit exists between man and environment takes the form of Canaan, sensible of its own joyousness, a state of freedom where "natural innocence / Would dance like sunlight over the delighted landscape" (*Brother to Dragons*, 41).

Next to *All the King's Men*, the best-known of Warren's novels is *World Enough and Time*. In his youth, Kentucky was for him world enough, as it remains in memories and dreams, an Eden to which he occasionally returns, only to be saddened by its decline: "The World of Daniel Boone," which he contributed to the December, 1963, issue of *Holiday*, describes it as "a beautiful country even now. It was once thought to be Eden" (160). When tracing the advance of the Kentucky pioneer's party into Blue Grass territory he says: "They were moving into the Promised Land." But the aboriginal glory vanished: "In the

---

3. Robert Penn Warren, *Brother to Dragons: A Tale in Verse and Voices* (New York: Random House, 1953), 204.

heart of Eden the palisades were rotting down. Soon Boonesborough itself, the first incorporated town in the commonwealth, was to disappear, that 'land of heart's desire,' Boone's dream" (*In the American Grain*, 139).

Warren often sets poems around his birthplace—Guthrie, Kentucky—subjecting them to the many transformations of the light after the manner of Giovanni Bellini in treating the Italian *paese*: "Bellini's landscapes are the supreme instances of natural facts transfigured through love" (*Encyclopedia of World Art*, IX, 15). At times he uses light, especially that at day's end, to express a complex affection for his native soil and to translate into a universal language various truths that in boyhood he half-comprehended and in manhood came to understand: such wisdom underlies the choice of title, *Incarnations*, for his 1968 collection of verse. In other instances, light becomes a tool of irony to render foreboding, as in *Brother to Dragons*, which notes "a trick of light on the late landscape" (7), *late* possibly meaning dead.

Once we have fully "received" a landscape, Warren believes, it lives forever, or at least as long as we do, captured in the "impeccable unspeaking line of art" ("For a Self-Possessed Friend," *Thirty-Six Poems*, 61). Stevens voices the same intuition about permanence in Part Three of "Peter Quince at the Clavier"; Yeats, in "Sailing to Byzantium"; Keats, in "Ode on a Grecian Urn." Unfortunately excised from the Bollingen Award book, "The Cardinal" of the Kentucky Mountain Farm series sets to dignified music a Promised Land unthreatened by change:

> Here is a bough where you can perch, and preen
> Your scarlet that from its landscape shall not fall,
> Lapped in the cool of the mind's undated shade,
> In a whispering tree, like cedar, evergreen. (*Ibid.*, 8)

Here the cardinal is addressed in Marvellian terms as "lover of cedar and shade." Warren contrasts its flamboyant "vision of scarlet" with "Rock and gold is the land in the pulsing noon," a hostile backdrop from which his mind, like a tree, will perennially shelter the bird after summer's lizard, "carved" on the lichen-covered limestone, has fled like the last breath of the season. Thus he himself becomes the cedar casting shadows, the blue tones of memory. Here four concentric images constitute the landscape of oasis: (1) its heart, the tiny reptile as sacred icon; (2) the actual Kentucky scene as an artistic whole; (3) the depiction of this scene in "The Cardinal"; and (4) Warren's mind as origin and Omega.

Typical of the Judaic Promised Land is the Garden, inseparable from its serpent. Part Four of "Boy's Will, Joyful Labor without Pay, the Harvest Home (1918)," like the story "Blackberry Winter," flings an adolescent up against the problem of evil, here the stoning of a black snake by farmhands. The aftermath is chilling:

> Against the wounded evening matched,
> Shagged high on a pitchfork tine, he will make
> Slow arabesques till the bullbats wake.

The action of these scriptural vultures focuses the ugliness of a boy's awakening to cruelty, pain, the destruction of beauty. Taking, like Judas, his earned silver, the protagonist goes to bed only to toss about imagining the blameless creature being torn to pieces while still alive. He continues to see this down the years, more vivid than the tangible things about him. Even the brilliance of the European vacation land wherein he composes the lyric cannot distract him from this gruesome object lesson, softened though it be by the starlight over the barnyard after the havesters' departure:

> And I shut my eyes and I see that scene
> And name each item, but cannot think
> What, in their urgency, they must mean,

> But know, even now, in this foreign shore,
> In blaze of sun and the sea's stare,
> A heart-stab blessed past joy or despair,
> As I see, in the mind's dark, once more,
> That field, pale, under starlit air.

The boy (later, the man) re-creates this autumnal landscape, analogous in its symbolism to Albert Pinkham Ryder's *Death on a Pale Horse*, where a skeleton rides a dark steed around a race track while a snake undulates in the foreground. In his Mediterranean landscape the sea flames up as his child's joy did; at the same time, like a threatening monster, it stares at him, lying in wait to strike. The poet recalls how the farm looked after the snake kill: the cooling tractor under that tree of death, the cedar; the work mule described as saurian, drooping under the night's splendor. "White now, the evening star hangs to preside / Over woods and dark water and countryside," shining on in his thoughts long after "The little blood that smeared the stone" has dried. Forever and forever, "In the star-pale field, the propped pitch-fork lifts / Its burden, hung black, to the white star." Bethlehem and Calvary, the star and the cross, haunt the pilgrim-poet as he searches his way back to the paradise he once inhabited, before the scene that has acquired for him the horror of a ritual murder.

Another remembered landscape of man's involvement in the mystery of original sin comprises "Small White House," a poem which, as if it were the painting its title suggests, remains stark and unchanging in the gallery of Warren's private past. Possessed of all the details, he even so cannot remember "where, in what state" (ambivalently, mind or place) he encountered the house upon which the July sun beats down until it "Swims in that dazzle of no-Time," the world of retained sensation. The second line touches greatness: "The pasture is brown-bright as brass, and like brass, sings with heat": chiasmus and synaesthesia heighten the sense of an unbearable metallic midsummer drought. Behind the house, the hills "shudder, withdraw into distance," to which Warren adds "Like paranoia," an instance of the Auden influence he has never quite shaken off. While this yoking of abstract and concrete (hills, paranoia) is as old as Pope ("And sometimes counsel takes and sometimes tea"), it seems slightly contrived here where no witty effect is intended but rather a Münch-like horror. Again the omnipresent cedar appears: "—And the wax-wing's beak slices the blue cedar-berry, / Which is as blue as distance," that death into which the hills have retreated. Subtly, Warren introduces the color of the horizon as identical to the blue cedar-berry's. The river, tiny because of its remoteness in the background, is patently symbolic: "The river, far off, shrinks / Among the hot boulders, no glister, looks dead as a discarded snake-skin"; the simile condenses not only time, the serpent-river, but also lost innocence and everything else signified by the dark portent of the snake in the harvest poem above.

Less merciless, though still in a somber vein, "Picnic Remembered" returns us to a Promised Land, even though its existence belongs to an unreachable tense. A luminous conversation with self held long after the joyous outing, these seven stanzas of Warren's seem more intricately woven than they actually are. A certain freedom in rhyme reduces that Marvellian symmetry which dominates a first response, though diction throughout remains more seventeenth-century than contemporary. Its three chief landscape features—leaf, hill, sky—gain structural harmony as the two picnickers look upward through waves of light, hungering for an impossible retention of joy. In the October, 1948, *South Atlantic Quarterly*, John L. Stewart connects agrarian primitivism with Freudian psychology in commenting on Warren's submarine landscapes, wherein water represents "the state of innocence for which man longs" (568). "Picnic Remembered" is executed as a poetic canvas of an underwater episode ("We stood among the painted trees: / The amber light laved them, and us"). Then, suddenly, stasis—the artist conceives the light as being so solid that the human beings are flies in amber. In the third stanza he releases his characters into motion again, further developing the seascape:

> Joy, strongest medium, then buoyed
> Us when we moved, as swimmers, who,
> Relaxed, resign them to the flow
> And pause of their unstained flood.

Warren's first book-length critic, Leonard Casper, couples this lyric with "Bearded Oaks"—a poem a man might be born to write—in which "the lovers lie submerged in the diminishing sea-light beneath the trees, symbolic of the urge to be unborn, unbothered, unnamed" (*The Dark and Bloody Ground*, 65). The day, like all days, ends:

> But darkness on the landscape grew
> As in our bosoms darkness, too;
> And that was what we took away.

Light will come again to the natural landscape but not to their hearts, where the darkness that ebbs before sunrise in "the region happier mapped" streams into the bosoms of these picnickers once night has dropped in front of their view like a black stage curtain, turning the amber light that laved them into "that brackish tide." Yet were these persons to return, seasonal conditions being equal, to the Promised Land, the light would still be as purely gold as in Warren's translation of their bliss into art which is the poem.

Another use of the submarine landscape occurs in "Fall Comes to Back County, Vermont": the lounging eagle "Shoulders like spray" the last light before his dive to the mountain. Wherever Warren goes, from the Louisiana of "Bearded Oaks," with its meadow over which currents of bright air roll, to the secluded retreat of Stratton, Vermont, focus of more recent poems, he experiences moments when place takes on the Edenic qualities of Atlantis. First mentioned by Plato in the fourth century B.C., this sunken continent has, according to a favorite theory, long been believed to be the location of the biblical Paradise.

Robert Penn Warren rewrites the Fall in "Composition in Red and Gold," which belongs securely to submarine landscape through its splendid image of the tail of the cat (an animal traditionally used by the devil as a disguise): "gold plume of sea-weed in that tide of light." Its pictorial character is established in the title, reminiscent of Demuth's abstract portrait of William Carlos Williams, *I Saw the Figure Five in Gold*. Its author accents the importance of this lyric by including it in the series "Notes of a Life to Be Lived." Color effects build up, beginning with the general word *light*, through *sunlight* (used twice), *golden* and *flame* (twice each), *gold* (eleven times) to *red-gold*, until they climax in *flame-gold*, which "Completes the composition." Warren emphasizes how the landscape is an actor in his drama by humanizing the brook, brown-gold like the hair of the watching little girl who sees the cat kill the chipmunk, which braids its waters as if they were tresses. The mountain in the background, deserted by its solitary eagle after the crime, may possibly be a symbol of Calvary at the end of Good Friday; the fish leaning hidden against an icy current in the alder-shaded stream, a reminder of Christ. Here, the Promised Land ironically wears a garment of flooding gold, just as the earth in Rilke's "Evening" wraps itself in a vesture of darkness.

The psychological equivalent of a terrestrial heaven is emotional delight. In the series of lyrics so named, Warren telescopes time, as he has done elsewhere, in a way typical of medieval masterpieces. He transforms the past considered as landscape into the present moment, *then* becoming *now* in a manner impossible to a society manipulated by clocks and calendars. The poet in "Delight," Part V, addresses some children, possibly his own, possibly vanished companions of his Guthrie boyhood:

> . . . Oh, children,

> Now to me sing, I see
> Forever on the leaf the light. Snow
> On the pine-leaf, against the bright blue
> Forever of my mind, like breath
> Balances.

His memory of a certain winter scene resembles a canvas painted
a shocking blue behind its snowy pine trees. This landscape, like Ed-
ward Hopper's relentless *Cape Cod Morning*, will not change. Both this
excerpt from "Two Poems about Suddenly and a Rose" and the recollection from which it springs have a permanence beyond leaves, snow,
sunlight—matter in general. Warren calls to the children to look at
the dew, a symbolic bead of light on the bloodred petal, the same jux-
taposition as in "Composition in Red and Gold":

> . . . Light,

> Suddenly, on any morning, is, and somewhere,
> In a garden you will never
> See, dew, in fracture of light
> And lunacy of gleam-glory, glitters on
> A petal red as blood, and

> The rose dies, laughing.

The verb *is* predicates of light a universal present: this gardenscape
will exist independent of addressee and artist. The four closing words
constitute a poem in themselves: "The rose dies, laughing."

The total impression of "Delight," Part V, recalls Flannery O'Connor's death scenes, wherein the characters do not wholly die. We tend
to feel as we grow older that whatever awaits us beyond the grave is
better than what we used to suppose, a truth which the rose has pene-
trated, if only we could come upon its secret. The participle *laughing*
stands for the exultation (hilarity in the Poundian sense) of Hopkins
in dying: "I am so happy, so happy!" Part VI of "Delight," if it retracts
the Jesuit's affirmation, does so only to return to it again in a meditation where Warren, gazing at a marine landscape, inquires:

> If this, now, is truly the day's end, or

> If, in a new shift of mist,
> The light may break through yonder
> To stab gold to the gray sea, and twist
> Your heart to a last delight—or at least, to wonder.
>   ("Finesterre")

The mark of Gerard Manley Hopkins lies upon these last two lines, as
well as on the diction and prosody throughout the three most recent
Warren books.

Two of the ten "Notes on a Life to Be Lived" have been discussed.

The third in this opening section of the Bollingen award winner, "Blow, West Wind, Blow," is one of the best poems of the century, destined to rank with its author's "Bearded Oaks." The cedar tree in it, besides presaging grief, serves as Aladdin's lamp to summon up from the past three crises, two of which appear as painted landscapes. Like the blackbird looked at thirteen ways by Stevens, the cedar tree remains a crucial symbol from poem to poem even when these are not explicitly joined. In Warren's ode to the west wind, his allusion to it is redeemed from gloom by the fact that besides physical death it connotes, as Michel Jacobs remarks in *Colour in Landscape Painting*, the positive values of faith, victory, contemplation, and immortality.

The first two lines condense the theme: "I know, I know—though the evidence / Is lost, and the last who might speak are dead." What the speaker knows is human transience, forgotten so quickly, with the evidence lost. We don't really believe that we shall die, except in moments of heightened awareness, symbolized here by wind and cedar imagery, when we are possessed by a simpler process than rational conviction:

> Blow, west wind, blow, and the evidence, O,
>
> Is lost, and wind shakes the cedar, and O
> I know how the kestrel hung over Wyoming,
> Breast reddened in sunset . . .

Coming from the direction of death, the west wind shakes the cedar, that "golden bough." Warren's whole lyric is a highly melodic tissue of vowel identities or approximations: by ending his third and fourth lines with "O" and repeating the cry in the sixth, he communicates a triple anguish. The sound of the west wind brings back to him that setting in Wyoming when the sun wounded the breast of that gallant bird suspended, but not for long, over the landscape. With the second rub of the lamp, the cedar trembling in the wind returns with the remembered sensation of a final kiss: ". . . and I know how cold / Was the sweat on my father's mouth, dead." Finally, the wind and cedar reinvoke his Kentucky childhood at a moment fraught with a significance which then was out of his range of prophecy, considered as the gift of looking deeply into the reality of the present:

> Blow, west wind, blow, shake the cedar, I know

> How once I, a boy, crouching at creekside,
> Watched, in the sunlight, a handful of water
> Drip, drip, from my hand. The drops—they were bright!

The evidence—kestrel, sunset, Wyoming skyline, shining creek—
is gone because of the irreplaceable uniqueness of every instant, the
remoteness of the poet, the subsequent deaths of any other persons
who might have been participants in this three-act drama. Only the
constants, west wind and cedar, persist, with their variations on the
theme of time: to all appearances permanent, they function as warn-
ings of impermanence. Expanding his skepticism through the pro-
noun *you*, Warren concludes: "But you believe nothing, with the evidence lost."

"Blow, West Wind, Blow" exemplifies what J. B. Leishman says
about Rilke in introducing a group of translations: "More and more
his poetry became the expression of a kind of interior landscape, the
'transformation' by inwardness, into a kind of higher *visibility*, of an
intensely seen outwardness" (Rilke's *Poems 1906–1926*, p. 33). Contemplation to the point of trance changes a windblown tree (the only
object indisputably "there") into first a sunset mountainscape, then a
deathbed scene, and thirdly, a Kentucky brookside. All of these meta-
morphoses catch at the fleeting nature of life while at the same time
implying a radiance just beyond the tangible which teases us out of
thought, like a glimpse of the Promised Land.

"A Vision: Circa 1880" is a sort of elegy wherein Warren sees his
father as a boy in Trigg County, Kentucky. The season is spring,
though he himself recalls only the scorching summer or the fall, times
when outside this "apparition" he tries to visualize the region where
it transpired:

> . . . and so the scene
> I had seen just now in the mind's eye, vernal,
> Is altered, and I strive to cry across the dry pasture,
> But cannot, nor move, for my feet, like dry corn-roots, cleave
> Into the hard earth, and my tongue makes only the dry,
> Slight sound of wind on the autumn corn-blade.

As if through binoculars ("Down the tube and darkening corridor of
Time"), the son stares at that "sunlit space" between woods ("green
shadow") and pasture ("sun-green"), an immortal landscape inhabited by the father-as-child whom he never knew.

In "The Ballad of Billie Potts" the narrator defines Time as "the new place," "West," all of which can be related to the Canaan symbol. *Brother to Dragons* also conceives Time as a setting, with its characters meeting at "no place," "any time," the alternation of personae held together in the mind of a storyteller who spins reflections about a labyrinthine landscape:

> Deep in the world of winter, snow on the brown leaves,
> Far in Kentucky there, I raised my eyes
> And thought of the track a man may take through Time,
> And how our hither-coming never knows the hence-going. (209)

As Warren writes earlier in this play for voices, his father, Moses-like, had climbed his years as if they were mountains, giving those who followed him an example impossible to evade:

> But still, despite all naturalistic considerations,
> Or in the end because of naturalistic considerations,
> We must believe in virtue. There is no
> Escape. No inland path around that rocky
> And spume-nagged promontory. (29)

Just as writers construct the anti-Utopias competently dissected in Kinglsey Amis' *New Maps of Hell*, so do they create warped Canaans. Warren's "Place and Time" is given over to his Richard Cory, Dr. Knox, who mysteriously commits suicide. Its landscape in whites conveys the nightmare terror of German Expressionism, the sun filling the sky with a scream of whiteness. Two moments unite into a single flare: that immediately before the event which happened when the poet at nine was walking along a dusty road daydreaming, and a hallucinatory moment during a return visit as an adult to this town aptly called Cerulean Springs:

> But to resume:
> heat-dazzle, dust-whiteness—an image in sleep,
>
> or in the brain behind the eyeball,
> as now, in the light of this other day,
> and year, the eyeball, stunned by that inner
> blaze, sees nothing, can nothing see
>
> outward whatsoever—only
> the white dust of that street, and it
> is always August, is 3 P.M.,
> the mercury 95 . . . .

Both moments lack the "water to wash the world away" ("And All That Came Thereafter"), mentioned in the series probing into the reasons behind the doctor's death. Here, the cleansing, sacramental waters are symbolized by the child's anticipated swimming haunt shaded by silver willows. When Warren the boy asks his grandfather why Dr. Knox hanged himself, the Civil War veteran begins a reply but breaks off his discourse to gaze out beyond the fennel, the peeling fence, and the cedars:

> The land, in sunlight,
> swam, with the meadow the color of rust,
> and distance the blue of Time . . . .
> ("A Confederate Veteran Tries to Explain the Event")

Rust is one of the many scriptural allusions in Warren: in comparison to timelessness, the meadows that hypnotize the old man belong to the things that rust corrupts.

In taking Time as a landscape, Warren resembles his friend and younger contemporary Randall Jarrell, an affinity especially clear in their dreamscapes. "Vision under the October Mountain: A Love Poem," one of his newer achievements is set near Stratton, Vermont. The mountain appears to his uplifted eyes to drift slowly through the sunset so beautifully that he thrice asks his companion if it springs from a shared prenatal dream:

> . . . did we
> once in the womb dream, dream
> a gold mountain in gold
> air floating . . . .

Here he restricts the meaning of the mountain, almost making it an emblem rather than a symbol: "it is the image of authority, of reality." Though doubt of its power immediately intrudes ("oh, is it?"), the mutual gaze of the watchers drives it away.

Brother to Dragons, which has so many fine passages, includes among them the anti-paradisial dream of Lilburn's wife, Laetitia, who after Lucy's death sees him in terms of a landscape—again such as Ryder might have devised, Ryder with his grotesque forms and limited palette:

> I turned and saw him—something on his face
> Grew like a stain in water, and it spread,
> And grew like darkness when the moon sinks down

> And creeks and valleys dark, and the trees get black,
> And grew like recollections in the night
> When you wake up cold and all you did seems awful. (86)

Lilburn's father also thinks of him as if he were a nocturnal painting: *"I have looked in the eyes of my first-born son and have seen / The landscape of shadow and the shore of night"* (98). Lucy herself, just before or after she has entered eternity, views her child in the same way. *Brother to Dragons*, like *Our Town*, regards life and death as more flexible conditions than the rigidly separate ones we know, thus leaving open the interpretation of her state:

> But I, I made the repudiation. I died.
> I lay and knew the end, and then I saw
> His face. But a wide world between, like a valley,
> Like a wide valley, and the rain fell steady between,
> So steady and gray and you hardly see beyond,
> Where the far hill is, and far across the valley
> So full of the rain falling, I saw his [Lilburn's] face.
> It was big as the hill, but the hiss was small with distance,
> And distance was dim and the rain without ceasing.
> The distance was but to the bed-foot, but a great
> Distance, and a wide valley where the rain fell. (73–74)

Babette Deutsch in evaluating the tale for the *Yale Review* calls its symbolic background, of which the above may stand as "a figure in the carpet," a witness to, even analogue of, the human condition itself (XLIII, 278).

When Billie Potts, in the second longest of Warren's poetic narratives, rides back whistling in the sun toward his birthplace after ten years out West, it is the narrator who sees the white peak beneath which Billy as prodigal son dismounts to stand and spit, sees it as the Hebrews did the Promised Land "that glittered like a dream." When Billie's parents in their greed unwittingly murder him, a Sophoclean "messenger" (frontiersman Joe Drew) reveals to them their macabre mistake. Looking into the dark mirror of the forest pool after his ugly slaying, the narrator, true prophet who penetrates happenings, drinks at its waters of experience but rises without the innocence he seeks: "And years it lies here and dreams in the depth and grieves / More faithful than mother or father in the light or dark of the leaves," innocence here personified as cursed by what "Letter to a Friend" calls the "dream without fruition."

Bearing in mind Warren's distinction between allegory as generated in the understanding, and symbol as constructed by the imagination, one can discern in this excerpt from his famous essay on Coleridge why he chose the dream-device for landscape epiphanies:

> In his swound the Mariner receives a fuller revelation of his situation and of the nature of the forces operating about him. He learns these things, it is important to notice, in the dream—just as the fellow-mariners had received the first intimation of the presence of the Polar Spirit through dreams. And the symbolic significance of this fact is the same: The dream is not at the level of the "understanding," but is the mode by which the special kind of knowledge of the imagination should be revealed. (97–98)

The Oriental scenery of "Kubla Khan" demonstrates such a revelatory character, a controlled imaginary fabrication far from the phantasmagoria of surrealism.

Though as a child in Kentucky Warren briefly took art lessons from a Sister Luke, he has never been a practitioner; yet he has cultivated "the painter's eye" to the extent that he regularly sees Nature as landscape. "Aubade for Hope" conceives sunrise to be a view from a window out of which no one is looking:

> And now they stir, as east
> Beyond the formal gleam of landscape sun
> Has struck the senatorial hooded hill.
> (*Thirty-Six Poems*, 47)

More appropriate to the Canaan theme is Jefferson's "vision" of Kentucky in *Brother to Dragons*:

> I saw all,
> Swale and savannah and the tulip-tree
> Immortally blossoming to May,
> Hawthorn and haw,
> Valleys extended and prairies idle and the land's
> Long westward languor lifting toward the flaming escarpment at the end of day. (11)

Jefferson's dream of the Promised Land ends in a nameless paradisial isle in the Pacific (counterpart of Saint Brendan's, west of Ireland), where the black seal barks, knowing that eventually the seekers will arrive ("And on the western rock, wracked in the clang and smother, / The black seal barks, and loves us, knowing we will come.")

Warren in the first twenty years of his lifespan drew less heavily, if at all, upon a Kentucky which was perhaps then too close to be seen as source material. "The Garden" is subtitled "On prospect of a fine day in early autumn," placing it in the category of landscape art where *prospect* is a common if archaic term. Modeled on Marvell's lyric of the same name, it shows the Fugitive reaction from Georgian verse, as well as movement toward metaphysical stanzaic tightness and a severely concentrated diction. Despite the absence of a focus of narration, the reader gets the impression of someone enjoying the sight of a garden, sparkling with frost, wherein leaves have become blossoms, his vantage point that best suited to "prove" or test aesthetically "The grace of this imperial grove":

> But branches interlace to frame
> The avenue of stately flame
> Where yonder, far more bold and pure
> Than marble, gleams the sycamore. . . .

The other trees, bent to a fiery arch, precede the sycamore, the shining trunk of which duplicates the cold but beautiful effect of a cathedral: "Of argent torso and cunning shaft / Propped nobler than the sculptor's craft." No one acquainted with Yeats can help thinking of that writer's Galway "laboratory," Coole Park.

In summer, lovers before kissing could see the consummation of their relationship portrayed in the ripe peach:

> The hand that crooked upon the spade
> Here plucked the peach, and thirst allayed;
> Here lovers paused before the kiss,
> Instructed of what ripeness is.

Edenic overtones inform the quarrel of Warren's familiar jay and cardinal, as these dispute over the ruined garden, its Adam and Eve departed. To the beholder, standing alone at the entrance, autumn is more rewarding than the sensual summer or the ominous winter, even though he is not happy: the garden, once a "rank plot," is referred to as "precincts," the first noun suggesting some traitorous conspiracy and the second its prison dénouement. A milder sun than August's will bring its blessing of peace:

> Only for him these precincts wait
> In sacrament that can translate

> All things that fed luxurious sense
> From appetite to innocence.

Purified sacramentally, the protagonist can here recover the "lost country" of his youth, akin to the virgin Kentucky of frontier America.

Though Jefferson's portrayal of a vista within the Louisiana Purchase in *Brother to Dragons* is perhaps the most prominent nature description turned landscape by heroic perception, other passages treat settings as synecdoche. At times the "golden glade" figure gleams more brilliantly because of a juxtaposed foil, as in Laetitia's thoughts after Lucy's death. It is dusk, "With night coming on and the gray light filling the land," which only the day previous was gold from the sun on the sweetgum:

> . . . and I could see out the window,
> Way down the bluff and over the flat land, way off.
> The river was there and had a kind of gleam-like,
> Not sun, for the sun was shady and night nigh,
> But just like the river gave off some light and it cold,
> Like a knife that lies in the shadow and the blade
> Gives off a light with a gleam-like, so still and cold,
> And grayness was slow over all the flat land,
> And I tried not to think but be still like the land and the gray
>   light. (76)

Laetitia (what name could be less appropriate?) finds in this gray light not only an exact replica of her emotional state but also some sort of answer to the riddle of existence. Desolate as she is, she remembers "yesterday / When sunshine made the sweet-gum tree all gold," and even though the river has become for her a knife lying ready in shadow, in her subconscious she expects the apotheosis of this gray light, remembering that "light changes old landscape," as Warren has affirmed in "A Real Question Calling for Solution."

Another instance of exterior landscape turned interior in *Brother to Dragons* is a double presentation of a certain Kentucky scene. In July heat, the narrator toils up a hill, struggling through plants and shrubs tangled "like a dream," until suddenly green serenity breaks upon him. The only *locus* such a place now has is *dove sta memoria*: it has become "that landscape lost in the heart's homely deep" of "Moonlight that Lingers." When he revisits it in cold weather, the bluff does not look so high. Out of the past there rises the way it used to be:

> July it was—and I damned the heat and briar,
> Saw-vine, love-vine, and rose, then clambered through
> The tall, hot gloom of oak and ironwood,
> Where grapevine, big as boas, had shagged and looped
> Jungle convolvement and visceral delight.
> For that's the way I had remembered it.
> But no, it's not like that. At least, not now,
> And never was, I guess, but in my head. (207)

One reason we can't go home again is the unlikelihood that the home we think we came from ever existed.

What the speaker sees before him on the second trip matches the first landscape point by point, except for seasonal change:

> There is some thicket, yes, and grapevine, sure,
> But scraggly-thin and hanging like it's tired
> From trees gone leafless now, and not so tall.
> So I'm prepared for what I find up yonder. (207–208)

His discovery upon reaching the crest is that the Promised Land has withered into the Waste Land:

> The ruin all shrunken to a little heap
> Of stone that grass and earth pre-empt again.
> And those fine beech trees that I'd celebrated—
> They just aren't there at all, and all I find
> Are piddling shag-barks, walnuts, two or three,
> And two oaks, scrub to middling, not to brag on.
> So winter makes things small. (208)

On the dead leaves rests a little covering of snow. The climber meditates, raising his eyes beyond the bluff and plain to the river, which in a younger year was another river. Then comes the miracle: the happiness he has known between the summer of scene one and the winter of scene two allows him to endure this parody of Eden with a mature and tranquil courage ("Since then I have made new acquaintance with the nature of joy"). He has learned that the kingdom of God is within him.

Not always is an "examination of conscience" in terms of life as landscape dominated by the peace of this passage from *Brother to Dragons*. Also in the valley-orchard-garden pattern, "Aged Man Surveys the Past Time" shows a man weeping over missed opportunities as he contemplates the western view of his unfruited trees at sunset, his tears like twilight rain—a touch of sentimentality which, together with strained inversions, may have prompted Warren's later rejection of this lyric published in *Thirty-Six Poems*. As the protagonist stands there "in diminished light," he reads his entire autobiography in the farm before him. It is winter. The catbird, counterfeit of spring's songsters, mocks him. Gazing out at his barn, he notes how the light pales behind it, even as it has died out in his own career, and he sees himself as a lightning-struck oak: "Light fails behind the barn and blasted oak." Like a strumpet, April with her spray of green and her crocuses has deceived him, as she will again in the year to come. All his days have been a journey downward into a private hell: "Time has no mathematic. Could Orpheus map / The rocky and bituminous descent?" The concluding words ("Thy godless summer and the dusty road!") summarize the misery of this modern Pontius Pilate, to whom the poem has compared him.

In "Garden Waters," all night, "Noisy and silver, over the moon-dark stone," a stream falls, unlike the waters of dream in that it possesses sound (*Selected Poems, 1923–1943*, p. 101). In contrast to this silver-streaked fantasy, outside this superficially Edenic nocturne lies a world where "men by crags have stopped against the loud / Torn cataract or hollow-bosomed flood," appalled by the similarity to the sea of the tumult within their veins, just as violent but "voiceless." The longest study of Robert Penn Warren's poetry to date is Victor Strandberg's *A Colder Fire*,[4] which finds rich meaning in these microcosm-macrocosm landscapes:

> This complexity of water imagery in "Garden Waters" shows the deepening complexity of Warren's perspective in his search for identity. His effort to define the self, as this poem demonstrates, employs both the inward and the outward look, both the groping downward through the inward labyrinth, wherein Warren most affirms the Romantic tradition, and the venturing into the outer landscape, so as to measure and evaluate, in the Classical tradition, the civilization that has shaped the raw material of self. (70)

The speaker in "Garden Waters" and the aged man surveying his land recognize catastrophe in the "dead leaf." They must mourn their

4. *Editor's note*: Since this essay was published, Victor Strandberg's second book on Warren's poetry has appeared: *The Poetic Vision of Robert Penn Warren* (Lexington: University Press of Kentucky, 1977).

failures in silence, like the blood within the body, denied the release of the ocean: "More terrible breaks the torrent with no song."

All of the poems analyzed thus far are in the mainstream of literature, which since Coleridge has leaned more and more toward *paysage moralisé*, as Herbert Marshall McLuhan has pointed out in his essay "The Aesthetic Moment in Poetry": "Beginning with Thomson's *Seasons* the poets appropriated landscape as a means of evoking and defining states of mind" (*English Institute Essays*, 1951, p. 171). Rimbaud, Poe, Eliot, and Crane are examples. Conflict within the mind resulting from original sin, a concept which can rise from either secular or sacred convictions, runs through both the fiction and the verse of Robert Penn Warren. His great exegesis of *The Rime of the Ancient Mariner* is based on the Fall of Man. In the old sailor's narrative, the sun and moon share the adventures of the crew: mirrors of mood, malevolent or beneficent influences. The cause of estrangement from grace and token of reconciliation is the sacramental Albatross, which Warren defines as a "moon-bird" (91). His trial over, the Mariner "gets home, in the moonlight, which, we recall, is the light of imagination, and in the end he celebrates the chain of love which binds human society together, and the universe" (104). Naturalistic novelists lower man to the level of nonrational animals through symbol; Warren, on the contrary, elevates even the non-organic as a result of his belief in the oneness of the universe in the redemptive plan, as it links the first Paradise to the final.

By associating himself (a figure of Everyman, though retaining uniqueness) with Billie Potts the outlaw, Warren affirms again the solidarity of the race. Like Faulkner, he thinks of a unity, vertical and horizontal, among men, so that guilt incurred by a segment, as in slavery, affects all. Thirteen times "The Ballad of Billie Potts" mentions its setting in the land "between the rivers," as Kentuckians know the region separating the Cumberland and Tennessee. Sometimes Warren returns here in dream to contemplate the terrain. The remembered shagbark and tulip tree have vanished, along with an old cabin, but the low hills, the oak, the slough, the tangled cane, the muskrat, and the bluejay remain:

> But the land is still there, and as you top a rise,
> Beyond you all the landscape steams and simmers
> —The hills, now gutted, red, cane-brake and black-jack yet.
> The oak leaf steams under the powerful sun.

Throughout the yarn, Billie is the storyteller's double: "Think of yourself at dawn: Which one are you?" When Billie returns to die at the hands of his parents in a landscape of evil, Warren balances against this scene the innocent pasture so prevalent in his writing: "The stars are shining and the meadow is bright." The spring which had served as a mirror the morning Billie left home is now "black as ink." Terrible, and yet somehow regenerative, this father-son crime (like the mother-son horror in *Oedipus*) becomes a step in the drama begun at Billie's disinterment in the light of a pine knot, a ceremony which awakens the long-quenched tenderness of Big Billie and his wife for their only son. Billie himself dies kneeling at the symbolic pool "in the sacramental silence of evening."

"To a Face in the Crowd" brings this insight of man's solidarity up to date by inquiring quite simply of a passing stranger: "Where will you one day be buried?" Various landscapes which might serve are put in the form of questions:

> Brother, my brother, whither do you pass?
> Unto what hill at dawn, unto what glen,
> Where among the rocks the faint lascivious grass
> Fingers in lust the arrogant bones of men?

Moving backward in time, Warren speculates in terms of a marinescape what the nameless other will suffer during his life:

> Beside what bitter waters will you go
> Where the lean gulls of your heart along the shore
> Rehearse to the cliffs the rhetoric of their woe?

Both he and the stranger derive through the centuries from "the chosen people": "We are the children of an ancient band / Broken between the mountains and the sea," whose pilgrimage is recorded in *Tale of Time*, subtitle for the 1960–1966 lyrics in the Bollingen Award collection. They become pilgrims explicitly in the lines:

> Renounce the night as I, and we must meet
> As weary nomads in this desert at last,
> Borne in the lost procession of these feet.

The convergence of men in this procession which is history depends upon choice: to renounce the powers of darkness, to keep on toward the promise. "To a Face in the Crowd" must have unusual strength in Warren's opinion, since it ends his most complete book of verse to

date—must indeed, as he there says in the prefatory note, lie on the
main line of his impulse.

Since we come upon our goal while looking for something quite
different, Saul in one of the "Holy Writ" poems finds not his father's
asses, as he expects, but destiny when he encounters Samuel on the
desert's edge. Event and environment blend: "Fate is the air we breathe."
Saul's backdrop is a lion-colored landscape of noon-blazing stones re-
sembling the droppings of lions, a wilderness of dry thorns, and a
yelping wind. He walks toward the old man who will anoint him
king. Samuel as prophet sees them frozen in the ritual of consecra-
tion, the locale fragile as his sensory assimilation of it:

> The far hills, white light on gypsum, dazzle.
> The hills waver like salt dissolving in water. Swim
> In the dazzle of my eyes.

These hills do not waver any more than the ones in "Small White
House" shuddered: perception intensified by high emotion alters
their existence (cf. "Modification of Landscape"). When Saul leaves,
Samuel, watching him, thinks of how his own consciousness is the
desert through which the younger man travels:

> He moved from me in the white light.
> The black dwindle in the distance which now he
> Was, was upheld by
> White light as by
> A hand. He moved across distance, as across
> The broad palm of my knowing.
> The palm of my hand was as
> Wide as the world and the
> Blaze of distance.

Here, the ambivalent *palm* demonstrates Warren's mature skill in the
use of metaphysical conceit. In his mind, Samuel pictures the future
monarch arriving at the south shoulder of the pass in the greyness
before dawn, where a stone-grey stallion will stand to bear him to
Gilboa, the place preordained for his death.

No object in Creation exists in isolation: man and Nature are
looped together by a band of light which symbolizes the common
destiny of a mortal world awaiting its fulfillment. Robert Penn Warren's vision, including *Incarnations* and *Audubon: A Vision*, is basically
affirmative. "The Last Metaphor," from *Thirty-Six Poems* (52–53), opens

with one of his least hopeful statements; though the end brightens, it is with a facile optimism which perhaps led to the exclusion of this lyric from later collections. In it, a man goes out in a chilly twilight to seek bare trees, shadow-colored rock, a lonely wind, rather than the soaring birds of a gentler day:

> He passed by a water, profound and cold,
> Whereon remotely gleamed the violent west.
> Stark rose a wood above a rocky crest.

Unlike the stripped trees of this grove, he is a tree from which tenaciously hang "memories of the phantom spring's decay." The real trees on the horizon represent the stoicism he desires:

> How flat and black the trees stand on the sky
> Unreminiscent of the year's frail verdure.
> Purged of the green that kept so frail a tenure
> They are made strong; no leaf clings mortally.

Alternately the man looks up at the grim hills or down at "the violent west" (the adjective not promising) gleaming across the icy depths of water, as if mocking him by Nature's indifference. His heart counsels him to be instructed by this bleakness, and in the end he is:

> Before he went a final metaphor
> Not passionate this, he gave to the chill air,
> Thinking that when the leaves no more abide
> The stiff trees rear not up in strength and pride
> But life unto the gradual dark in prayer.

In spring it is easy to feel a joy of renewal; in summer, of triumph and mastery; when not only wind and dark but also cold come on, the spirit faints. In "The Last Metaphor" the plea for supernatural help as assuagement for grief is unconvincing because unprepared for.

The moods of this lyric are incidental, however, as against the cumulative Promised Land of Warren, a writer thoroughly conversant with the Bible as a source of symbol. Though the concept of Canaan is broader than Old Testament references to it, acquaintance with the latter helps, in the way that Genesis is relevant to a critic of *East of Eden*. The term began in Judeo-Christian tradition with Abraham's departure from Ur for Canaan. Centuries later the Hebrews, captive in Egypt, kept on trusting in God's pledge to him (Gen. 17:8) as to their ultimate joy. When Moses led them out of bondage across the

Red Sea, their entrance into the Promised Land might have been accomplished had not fearfulness over exaggerated reports of scouts
doomed them to wander until Moses, at the age of one hundred and
twenty, died within sight of his dream and was replaced by the war-
rior Joshua. Gradually, the entire twenty-six thousand acres west of
the Jordan came to be considered the Promised Land, under the name
of Palestine. The second stanza of "Swing Low, Sweet Chariot,"—"I
looked over Jordan and what did I see, / Waiting for to carry me home,
/ A band of angels coming after me"—reflects the transfiguration of
this small nation into Paradise itself. (Its phrase *band of angels* brings to
mind Warren's novel of that title.)

"History" concerns itself directly with this Promised Land:

> And now
> We see, below,
> The delicate landscape furled,
> A world
> Of ripeness blent, and green,
> The fruited earth. . . .

Throughout Warren's verse, Canaan, as in this passage, takes on the
character of an "innocent pasture." The religious tone of this episode
in the migration toward the West, as recorded by an eyewitness, has a
Psalmist ring. "Much man can bear," the poem says, listing the chas-
tisements of the Bride: arduous travel, hunger, no water or fodder,
cold, ulcers, cracked lips. The travelers descend to take the Promised
Land by storm, but not in anger.

The lyric "The Letter about Money, Love or Other Comfort, If
Any" treats of a personal, not a communal, Promised Land. Its biblical inspiration is clear from the metonymy of its subhead: "'In the beginning was the word,—THE GOSPEL ACCORDING TO ST. JOHN.'" The
"word" is a letter marked BY HAND ONLY which the protagonist in a
Kafkaesque tragicomic series of attempts, delivers for a stranger re-
sembling the one in "Blackberry Winter." He goes on and on, everywhere meeting trials but persevering until he climbs a high cliff,
where he buries the letter like a body. His mission over, he plunges
back into the darkness of trees, to emerge into an enchanted sunrise:

> I stand, bewildered, breath-bated and lame,
> at the edge of a clearing, to hear, as first birds stir, life lift now night's
>   hasp,

then see, in first dawn's drench and drama, the snow peak go gory,
and the eagle will unlatch, crag-clasp,
fall, and at breaking of wing-furl, bark glory,
and by that new light I shall seek
the way, and my peace with God. . . .

Among Warren's Eden enclaves, "Gold Glade" is unquestionably
one of the most exquisite. The poet thinks of the landscape with a
sense of "Is this real or imagined? What state (even literally, as on a
map of the United States) is it in?" The splendor of "Gold Glade" resembles that surrounding Stratton, Vermont, or the magic mountain
of "October Vision." Yet, actually, the spot exists in a Kentucky remembered from his boyhood, when he was not as yet capable of realizing that his aimless hunting expedition had brought him right to the
edge of a woodland beauty which was Canaan in symbol, a place
looking backward to Eden and forward to Paradise. After spending
his holiday climbing under the black cedars, the young huntsman
gains the crest of a limestone ridge from which he can gaze down and
picture in his mind's eye the hidden "white water tumbling" over
"stone wet-black." This landscape of gorges, seen at the start of evening, is "sublime" and perhaps to some extent more a source of the
fright the boy feels than the danger facing him in clambering down
slick boulders: it is hazardous to approach perfection.

Between the lad and the Promised Land is a level beech grove;
after he has crossed it he comes out upon a magical "theater in the
round":

The glade was geometric, circular, gold,
No brush or weed breaking that bright gold of leaf-fall.
In the center it stood, absolute and bold
Beyond any heart-hurt, or eye's grief-fall.
Gold-massy the beech stood in that gold light-fall.

There was no stir of air, no leaf now gold-falling,
No tooth-stitch of squirrel, or any far fox-bark,
No woodpecker coding, or late jay calling.
Silence: gray-shagged, the great shagbark
Gave forth gold light. There could be no dark.

The gold-gleaming midpoint of this circle is a beech. Unlike Hopkins'
golden grove, these trees are too still for unleafing, holding themselves separate from the sorrows of a beholder's heart or the tears in

his eyes. Typically, the landscape of this moment is silence: the highest landscape effects in Warren occur in scenes devoid of sound or motion. A deleted version limits the Promised Land here to a definite place, not an elusive dream such as Poe's Eldorado or Yeats's garden of the golden apples of the sun and silver apples of the moon, but a particular glade the location of which he has forgotten:

> No, no! in no mansion under earth,
> Nor imagination's domain of bright air,
> But solid in soil that gave its birth,
> It stands, wherever it is, but somewhere.
> I shall set my foot and go there.
>   (*Promises*, 25)

Warren's dropping this passage might be interpreted as a loss of faith in a certain form of primitivism. No longer does he expect to recover the pure bliss of natural loveliness which thrilled him in boyhood and young manhood. Moreover, with the lengthening of the river of consciousness, he finds it increasingly difficult to distinguish reality from imagination. Yet though he comes to such things colder, this Kentucky landscape recollected embodies a revelation too piercing ever to be lost.

The speaker in "Gold Glade," unable to decide whether its perfection belongs to Tennessee or Kentucky (and if the latter, to Montgomery, to Todd, or to Christian county), ends by wondering: "Is it merely an image that keeps haunting me?" In symbolism the *paysage* is very near to Frost's "Nothing Gold Can Stay," which I have analyzed for landscape meaning in the *English Journal* (LV, 621–24). *Gold* is Warren's favorite word, as a concordance will one day substantiate. What he says about Frost in *Selected Essays* might just as easily apply to himself:

> The poet has undertaken to define for us [in "Birches"] both the distinction between and the interpenetration of two worlds, the world of nature and the world of the ideal, the heaven and the earth, the human and the non-human (oppositions which appear in various relationships), by descriptive level or reference to the symbolic level of reference. (135)

Gold is as symbolic for Warren as for Saint Matthew in the text concerning the gifts of the Wise Men.

"Gold Glade" looks to the west for its transfiguration. The American West started much farther from the Pacific Ocean than the twentieth century thinks. Its Moses was Jefferson, who led his people to Canaan though he never entered it, possibly because of the confusion in morals dramatized by William Wells Brown's novel *Clotel*. In *Brother to Dragons* he presents himself in that biblical role:

> It was great Canaan's grander counterfeit.
> Bold Louisiana,
> It was the landfall of my soul. (11)

From the top of Mount Nebo, God showed Moses a panoramic view of the Israelites' terrestrial paradise. Jefferson identifies Kentucky and beyond with what Moses saw:

> But it was my West, the West I bought and gave and never
> Saw, or but like the Israelite,
> From some high pass or crazy crag of mind, saw . . . .

More fortunate than Jefferson, the narrator, R. P. W. (in *Brother to Dragons*), crosses the frontier:

> There was the quiet, high glade.
> Blue grass set round with beeches, the quietest tree.
> The air was suddenly sweet, a hint of cool,
> And even the sun's blaze could abate its fervor,
> And I stood in the new silence while my heart was beating.
> Some cattle gazed like peace from the farther shade. (32)

As in a "picturesque" painting, the ruined dwellings of departed farmers only enhance the Romantic art of this day in a vanished July.

Toward the end of *Brother to Dragons*, Warren introduces as a last "voice" Meriwether Clark, companion of Boone, who experiences the same exhilaration as Jefferson as he looks out over the virgin landscape: "We entered the land of the enormousness of air. / For a year we moved toward the land of the Shining Mountains" (178). The excitement of Cortez vibrates through his response to unbelievable serenity:

> And the snow on the far peak glared blue
> In excess of light, and no track of beast on the unruffled
> White of the high plain, no wing-flash in high air,
> And in that glittering silence of the continent
> I heard my heart beating distinctly, and I said,
> Is this delight? Is this the name of delight? (179)

The word *delight*, title of a seven-poem sequence in the 1966 volume, relies upon its second syllable to render visible the ecstasies which, unannounced, pierce man the explorer.

Incarnations, although it contains "Treasure Hunt" with its proclamation that all promises are kept, even happiness, has nothing to offer by way of explicit Canaan imagery. *Audubon: A Vision*, too, does not develop this figure directly: only its hero binds it to Kentucky, where the bird artist knows the most supreme of emotions, caught up in a state in which dream and reality are indistinguishable. In a letter of September 20, 1969, Warren has given Eudora Welty's story "A Still Moment" as in all likelihood the germ for this latest book: after twenty years, even he can't be positive. Miss Welty imagines Audubon thus:

> Coming upon the Trace, he looked at the high cedars, azure and still as distant smoke overhead, with their silver roots trailing down on either side like the veins of deepness in this place, and he noted some fact to his memory—this earth that wears but will not crumble or slide or turn to dust, they say it exists in one spot in the world, Egypt—and then forgot it. (*The Wide Net*, 82)

Even closer to Warren's overall intentions in his vision is the excerpt a few pages on:

> O secret life, he thought—is it true that the secret is withdrawn from the true disclosure, that man is a cave man, and that the openness I see, the ways through forests, the rivers brimming light, the wide arches where the birds fly, are dreams of freedom? If my origin is withheld from me, is my end to be unknown too? Is the radiance I see closed into an interval between two darks, or can it not illuminate them both and discover at last, though it cannot be spoken, what was thought hidden and lost? (85–86)

The Middle Ages looked on Nature as the Book of the Creatures. Audubon, Warren, all of us in these still moments of *shalom* come close to reading its secret. The closest analogue to such a "dream / Of a season past all seasons" (29) is a reappearance of the golden glade:

> The spring is circular and surrounded by gold leaves
> Which are fallen from the beech tree.
>
> Not even a skitter-bug disturbs the gloss
> Of the surface tension. The sky

Is reflected below in absolute clarity.
If you stare into the water you may know

That nothing disturbs the infinite blue of the sky. (21)

George P. Garrett has said of this poet: "He stands almost alone in the sense of continued growth and change in his poetry."[5] In the years ahead, Warren's readers can logically expect that each lyric, by the keeping of its unique promise, will be a step forward toward its maker's Promised Land.

5. George P. Garrett, "The Recent Poetry of Robert Penn Warren," in John L. Longley, Jr. (ed.), *Robert Penn Warren: A Collection of Critical Essays* (New York: New York University Press, 1965), 223–24.

Psychology and Theme in *Brother to Dragons*

Frederick P. W. McDowell

Warren's novel in verse, *Brother to Dragons*, is most notable in its philosophy and psychology and summarizes vividly his continuing metaphysical and ethical themes. Aware in his moralist's zeal "that poetry
is more than fantasy and is committed to the obligation of trying to
say something about the human condition," Warren is in this work
more than ever haunted by an anguished sense of the disparity in
man between recurrent beatific vision and the ubiquitous evil which
blights it. Accounting for the force of the book are Warren's realization of character, his flair for the arresting image and apt phrase, his
evocation of situation and atmosphere, and his instinct for the telling
structural contrast. Indispensable as are these aspects of literary talent
to the precise rendition of value through form, they are all subordinate to Warren's tense brooding over human motivation and human
destiny.

Despite his cavils against oversimplified abstract thinking in his
critique of "The Ancient Mariner" and elsewhere, abstract speculation has come to absorb Warren. He has, however, eschewed the dan-
gers he warns against—the abstract, the general, the universal is always related forcibly, even violently, to the concrete, the particular,
the local. Warren achieves a sensible, sometimes drily pragmatic balance, then, between the relative and absolute, the mutable and the
permanent, the fact and the archetype. In *Brother to Dragons*, the combined reflections of the several interested persons, including the author as R. P. W., yield a valid disinterested truth, since its roots are in
their immediate experience. The localizing of his narratives in history
achieves a similar purpose. Viewing dispassionately the dilemmas of

"Psychology and Theme in *Brother to Dragons*" by Frederick P. W. McDowell. From
PMLA, LXX (September, 1955), 565–86. Copyright © 1955 by the Modern Language
Association of America. Reprinted by permission of the Modern Language Association
of America.

individuals in history, Warren has a specific perspective upon which to focus his ranging intelligence. To reach exact definitions of elusive moral and metaphysical values, to reach befitting conclusions as to the provenance of good and evil. Warren also utilizes in *Brother to Dragons* an incident from out of the past, one drawn from the annals of the Jefferson family.

The central figure in this episode is Jefferson's nephew, Lilburn Lewis, who, after his mother's death, butchers his Negro valet, George, when the latter breaks a pitcher once belonging to the mother. Since a maniacal self-love and a maniacal Oedipus complex consume him, Lilburn must at all costs secure vengeance for an imputed spiteful violation of his mother's memory by George and the other household Negroes. The senselessness of Lilburn's crime and the sinister forces it epitomizes all but overwhelm the hapless idealist, Thomas Jefferson, who had not, in his aspiration, fully considered the evil in all men. With his eventual if somewhat reluctant attainment of a more valid knowledge—presupposing right reason, infused by the spirit, or else creative imagination, informed by the sense of fact—he is then able to effect a fruitful reconciliation between aspiration and reality, between the disparities, in general, of his experience. As a result, he achieves wholeness of spirit.

Warren is even more insistent in *Brother to Dragons* than in his other work upon the transforming influence of the true spiritual principle and the nefarious influence of perverted spirituality. Both Lilburn and the early Jefferson illustrate a familiar pattern in Warren's work: the individual's search for spiritual peace by side-stepping his inner difficulties and by subservience to an abstract ideal only indirectly related to them. Unable to find peace within, through his lack of internal resources and through his too easy disregard of the truths to be found in religious tradition, such an individual searches for it too aggressively outside the self—in the empirically derived configurations of his experience or in nature. From these sources, he seeks some kind of absolute which can always command allegiance, but an absolute personally defined and designed to further his own interested motives, whether he will admit to this tacit hypocrisy or not. Such anodyne for inner insecurity is only temporary since too much is expected from it. Unless conversion to a different mode of being has finally occurred, disillusionment and violent rather than meaningful insights into reality result from a quest thus histrionically self-centered and self-sufficiently pursued. The aborted spirituality which may derive from such activity often has dire consequences, since if prideful man alone provides the measure for all values there is nothing to prevent him from going to any length, even to crime, to make his vision prevail. Barring a conversion from such self-righteousness, the typical Warren character is unable—or unwilling—to lose his soul to find it.

In purport *Brother to Dragons* does not depart markedly from Warren's previous work, but its exacerbated tone and persistent undercurrents of violence reveal Warren's increasingly urgent sense that the provenance of original sin is universal and that it is inescapable. The potential acedia of spirit resulting from our possible despair at such a prospect Warren condemns, however, at the same time that he shows how little room there can be for complacent acceptance of human nature as it is. If human nature in itself is seen to be ultimately monstrous, and if we are lost in its labyrinthine fastnesses, there can also transpire, through the accession of Grace, an enlargement of our possibilities beyond those predicated by any superficially optimistic philosophy. The succinct definition of these possibilities and of the positive values that man, in his fallen condition, may yet embrace is Warren's most distinctive achievement in *Brother to Dragons*.

* I *

A psychology which distorts the facts of experience by assimilating them into a self-generated obsession betrays Lilburn Lewis. Consumed by Oedipal attraction, he idealizes Lucy Lewis and makes of mother-love a worshipful abstraction, to be put forward regardless of the consequences. This intense, abstract benevolence ultimately leads to crime, enforcing Warren's judgment that this is a tragedy of "our sad virtues." In Lilburn we see the most frightening aspect of our moral history, that all too often "evil's done for good, and in good's name" and that a single-faceted idealism can be tragic. Lilburn has made no compact with the devil, Warren says—he has not had to go that far afield. He has only had to follow the good impulse, love of his mother, to be corrupted. If, after his mother's death, Lilburn had been humble in his sufferings, he might have escaped the degradation which ensues when he insists that all others revere his mother's memory as he does. When the household Negroes, in particular, seem to forget Lucy Lewis, Lilburn's fury works at odds with the affection that prompts it. He finds to his horror that love diminishes to the degree that he asserts it strenuously and desires to preserve it intact. In its place, injured pride and fear lest the organizing principle of his life be destroyed now fanatically motivate him. Like the Ancient Mariner in Warren's interpretation, Lilburn is the victim of self-deception as to his own motives, judging the morality of an act in terms of its advantage to him while pretending to be dispassionate. The good impulse, conceived in self-interest apart from Christian restraints, can become through its induced intensity more uncontrollable than calculated evil and eventually more destructive. When self-knowledge or "definition" eludes Lilburn, he adheres to his mistaken idea of the good and does the worst. Following a reductive principle, Lilburn tries, with fearful results, to define the human, to give order, violently, to chaotic flux. In such wrenching of the spirit to preconceived ends, all hint of humility evaporates. Such eager defense of his self-locked love for his mother from contamination in the outside world blinds Lilburn to his mother's greatness of soul and causes him more and more to fix upon the letter of his affection for her.

To implement this ruling devotion to his mother's memory, Lilburn develops a passion for the pure act motivated by the pure idea and untouched by embarrassing reality. Afraid that the facts might rout his cherished ideal, he raises it above them to an absolute and assures himself that its importance justifies his realization of it beyond the limits of the ethically permissible. "The dear redemption of simplicity" in such abstracted activity becomes his solace despite its untruth and the anguish it fosters. To others, the gratuitous act inspired by unreasoned fervor is forcible but not ethically justifiable. When they then react sharply against it, Lilburn is only the more confirmed in his self-righteous vision.

Lilburn's desire for others to meet his impossible standards prevents, first of all, a normal sexual relationship with Laetitia. Something she describes as "awful" transpires in their relationship shortly after their marriage. Though we are not told definitely what has happened, some sort of sexual violence has undoubtedly occurred. Lilburn seems to force the apparently inexperienced Laetitia against her will and then holds this fact against her, particularly after he compels her the next night to tell what she thinks has happened. Irrationally, he resents the fact that she is spoiled at his own hands and would not remain "pure" despite her helplessness before his violence. His "angelic" Laetitia is an ordinary mortal after all; she has, he is sure, liked stepping in "dung." Shock from her violent experience deepens in Laetitia to frigidity, so that, after the mockery of their marriage, she cannot respond to the husband whose contempt for her increases nor help him when he most needs her.

Because obsessive love for his mother excludes the possibility of other emotional commitments, Lilburn uproots the love that might have steadied him after her death. After he spurns Laetitia, he becomes yet more tortured, more unfeeling, more inhumane. He beats his servant George, whom Lucy sent out to bring him home following a three-day drunk when Laetitia had disappointed him. Having resisted the affection of Laetitia and George before Lucy's death, he is led, in his overwrought fixation upon his mother, to repudiate, after her death, both Aunt Cat and his hound. Since these two love him most unquestioningly, he derives sadistic pleasure from senselessly repulsing them. Poetic justice is served when they betray him after his crime—though such betrayal is paradoxically also Lilburn's "deepest will"—the dog unwittingly, Aunt Cat by clever design. By killing love, Lilburn attains "the desiderated and ice-locked anguish of isolation" which then frightens him, a security breeding insecurity. He asks love, yet he cannot bear to be loved, since it magnifies his guilt; he must then destroy what disturbs him. Symbolic of his confusion and incipient degradation is Lilburn's hatred at his mother's grave for the encroaching grass which destroys her memory among men. In view of the raw, cold, cruel, pure fact of his love, he wishes her grave to remain bare and open as a fresh wound to be a perpetual reminder to him of his loss.

In order to break through to a reality whose force, however, diminishes in proportion to his frantic efforts to reach it, Lilburn is led, Macbeth-like, from one crime against man and nature to others still more harrowing. Now that any other love except that for his mother seems desecration to him, he instinctively kicks the hound which comes fawning to him at the grave. The resulting rapture of conflicting joy and sorrow brings catharsis in cruelty for his festering grief. When he kicks the hound for the second time, Lilburn is not surprised but soothed. Distraught by his mother's image, he feels no joy "of the soul's restoration" in reconciliation with the hound. Terror and violence besiege the homestead, while the Negro victims counter with supernal cunning. He rages inwardly and broods upon insatiate revenge, trusting that inward force will vindicate the self by vindicating what the self most reveres.

At no time does Lilburn question the rightness of his acts, since their absolute rationale forbids any vacillation. The only necessity he now feels is to remain true to the light within, to a self-appointed destiny. Defining thus expeditiously his own necessity, Lilburn resembles Warren's other uncritically self-confident characters like Slim Sarrett in *At Heaven's Gate*, Willie Stark and Adam Stanton in *All the King's Men*, and Jeremiah Beaumont in *World Enough and Time*. Like them, once Lilburn tastes the spiritual security inherent in a self-generated absolute principle, he has no power to remain aloof from its demands. To compensate for deficient inner resources, which had earlier made him discontented with the frontier, he now enshrines at all costs the ideal which orders his life. In contrast with his previous states of incertitude, Lilburn is now perfectly adjusted, if occasionally still unsure of himself. As he waits for the "thrilling absoluteness / Of the pure act to come," Lilburn is unaware of the price he has paid for this assurance, the snuffing out of intervening benevolent instincts. Forcible and self-willed, he abrogates the intelligence and attains to a ruminative peace like that which any monster might feel, sunk deep in nature, such peace as Warren depicts in his poem "Crime" as "past despair and past the uncouth / Violation." Linked to Lilburn's suprahuman surety is the motionless, insensate catfish with its brute face and complacent adaptation to the channel-mud as it hibernates under the Mississippi ice. In his complete harmony with amoral nature, of Lilburn as well as of the catfish it might be said, "How can there be / Sensation where there is perfect adjustment?" The result is that Lilburn is unconscious of the barbarity of his crime, since his own nature justifies it.

His crime moves him one step nearer a more perfect realization of self as he has been able, delusively, to define it. The fact that he has now completely left the world of actuality behind him is implied in his inability to kill a huge moth which comes in the window and which distracts him only momentarily from concentrating upon his vision of his self-imagined destiny. With the help of Isham after the crime, he awaits then, in his half-joyful abandonment to the currents of the self, the grand hour when he can still more completely fulfill his nature, "the hour of the Pentecostal intuition." In his impatience, he moves to bring this time about more quickly when he gets Isham to agree to a

mutual death pact. Because Lilburn savors the full pleasure of this abstracted moment—the grandest of moments because the farthest removed from the distracting realities of life—and because he wishes to
enjoy to the full his "sweet alienation" and the sense of injustice done
him previously, he counts slowly while Isham stands before him with
a pistol. He then betrays Isham by himself not firing, since he knows
that the law will take care of Isham. Monomania induces the "death
of the heart," despite the fact that a heart too sensitive to confront the
reality had induced the monomania.

* **II** *

At a more intellectual level, Thomas Jefferson in Warren's view is also
initially motivated by the oversimplified abstraction. His ruling passion is the idealistic destiny he foresees for man, for he grasps the fact
that man in his median position between God and beast aspires to the
God-like. He is too anxious, however, to believe this aspiration exists
pure, and he discounts too readily and vehemently the beast-like
within man, as he himself admits later. Subscribing to this self-defined
"rational hope" and leaping beyond man's "natural bourne and con-
stitution" to envisage his glorious future, Jefferson denies, until too
late, the discomfiting reality. At first, he looks upon the evil in man as
a blot upon his shining nature, which the centuries have all but erased.
With its clean lines and simple harmonies, the Romanesque cathedral
at Nîmes is a symbol of ideal human fulfillment and of Jefferson's noble vision. If man would but strike off his shackles, his divine innocence would then "dance" amid the oppressive realities of the world
which tend to stifle it. Because one must struggle with some of the
realities of the world to attain to inner integrity, one cannot, as Jefferson tends to do, deny them all. "The eternal / Light of just proportion
and the heart's harmony," which Jefferson so insatiably hungers for,
is, accordingly, ironically extinguished in his fanatical craving to achieve
it. As Warren presents him, Jefferson is, in his early phase, as fervent
in his idealism and as insensitive to pragmatic realities as Jeremiah
Beaumont in *World Enough and Time*. As a result, Jefferson cannot see
that he desires too unmixed a good, impossible under the imperfect
conditions of this world, just as Jeremiah Beaumont cannot see that if
his antagonist, Cassius Fort, once did evil he might yet be, on the
whole, a good man. Neither character realizes until he has been inex-

orably reoriented by tragedy that beatitude for man—a partial realization at best of all that he aspires to—is possible only through humble contrition and dispassionate love. Such a transcendence of reality must be earned through suffering, through divine Grace, instead of merely being asserted by the intellect as a cherished aim.

Warren shows how close Jefferson's psychology is to Lilburn's, despite their different purposes in life. Both seek to define the human through the self-determined abstraction, and both wish to assert an innocence consonant with it. Both lack in large part a sense for tangible realities, and both become enslaved to an overpowering vision. Both are romantic in that they tend to transform by wishful thinking things as they are into what they are not. As with so many of Warren's misguided characters, they both wish a too easily attained coherent explanation for an essentially incoherent world. Hate, the result of a naïve emotionalism in Lilburn's case, and nobility, the result of a misguided intellectuality in Jefferson's, are, as Warren explains, but different "thrust[s] toward Timelessness, in Time." The only valid motivation, Warren implies, is just the opposite: with one's intuited sense of the eternal, one must work toward time, the actual, the objective, and bring one's sense of the ideal always back to the reality. Life without saving illusion is a mockery, but a life given over to furthering at all costs the self-righteous illusion can be calamitous. Neither Jefferson of the early hopeful stage nor Lilburn could realize that the "impalpable" is not the ideal and that the ideal, in becoming too nebulous and disembodied, is in danger of being distorted.

The difference between Jefferson and Lilburn is in sensitivity, the contrast Warren had made memorable in *World Enough and Time* between Jeremiah Beaumont and Skrogg. Despite the fact that he meets a violent death, Jeremiah could ultimately be saved in a spiritual sense after a wasted life because he has spiritual receptivity, whereas Skrogg had deliberately snuffed out his soul. This kind of sensitivity also underlies the bluff exterior of Jack Burden in *All the King's Men* and allows him finally to decide between the conflicting claims of the illusion and the reality, of the self and the world of other men. The education of a misguided protagonist to the truth is thus a constant theme in Warren. In *Brother to Dragons* both Lucy Lewis and Jefferson are educated by tragedy, Jefferson the more slowly because his mistaken vision is so inflexible. Jefferson's conversion from a restrictive idealism to a more integral view of life is the chief situation explored in this verse-novel. It is significant that Lucy Lewis, reborn through her death—the result of her inability to cope with reality—redeems Jefferson by making him aware of realities outside those apparent to the intellect when it perceives only what it is interested in perceiving. For most of the verse novel, Jefferson is in the first period of his redemption—when he has become disillusioned with his earlier ideals and has come to realize the universality of evil in men. Only at its end, through Lucy's intervention, does he reach a decisive spiritual poise and the second period of his redemption—when he can acknowledge original sin without recrimination.

In the first stage, Jefferson is haunted by the fact that human nature too often turns its back upon the glories of which it is capable to revel instead in the evil act. Like Lilburn, Jefferson lacks to a large degree the spiritual reserves, the stabilizing philosophy he needs to combat the evil which destroys his perfectibilist vision. Heartfelt joy in his vision leads to Jefferson's sense of betrayal,then,when one of his own blood, through the absolutely evil act, extinguishes it. Trying to order reality according to his own ideals, Jefferson continually fails to grasp the circumstances under which it may be ordered. Like Jeremiah Beaumont or Adam Stanton, Jefferson at this point both overemphasizes and underplays the intellect: he worships an intellectualized abstraction while disregarding the critical function of reason except as it reinforces his interested idealism. Jefferson becomes bewildered, disillusioned, almost cynical in outlook. In this phase, this induced pessimism is so powerful as to becloud his earlier humanism. In a world where evil is apparently supreme and obliterates by greater force the serene good, Jefferson even comes to feel that violence alone gives truth. He now assumes that "all values are abrogated in blankness," and he reproves his sister for not having struck George after he had returned from Lilburn's beating. At this stage, Jefferson does not understand how close this counsel is to that suggested to Lilburn by his own unleashed nature before the crime. From Lilburn's brand of violence Jefferson had, indeed, recoiled in loathing. The fact that redemption often derives from violence through the polar connection existing between a strongly negative evil and a strongly positive good does not justify this counsel of Jefferson's to Lucy, although he is right in feeling that the violence he recommends is preferable to the inertia of Charles Lewis, for example. Jefferson does not perceive, moreover, that Lucy's inability at this point to conquer pride and assert the love which inwardly prompts her is her real sin and the ultimate cause for her son's tragedy.

In his first stage of regeneration, Jefferson cannot see past the fact of human evil, which has paralyzed his soul. In his obsession with its prevalence, he is as unreasoning in his denial of aspiration as he had been devoted to it previously. At a time of crisis, the inflexible philosophy of life, whether it stresses demonic pride in Lilburn or angelic aspiration in Jefferson, fails to comprehend the complexities of experience. In recoil from the reality he misunderstood, Jefferson now condemns love as "but a mask to hide the brute face of fact, / And that face is the immitigable ferocity of self." Unrealistic also is his present despair over humanity itself: "I'd said there's no defense of the human definition." This agonized pessimism is actually as intense and as uncritical as the optimism of his unregenerate days had been.

Since he has had to relinquish the perfectionist enthusiasm which motivated him at the First Continental Congress, Jefferson now recognizes "the darkness of the self" and its labyrinthine wilderness. At the height of his dreams, he had been realist enough to acknowledge the fact of evil, but he had tried to minimize it. He knew from his reading of history, for instance, that there lurked horror in its "farther room" and that the act and the motive are not always ballasted by the good deed and the good intention respectively. He also had known that all men are not innocent despite his belief in Innocence as an ideal. His disillusion, however, makes him perceptive where he had been merely suspicious. Correctly but reluctantly gauging evil, even if unnerved by it to an unreasoned denial of the good, he now sees that it can be passive, since all things come to it and seek it out in magnetic attraction. He sees the lurking beast within us all, a minotaur to be found at the last turn of the spirit's labyrinth. This beast, "our brother, our darling brother," is not, in Warren's view, to be denied by any mere effort of the will; his insidious promptings can be finally overcome only by effort of the will if one can force himself to make it. Like Pasiphaë with her unnatural lust, we can become enamored of our evil. This Jefferson now sees. At the height of indulgence, we catch, like her, in the same sneaking way, a glimpse of our beatific innocence in childhood, and thereby rationalize our evil acts. Except for the reductive premises in each case, Jefferson's initial vision of man's preternatural innocence was the obverse of Pasiphaë's. She was evil but rationalized her evil by the fleeting vision of the innocent good, while

Jefferson thought of man as innocent only to find him besmirched with evil. Thus the lie was given to Jefferson's earlier "towering definition, angelic, arrogant, abstract, / Greaved in glory, thewed with light." That earth's monsters are innocent in their lack of knowledge Jefferson had always realized; but that man, capable of knowledge and self-definition, could be a "master-monster" and exhibit only a black, ignorant innocence Jefferson had not realized. Neither had his nephew, Meriwether Lewis, comprehended "the tracklessness of the human heart" until the facts of experience forced him to do so.

Now that his original conception of man has been proved wrong, Jefferson would have stressed the truth about man at all costs, he asserts, had he known then what he knows now: he would have run with "the hot coals" of that truth till they had burned through his flesh to the bone. That evil is progressive, that one deed of horror can poison all else, is Jefferson's sickening conclusion. When he still tries to cling tenaciously to "the general human fulfillment," he finds that violent evil obtrudes in his thoughts and proliferates emotionally. In his near-hysteria, therefore, Jefferson looks upon Lilburn's deed as the reigning archetype of human psychology, as the microcosm of the evil which infects all hope and which lies like a cloud and curse over the land he had once loved. To Jefferson, all social injustice and all crime are, in fact, somehow inherent in the fall of the meat-axe, in the fact that his nephew could commit his crime and that other people might commit similar crimes. That one must not only shudder at evil but try actively to understand it Jefferson doesn't realize until later, nor the fact that suffering, in some degree, atones for it. He is impatient at its persistence, failing to see that it can be only partly overcome and that one must not shirk the struggle to master it.

The second stage of Jefferson's education provides the poem with its central meaning. Under the guidance of Lucy Lewis, Jefferson accommodates his original resplendent vision of man's nobility to the actual facts of human existence, especially to the cardinal fact of original sin, and mitigates the harsh abstractness of this ideal with the exertion of his sensibility. A grander nobility than Jefferson's initial conception consists, Lucy claims, in testing that conception in the world. His redemption is assured when his faith in the Idea is renewed, once a "deep distress" has humanized it and once he relates it to mankind. The dream—or idea—of the future, Jefferson concludes, requires for complement the fact of the past:

> Now I should hope to find the courage to say
> That the dream of the future is not
> Better than the fact of the past, no matter how terrible.
> For without the fact of the past we cannot dream the future.

Since lack of self-knowledge is original sin in either Lilburn or Jefferson, and since complete self-knowledge is impossible, original sin is universal, and we are all implicated in it and with each other. As a gesture indicating he now understands that he and all men are involved in Lilburn's crime, Lucy insists that Jefferson take his hand. Evasion will no longer do, for Jefferson can't escape our universal complicity in sin, "our common crime," as Warren phrases it in "End of Summer." As commentator on the action, "R. P. W." stresses throughout our complicity in the tragedy. It contains us, he says, and it "is contained by us," for we in our fallen condition are all guilty of it in being human. We are guilty, furthermore, in being too complacent about evil, since we are only too anxious to adjust ourselves comfortably and snugly to it. As to the crime which so unnerves Jefferson, R. P. W. explains that it is not so special as he thinks. It is but one episode in the long pageant of man's sinfulness down the ages and is "impressive chiefly for its senselessness" as all evil acts tend to be. The earthquake which followed the crime struck fear into the hearts of guilty men who had had no knowledge of Lilburn's act—they were simply guilty of it by extension, by being human, and by being capable in their worst moments of kindred atrocity. Guilt is common enough, therefore, to make any one day appropriate for the Judgment, even as this present hour would be. R. P. W. expresses, however, the ironical fear that the modern age might be too "advanced" to pray for deliverance from its guilt or to fear God's wrath, just as men in 1811 had got used both to the repeated quakes and to the "horror" of being men. In any event, Jefferson's complicity in original sin through his use of black labor to build that citadel of freedom, Monticello, is real, if at first unacknowledged by him. The fact that evil exists should not attract us nor repel us, but should interest us since we all are, for better or worse, involved in it. When the evil is done is the question R. P. W. would explore, for all who face up bravely to life must solve that question, must analyze the anguish and the agony involved in bringing the evil act to its full birth. Unless we have that curiosity, we can never attain to saving knowledge, R. P. W. would insist.

In a noble speech Lucy tells Jefferson that she in her love brought disaster to her son, just as he in his aspiration brought disaster to Meriwether Lewis. "Our best gifts," she says, carry some ineradicable taint, and we corrupt even as we freely give—Jefferson like Lilburn has done evil in the name of good by interfusing his altruism with pride of self. This burden of our shame should always confront us, and while it should not inhibit us, it should make us bestow our gifts with humility. Lilburn's face, Jefferson must realize, is but a "mirror of your possibilities." To the criminal we are linked by the terror we all must feel at our own demonic propensities which, without our careful scrutiny, will project outward into the evil act: Lilburn's last indefensible hour is simply "the sum of all the defensible hours / We have lived through." Jefferson has squelched his fear that he, too, might be capable of all evil in being capable of any evil. As R. P. W. expresses it, Jefferson had forgotten that even the wicked man seeks God according to his own lights and fulfillment as he can find it. Along with his disillusion and his cynicism, Jefferson is forced to see that his rejection of Lilburn is too summary. Now that his confidence in himself and in his Utopian dreams has been shaken through Lilburn's crime, Jefferson rejects his nephew principally out of pique. There is some truth, then, to Meriwether's charge that Jefferson had originally contrived his "noble lie" for his own comfort and to feed his own vanity. Jefferson has a sure sense for the horror of Lilburn's crime, but hardly sees, in his revulsion, its application to himself.

> For Lilburn is an absolute of our essential
> Condition, and as such, would ingurgitate
> All, and all you'd give, all hope, all heart,
> Would only be disbursed down that rat hole of
>   the ultimate horror.

In commenting upon the action and characters, R. P. W. insists that evil—at least its germ—is universal. Modern Smithland, a village near the site of decayed Rocky Hill, is to Warren a symbol for universal sin and universal suffering, by virtue of the sin and suffering it does contain. The minotaur-in-labyrinth image, so forcibly presented by Jefferson early in the poem, also becomes a symbol which dominates the poem in vividly suggesting the lurking evil in the dark heart of man. In greater or less degree, all the characters in the poem sin, and they all suffer because they cannot transcend their failings and emerge completely from the darkness of their inner selves. None of them are as wholly innocent and glorious as Jefferson had initially imagined the men at the First Continental Congress to be; rather they all resemble his colleagues as Jefferson describes them in a revised estimate:

> lost
> Each man lost in some blind lobby, hall, enclave,
> Crank cul-de-sac, couloir, or corridor of Time.
> Of Time. Or self: and in that dark no thread . . . .

Lucy Lewis, radiant as she is, is prevented by pride from making toward George in his suffering the spontaneous gesture which would alleviate it and result in her own fulfillment: "the small / Obligation fulfilled had swayed the weight of the world." Similarly, Laetitia is prevented from making toward Lilburn at Lucy's death the gesture which would gain his love forever through her willingness to forgive his past violence to her. Actually, Laetitia had in part willed Lilburn's violation of her, and in one sense, therefore, merits the scorn of her husband for imputed impurity—at least she could not, and hardly wanted to, tell Lilburn to stop. Betrayed by her innocence into a fascination with the evil she shrinks from, Laetitia in her psychology at the time of her defilement by Lilburn is not unlike Pasiphaë, as Warren describes her, at the time of her submission to the plunging bull.

Our common complicity in evil Warren elaborates upon still further in his analysis of Laetitia's brother, of Isham, of Aunt Cat, and of George. Laetitia's brother is indignant when he learns that Lilburn had forcibly used Laetitia, and he proclaims loudly how sweeping would have been his revenge if he had known. Laetitia acutely says that he would not have avenged her out of love, but out of pride at accomplishing the deed—at best, out of desire to protect the family honor. Aunt Cat, Lilburn's colored mammy, really loves him, but in her love there is calculation too, manifested for years in the silent but tense struggle between her and Lucy Lewis for Lilburn's affection. To a degree she also merits what she gets when Lilburn, in a fit of fury at the time of his mother's death, pretends to disgorge the black milk he had been nursed upon. Isham, too, is as guilty of George's butchering as his brother, for Isham knew instinctively what was going to happen and did nothing to prevent it. In that he seemed half-willing to meet his fate, George was, in some part, an accomplice in the deed.

He almost wills, with obscene pleasure, the fatal stroke, and seems more in love with the "sweet injustice to himself" than fearful of death. Even though he keeps running away, George is also drawn back hypnotically again and again to Lilburn in a continuing attraction-repulsion pattern. R. P. W. admits this notion of George's complicity is, in some degree, fantastical, since nothing can really excuse Lilburn's crime. But R. P. W.'s observations are true, he would assert, to the extent that "we're all each other's victim. / Potentially, at least."

*   III   *

Jefferson has failed to see, in short, that positive good presupposes positive evil, that the two are closely related, and that Lilburn's motivation is really the need, as R. P. W. maintains, "to name his evil good." That moral and psychological values are complex Jefferson is unwilling to admit, because of his zeal to preserve the integrity of his vision. That ambiguity is the indispensable feature of the moral life, that philosophical truth is to be measured in terms of an adjustment of the discordancies of experience, that illusion must be squared with a multiform actuality has somehow escaped Jefferson, as it had also escaped the unintellectual Lilburn. In describing the crime, R. P. W. had addressed the night as a symbol of the absoluteness of vision that Lilburn—and Jefferson—aspired toward. The night would obliterate in its uniform blackness "the impudent daylight's velleities," that is, the concrete actualities of our experience. Once they are obscured, it is tempting to define the Absolute by an interested exertion of the will alone rather than by the vigorous reconciliation of the Many to the One. The mixture of good and evil in humanity is something that Jefferson had realized in his intellect, but he had not given the concept his emotional assent. Jefferson's psychology is essentially too simple—in his disillusion he rejects, for instance, the innocence of the newborn babe because of the evil that human nature can also perpetrate. He then denies the generous act because it can never exist pure, because it is always tainted inescapably by the self. The omnipresence of malignant evil disturbs his inner poise to the extent that he all but denies the worth of the ideals he had once cherished. Though love, for example, has an admixture of pride in it and is scarcely ever disinterested, Jefferson fails to see, notwithstanding, that it is truly estimable. The all-or-none point of view is thus pernicious in overlooking the truth that every act and emotion carries within it not only its own impulsions but its contrary possibility. A fervently accepted good, therefore, has more possible evil in it than a lukewarm virtue, while an unabashed evil carries within it latent violences that augur the possibility of heartfelt conversion.

Every act, moreover, implies a choice among motives for it to become the act, implies a resolving of "the essential polarity of possibility" contained within it. The act has a finality "in the mere fact of achieved definition," therefore, a degree of purity and simplification at variance with its confused intent. Even though such choice among motives is made and a large degree of purity is thereby attained, the act still carries within its secret core other latent impulsions. If it represents a simplification of our swarming experience, the origins of the act are never clear-cut, but rather a "hell-broth of paradox and internecine / Complex of motive." It must, accordingly, be exhaustively analyzed, not merely accepted at its apparent value for the relief it brings the doer. Lilburn's evil deed, for instance, must be judged not only for its destructiveness but also as misguided creation. The wicked man, says R. P. W., is, after all, but seeking for his crimes some outward rationale which the man would term God.

The paradoxical substratum underlying all our acts is variously emphasized in the poem. One aspect of the tangled nature of reality is suggested by Charles Lewis—though Warren shows more contempt for him than for anyone else—the fact that madness is "the cancer of truth" and has more affinity with the actuality than has a deadened complacency. For this same reason, Warren values violence more highly than timid conformity to convention. Even Jefferson realizes this truth when in his disillusion he says that "all truth is bought with blood," except that he then is too much obsessed with the blood to realize that violence is only one avenue to renewal. At the very least, violence will exorcize unreality, will expose the fraudulence of "the pious mind" to whom "our history's nothing if not refined." Only when violence is pursued with self-interest, as with Lilburn, does it become the supreme evil. Since reality is thus elusive and multiple, R. P. W. maintains that a balance of qualities, educed by the supple intelligence, is the essential of wisdom. Grace, pity, and charity we all need from God, but that does not mean that free-will can be set aside. The glorious possibility acknowledges the despair which hems it round, and derives its strength from that honesty. But it does not give in to this pessimism. The complexity of existence is again emphasized when R. P. W. asserts that it is through isolation that we grasp "the human bond" and at length define the self—in "separateness," Warren has declared in his poem "Revelation," "does love learn definition"—while at our peril we reject our fellow man completely. If we withdraw from society to gain a greater inner irradiation, we must, thus fortified, return to it and seek our place in it. Failure to see that a personally determined moral code has weight only when it comprehends the self in relation to other men was, after all, Jefferson's original mistake as it had also been Lilburn's.

Of the many ambiguities explored in the poem, the most striking concerns the natural world. On the one hand, Warren stresses the malignancy and impersonality of nature. The fact that the white inhabitants have unfairly wrested the land from the Indians places a curse upon it, so that moral unhealth hangs like miasma over the wilderness, and its shadows enter the souls of the pioneers. Both sons of Lucy Lewis come under its dark spell; both have become victims of "the ignorant torpor / That breathed from the dark land." After his crime, moreover, Lilburn feels only at home in "the unredeemed dark of the wild land." Raised on the edge of the wilderness, Jefferson had also come to feel over and through him "the shadow of the forest," sinister and foreboding. Even then, he had felt that man must redeem nature, for nature is too harsh and unfeeling for it to serve as moral ministrant to erring, aspiring man. As she did in 1811, nature will likely as not visit mankind with earthquakes, floods, and sickness to add to his discomfort and perplexity. As measure of her hostility to living creatures, she causes the dog-fox to drown in protracted agony in a flood, or she causes the oak tree, like Jacob, to struggle all night in anguish with "the incessant / And pitiless angel of air." In a perfect adjustment to nature, there is either overplus of misdirected feeling or inability to feel at all. In its "idiot-ignorance" nature obliterates the purely human and the moral law which alone can educe the human. Feeling strongly this need for other than naturalistic values in their undiluted form, Warren asserted in his poem "Monologue at Midnight" that "Our mathematic yet has use / For the integers of blessedness." The grandeur of nature, Warren maintains in the concluding lines of the verse-novel, can give us an "image" only for our destiny, but can in no sense give us a "confirmation" of it. That must be sought from within the soul itself.

If nature "as an image of lethal purity" is a symbol of evil, it is also a symbol of reality and truth; it is both malignant and beautiful, soul-benumbing and life-inspiriting, giving rise to heartfelt joy despite the infinite darkness at its heart, as Warren also tells us in "Picnic Remembered." The beauty of the springtide upon the untracked forest, its "heart-breaking new delicacy of green," is an emblem of such ambiguity. If we follow the promptings of nature too closely, we can lose our humanity; but, paradoxically, it can also assuage our sufferings deriving from the evils which follow the loss in others of that humanity. By making such men contemptible and insignificant in comparison with its power, it can comfort us for the violence and cruelty they may instigate. It can bedwarf even the monstrous and endow us with the vital energy that can alone enable us to transcend the "human trauma." Lilburn is as if driven onward by the raging wind, as if in the whirlwind of senseless force. Yet if he is so closely part of nature, it is only by escaping from him out into "the glimmering night scene" that we can regain proportion and sanity. After his crime Lilburn, so much a part of nature in his unrestrained violence, can no longer respond to its spiritual influence. He inhabits then a somber inner landscape "of forms fixed and hieratic," and abjures the promiscuous promise of joy in newly wakening nature.

Nature is in essence spiritual and a source for deep reality provided its power is used to strengthen the innately spiritual and not substituted for it. Warren can say, therefore, that in spite of "all naturalistic considerations" or because of them, we must believe in virtue—nature can both extinguish the human impulse and reinforce it. We ought not to regard nature abstractly by naming its objects out of their context, for they are more than mere names: they are symbols of inner spiritual facts, so that a snake is really a symbol of evil, violence, darkness, and terror, though science would call it only "Elaphe obsoleta obsoleta." Such a rationalist approach to nature impoverishes it, yet Warren's earlier emotional fervor for it, as recounted in the poem, is also unreal. The joy he had felt as a boy in holding tight the objects of the sense provides an easy faith that cannot last. Neither an easy nor an exclusive faith in nature is tenable, yet Warren does quote Lucretius to the effect that the order underlying nature, the ranging of natural phenomena under natural law, may dispel the "darkness of the mind" and lead to inner light. A true knowledge of nature, fortified by our sense of the human, can dispel our morbid fears and the darkness and terror that haunt the innermost soul of man, while an unconditioned emotional response to its promptings can intensify those fears and that darkness and terror. Man is at once part of nature and above it, and should, in his adjustments to it, be mindful of this paradox. A security or joy obtained, like Jefferson's, by a denial of inconvenient natural fact is as reprehensible as Lilburn's blind immersion in nature.

* **IV** *

More than any of his other poems, *Brother to Dragons* represents a mature if sometimes muted statement of Warren's own values. From his narrative Warren elicits certain conclusions about human life which he is always careful to clothe, however, in the specific symbol or to educe from the concrete situation. While for Warren the absolutes of tradition have an independent existence, he avoids sentimentality and provides for their inevitable definition by allowing them to emerge from a specific milieu.

Chief among these positive values is glory, which alone makes life worthwhile, fearful as the experience of it may become. It is a dynamic spiritual harmony, the exaltation attendant upon salvation, the sense of being attuned to both the natural and the supernatural. Failing to cultivate such a mystique as it illuminates his experiences, man fails to live as deeply as he could, Warren asserts. Despite this truth, it is with reluctance that we face the necessity of being saved, of surrendering ourselves to the radiance of glory and permitting it to determine the quality of our lives. As the chief reality in our lives to be reverenced, glory will, once its provenance is admitted, reorient us positively: "for it knocks society's values to a cocked hat." Glory is what the soul is best capable of, contrasting with the abstract idealism which becomes hardened to formula and withers rather than elicits the potentialities of the soul. If we are identified with all other men in guilt, we are also identified with them in their troubled aspirations after glory.

To know the farthest reaches of the spirit demands an emotional sensitivity toward others, a realization that it is fatal only to love and to love well, and not to love well enough. In these terms Lucy Lewis describes her own failure with respect to the family tragedy. Unable because of fear to extend her hand to George in kindness and love, she soon collapses physically and morally. Her death retributively follows her inability to live the life her instincts countenance. Because she fails in love toward George, she fails in love toward her son. She learns that love is the most valuable human trait and represents "definition"; once expressed it can never again be denied, unless one would die spiritually, the same point that Warren had made in his poem "Love's Parable." As we have seen, Laetitia does not love Lilburn enough, either, to minister to him at the time of Lucy's death. She is right in feeling that a change of heart in herself would have availed her husband; in her pride, however, she is unregenerate and cannot attain to selfless love. Lilburn is in a sense betrayed by the women who love him—Lucy, Laetitia, and Aunt Cat—because they do not love him strongly enough to stand by him when he needs them most and to instruct him in "the mystery of the heart." In the modern age, we also deny ourselves too often to others. As we speed down the highway, we can too easily forget, for instance, the loveless eye, which glares at us from a hovel and reminds us of our inhumanity; we merely press the accelerator "and quick you're gone / Beyond forgiveness, pity, hope, hate, love."

Closely allied to Warren's reverence for both love and glory is that for virtue and its concomitant, humility. There is no possibility of our not believing in virtue, for our conscience is always with us and will not be silenced, Warren asserts. Virtue is tougher and more "remorseless" than any of our other attributes, for it isolates the human amongst the other forms of life. Virtue, if disregarded, will lie in wait murderously, like "the lethal mantis at his prayer," to pounce upon the heart that denies it. It is also the necessary rationale for all human anguish. Without anguish, virtue could not be so clearly delimited as to command our absolute allegiance: anguish gives to virtue its local habitation so that it does not become intolerably abstracted from reality:

> I think I begin to see the forging of the future.
> It will be forged beneath the hammer of truth
> On the anvil of our anguish. We shall be forged
> Beneath the hammer of truth on the anvil of anguish.
> It would be terrible to think that truth is lost.
> It would be worse to think that anguish is lost, ever.

Virtue purifies from pride and induces in the more sensitive characters of the poem needed humility, a sacramental vision of the uni-

verse such as the regenerate Ancient Mariner also embraces in Warren's interpretation of the poem. Through thus dying to the self, real
selfhood alone will be achieved, says Warren in his own poem. As to
Jefferson, he remains cynical until Lucy can prevail upon him to cease
dwelling upon the outrage of Lilburn's crime and to accept him. When
he finally acknowledges Lilburn, the pride inseparable from the judging of another by one's own standards disappears. Jefferson then attains the humility needed for the inner balance his near-hysteria had
heretofore destroyed. The other chief characters, Laetitia, Lucy, and
Aunt Cat, are, as we have seen, all prevented by varying kinds of
pride from being true to their instinctive sympathies. Only when they
accept in humility rather than reject in pride are they serene. The
forms of pride, Warren argues, are many and treacherous. Even the
act of forgiveness stems in large part from injured self-esteem, and
allows us to placate the wounded self. Heroism, declares the knowl-
edgeful Jefferson, this time speaking for Warren, is more often motivated by pride in putting down the monster than by any altruism.
The usual hero is potentially more evil than the monsters he van-
quishes, because vainglory encourages him to reject normal human
limitations in an aggrandizement of self: "man puts down the bad and
then feels good," says Warren. The black snake that R. P. W. sees outside at Rocky Hill is not only the traditional symbol for the evil and
violence that have brooded there, but it is conversely a symbol of the
fact that by humility and love we gain wisdom to oppose the influence of furtive evil. Like man at his ideal moral and spiritual fulfillment, the snake both forgives and asks forgiveness.

An activist cluster of values also informs the poem. As members
of the human race, Warren insists, we must be morally responsible—
our connections with other men are so subtle and so pervasive that
we deny them at our peril. Because we are all in some degree the victims of history and of our environment, we have no right, Warren al-
leges, to disavow responsibility:

> For if responsibility is not
> The thing given but the thing to be achieved,
> There is still no way out of the responsibility
> Of trying to achieve responsibility
> So like it or lump it, you are stuck.

Jefferson's rejection of Lilburn is simply his rejection of what is un-
pleasant, says Lucy, Warren's mouthpiece. In his presentation of Charles

Lewis, Warren even more directly inculcates the need to assume gratefully and without evasion our responsibilities. Lewis had fled his moral obligations in Virginia in the hope of finding peace in a new land; but since he brought his inner weakness and hollowness with him, he is, if anything, more at loose ends on the frontier than he had been in Virginia. By his repudiation of family responsibility, his descendants are left, without light, to degenerate on the frontier.

Coming to Kentucky to seek reality, to become once more "part of human effort and man's hope," Charles does not find it because his soul is shrivelled. After Lucy's death, Charles in fact sometimes thinks he is empty so that he is surprised to find his footprint in the earth. At the time he feels relief, as well as sorrow, that he need no longer seek reality. It demands too much uncomfortable effort now that the one person to whom he was in any way real has gone. He hopes that her remains will rot quickly "into the absolute oblivion" and that she may soon be the nothingness he has already become. He goes back to Virginia to fulfill a barren, hollow destiny amid the artifices of civilization where the reality—as well as the stark evil—of the dark land will not so rudely challenge him, where he will be safe from disturbing violence, and where he can pursue, unimpeded, a materialist "success." Like his nephew Meriwether, Charles Lewis had also found that the foulness of savage men had more vitality than the artifice of "civilized" man, but Charles lacks the vigor to break out of his moral torpor. He cannot escape the lie he lives because he brings it with him from Virginia to the Kentucky wilderness. The milieu he fled, he sees, is intolerable simply because it had nothing intolerable in it. His desire to find some new "tension and test, perhaps terror" in the West is thwarted because he tells the only lie that a man cannot embrace and still live, "the lie that justifies." Lilburn and Jefferson—and in his wake, Meriwether Lewis—also tell the lie that justifies. Tragic violence, disheartening disillusion, and suicide are the respective results. This kind of lie is simply a rationale for irresponsibility: in each case, the critical sense, or, as R. P. W. calls it, "a certain pragmatic perspective," is lacking.

The effort of the will to achieve definition is ultimately necessary if the individual is to attain spiritual clarity. One cannot arrive at the reasons for George's anguish and Lilburn's degradation by thought alone, says the reborn Jefferson, but one must create the possibility for such a reason by a directed resolution, wherein strength is modulated by charity. This, the only knowledge worth possessing, is so

elusive as to be almost impossible to possess fully. Understanding—
even understanding a crime—requires an active exertion of the will,
not merely a passive analysis by the intellect. One cannot define abstractly the inscrutable, but one must participate, at least vicariously,
in its manifestations: "what is any knowledge / Without the intrinsic
mediation of the heart?" Above all, we have to realize that such intui-
tive sympathy demands that we also acknowledge, unflinchingly, the
worst that can happen:

> We must strike the steel of wrath on the stone of guilt,
> And hope to provoke, thus, in the midst of our coiling darkness
> The incandescence of the heart's great flare.
> And in that illumination I should hope to see
> How all creation validates itself,
> For whatever you create, you create yourself by it,
> And in creating yourself you will create
> The whole wide world and gleaming West anew.

To translate idea into action demands a courage which Warren's characters do not usually possess, though they may recognize its desir-
ability. Lucy and Laetitia, for example, are unable to realize in actuality what their hearts tell them is right. Warren says that bravery is
the quality which counts most, for only those who meet moral tests
without cowering have a true knowledge of life. The reasons which
prompt the Lilburns to evil will become apparent alone to those who
have striven, for they alone will be aware of the suffering involved in
translating the evil impulse into the actual evil act. Warren, as we
have seen, quotes Lucretius to the effect that, in dispelling the "darkness of mind," the law and aspect of nature is needed: this implies a
patient perusal and endurance of the tests it offers. Stoic endurance is
also necessary for the expunging of vanities: it is needed, for example, says Warren, in accepting our fathers' reconciliations to experience, which we can do only when we do not set ourselves above our
fathers and when we can accept our own failure to achieve their triumphs. Recounting his experiences in the West, Meriwether Lewis
stresses how greatly fortitude was required, a quality, moreover, which
eluded him in his own adjustments to life. His sentiment that "pride
in endurance is one pride that shall not be denied men" is surely, in
its clear emphasis, Warren's own. Aunt Cat also illustrates the tena-
cious fortitude that Warren values so highly, for she has the stability
which permits her to survive to a ripe old age, to outlast the rest of

the people at Rocky Hill who are either physically dead or blighted inwardly.

Warren is poised in his general view of things between an outright pessimism, which is most intense when due to self-dramatized frustrations, and a too easy optimism, which feels it can control to its own advantage the conditions of life. Warren is pessimistic to the degree that he feels life is possible only because we do not have to face realities too often. He condemns both Lilburn and the earlier Jefferson for not facing them at all, yet he knows also that mankind cannot stand too much reality. Life is possible only because of its "discontinuity." A partial glimpse of the truth is about all that we can ordinarily endure. Otherwise the pressures upon us might cause us to go mad. In the conduct of life, discretion is all-important, for it is an outward sign of inner balance. Jefferson's ultimate reasoned position and, by extension, Warren's own is a qualified optimism or a meliorative pessimism: "we are condemned to some hope," says Jefferson at the last to contrast with the fulsomeness of his earlier utterances and with the blackness of his intervening despair. The fact that Grace is possible, that a modicum of knowledge may be attained, that tentative definition is possible implies that a constructive point of view is, in part, valid. Extreme optimism or extreme pessimism are both false since they both falsify the facts. Warren is not sure, however, how far he ought to stand from either pole. Lucy Lewis is his avatar: the spaciousness of her personality, superior to both transient enthusiasm and soured despair, induced in the slaves under her control an enthusiastic loyalty which to them—and to Warren—represented a serenity that transcended in value their love for her and her love for them.

Warren as Poet

John M. Bradbury

One can best approach *Brother to Dragons* through the symbolic meaning patterns which are imbedded in the narrative. Jefferson's first long speech establishes the chief thematic poles and much of the major symbolism which clusters about them. The dream that Jefferson had cherished and lived for was that of man at length become perfect, his potentialities for good realized, an image

> angelic, arrogant, abstract,
> Greaved in glory, thewed with light, the bright
> Brow tall as dawn.

In a further image, he speaks of

> Green germ and joy and the summer shade, and I have said:
> Beneath that shade we'll shelter,
> Green grandeur and unmurmuring instancy of leaf.

Here, connotations of innocence and rapport with nature are added to the God-man, abstraction and rational aspects of the first image; and the green shade symbol amplifies the glory-light-dawn cluster. These groups establish the pre-poem Jefferson, and they carry over in varying combinations and extensions to the members of his family who are principals in the narrative.

A disillusioned Jefferson establishes the other pole in a group of Minotaur-labyrinth images:

> There at the blind
> Blank labyrinthine turn of my personal time,
> I met the beast.

Then,

No thread, and beyond some groped-at corner, hulked
In the blind dark, hock-deep in ordure, its beard
And shag foul-scabbed. . . .

The beast waits. He is the infamy of Crete.
He is the midnight's enormity. He is
Our brother, our darling brother.

The beast-man, natural malignancy, the dark and blindness, and ordure cluster at this pole, and are identified by Jefferson in the final
line with Lilburn Lewis, the murderer and Isham's "darling brother."
    Both symbolic groups are strongly reinforced as R. P. W. describes
his visit to the ruins of the Lewis house in Kentucky. It is summer,
bright, but hardly the light-and-shade summer of the pre-poem Jefferson:

        the sun insanely screamed out all it knew,
    Its one wild word:
    Light, light, light!
    And all identity tottered to that remorseless vibration.

The land which Charles Lewis would have redeemed from savagery is
rock and thorn and ruin; the shade he would have established is "The
tall hot gloom of oak and ironwood, / Canted and crazed," the cultivation
a huge grapevine, "hung in its jungle horror, / Swayed in its shagged and
visceral delight." But chiefly there are the heat and light, which prefigure
the central tragedy. For at the climax, the insanity, the scream, the wild-
ness, the tottering, the vibration from the "*light*" quotation are all concomitant elements of the murder scene. And the obsession with one
word, one idea, traceable to the "light" delusion, is the indicated motivation of the murder.
    Once at the ruin itself, Warren offers an alternate beast image in
the blacksnake which flows out of the dark pile, "as though those
stones / Bled forth earth's inner darkness to the day." The brilliant description of this encounter forms one of the two reference frames between which the main narrative is swung; the other, following the action, is a return visit to the ruin in winter. The beast element, like the
harmless snake, is itself innocent; only as it combines with the specifically human—the Minotaur symbol—does it become knowing and
therefore, in the Jefferson view, responsibly evil, with the "immitigable ferocity of self." Throughout the poem metaphors of coiling and
"humping" in the dark accent this element, and the earth itself humps

up or "heaves" in earthquake tremors at the climax. At the climax, too, the "jungle" image from the scene at the ruins reappears in the extended metaphor of a parasitical flower which "swells / From the blind nutriment of Lilburn's heart" as he approaches the murder.

All of these symbols of evil have further projections in the characters, but they are primarily emanations from the disillusioned bitterness of Jefferson. The innocent ones, personified chiefly in Meriwether Lewis, whom Jefferson sent West in the thought that "Man must redeem Nature," emanate from the pre-poem Jefferson. The mind of Jefferson, therefore, stands at the center of the poem; Lilburn's crime destroys his Rousseauism and the aspirations which accompanied the philosophy, and Meriwether's suicide confirms the destruction. The image of flames dances around the funeral pyre of Jefferson's hopes: first, the parasite which unfolds "foliage convolute like flame" within Lilburn, then the lurid fires which light up the meathouse scene and consume the victim's flesh. Lilburn's only appearance as a voice in the poem prefigures this destruction as he draws an image out of childhood: lying in the dark with "just one light, one candle flame"; then a cold gust, "and the flame snapped," and "put out the light." Jefferson finally clinches the symbol by his late discovery that man must provoke "in the midst of our coiling darkness / The incandescence of the heart's great flare" to illuminate his creative hope.

Lucy Lewis, then Jefferson and R. P. W., finally project beyond Jefferson's despair a new innocence born of knowledge, that which Warren first offered in "The Garden." Lucy tells Jefferson:

> my love and your aspiration
> Could not help but carry some burden of ourselves,
> And to be innocent of that burden, at last,
> You must take his hand, and recognize, at last,
> That his face is only a mirror of your possibilities . . . .

Then Jefferson sees that

> we must
> Create the possibility
> Of reason, and we can create it only
> From the circumstances of our most evil despair . . . .
> In creating yourself, you will create
> The whole wide world and gleaming West anew.

R. P. W. on his return to the ruins projects the same vision, and en-
dows it with a new set of images drawn out of the major clusters,
modifying them. Under a pale "lemon light" in the winter, when "all
things draw in," a snow "thin and pure"—of the new innocence—
covers the earth. (An earlier icy and stormy night image of "lethal purity" and "desperate innocence" has prepared the symbolic extension
here.) Then, there is the reflective moon, like a "mirror to the human
heart's steadfast and central illumination." And R. P. W. says:

> If there be glory, the burden, then, is ours,
> If there is virtue, the burden, then, is ours . . .
> The recognition of complicity is the beginning of innocence,
> The recognition of necessity is the beginning of freedom.

In this new illumination, the grapevine, once "big as boas" in a jungle
setting, is now "scraggly-thin and hanging like it's tired / From trees
gone leafless now, and not so tall." The snake has withdrawn to sleep
"in earth's dark inwardness," and the river below bears away the "Ordure of Louisville," becoming the image of "our history" and also of
"some faith past our consistent failure, and the filth we strew."

As a more personal *exemplum* and image of the final stage of reconciliation in responsibility, Warren introduces briefly another winter
scene, this time of a modern man and woman and their first cold kiss:

> We kissed in the cold
> Logic of hope and need. It was not joy.
> Later, the joy . . . .
> Since then I have made new acquaintance with the nature of joy.

It was "joy" that Jefferson first sought, and that others of the characters had desperately looked to find. The word is a constant reference
point through the poem, and a balance for the terror of the central
incidents. Now it becomes possible, and the ideological and symbolic
patterns have moved in unity throughout until they reach their earned
resolution.

Brother to Dragons is almost certainly, as several distinguished reviewers have found it, the most successful long narrative poem of our
era; it is in many ways also the most completely successful of all Warren's works. Its form seems better suited to his manifold talents than
those of the lyric, the drama, or the novel, all of whose specific effects

he is able to use without strain or violation of the form. The narrative constantly moves and holds the interest; the telling is varied by the voices which pick it up and add the dramatic conflict of differing points of view to the flow of the action. At the same time, the heightened pitch which the poetic medium requires affords a free release for lyrical flights and for the imagery which wells up spontaneously when Warren sits to write. Finally, the Eliot-like philosophic commentaries, which sometimes strike us as intrusive and overpitched in the novels, have dramatic place and a proper key in this form. There are occasional pieces of overwriting in this poem, and at least two breaks out of character in the voices, but the work as a whole is remarkably textured, as well as remarkably readable.

Much of the texture is gained by the variation of speech styles. Though the poem is written basically in a free blank verse, there are many tones of it. R. P. W.'s is naturally the freest voice. In its lower range, it moves from a short matter-of-factness:

> The sheriff came too late. He found it done.
> But that account's not true. Too bad, it's tidy . . .

to a homely slang, and to the raciness of a Kenneth Fearing:

> for virtue is
> More dogged than Pinkerton, more scientific than the F.B.I., . . .
> More remorseless than the mortgage or glitter of banker's *pince-nez*, . . .
> And that is why you wake up sweating before dawn
> And finger the cold spot in your side with no fancy now for the matitudinal erection.

In the high range, it has a number of lyric and dramatic tones, topped by the Warren "high rhetoric":

> Let now the night descend,
> With all its graduated terrors,
> And in its yearning toward absoluteness now amend
> The impudent daylight's velleities, and errors,
> And let the dark's most absolute shame
> Amend the day's finicking shamelessnesses
> And in that dark let the absoluteness of hate's dark flame
> Consume, like pitch-pine, the heart that had longed for love's timid and tentative caresses.

Jefferson is both quieter and more smoothly lyrical than R. P. W. in his innocence mood of reminiscence, and more violent—even night-marish, as Tate can be—in disillusion. All the rhetorical excesses in the poem are Jefferson in his over-violent reaction to the discovery of basic evil in "angelic" man. Against these two sustained extra-cast voices, major contrasts are sounded in Isham's early frontier dialect, fumbling for understanding—this reinforced by the Brother's queru-lous bumptiousness—and in the cadence and cultured dignity of his mother Lucy's intelligence. Somewhere between these two we hear Laetitia's homespun, gently baffled speech, while at the dialectal ex-treme sounds Aunt Cat's innocent-cunning Negro talk.

The characters built in these voices are not so fully blocked in as the characters in Warren's novels, but, in so far as the quasi-dramatic form allows, they are individual and often movingly realized. Of the principals—R. P. W. and Jefferson, outside the action proper, are dis-embodied reactive agents in the main—only Meriwether Lewis, whose narrative is an addendum, fails to come alive. Lilburn certainly is so darkly controlled, his historic actions so unspeakably sadistic, that he shakes our credibility, as does the Gran Boz of *World Enough and Time*, but we cannot fail to recognize his potential life in ourselves. The all but ineradicable weakness in Lilburn's portrayal, however, makes for the strength in Laetitia's. Her reactions to the incredible Lilburn's acts and moods establish a vital and affecting portrait. As Robert Lowell has noted,[1] Laetitia and Lucy are Warren's "triumphs" in this poem; where Lucy charms, Laetitia overwhelms. Isham, too, is a success, a dog-like, brother-worshipping ally in evil, whimpering for Lilburn's love and respect, stupidly baffled by the kicks and curses he inevita-bly receives.

Warren has dealt with history in this poem as he has dealt with it in all of his novels, accepting its facts and exposing them to the action of the imagination. Here, as always, he is concerned to probe out the meaning pattern and project it in terms of the symbolic patterns of imagery which the facts themselves suggest. The hazard in this method is in its liability to author imposition, and the one real weakness in *Brother to Dragons*—the major weakness of the novels also—is a nar-rowness of construction which the author's philosophical commit-

---

1. Robert Lowell, "Prose Genius in Verse," *Kenyon Review*, XV (Autumn, 1953), 622 [q.v., p. 166].

ments force upon the action. Both Lilburn's and Meriwether's stories are strained in the interpretation, though not in the presentation, so that they may be accommodated to the exposition of Jefferson's errors. Both of these characters must become embodiments of the Rousseauistic fallacy and illustrate, therefore, the deceptive principle which Jefferson advocated and America adopted to precipitate, finally, our modern cultural dilemma.

But Warren proves in *Brother to Dragons* that he remains a major American poet of our time. The lyric quality, which seemed threatened in the later poetry of *Selected Poems*, is still much in evidence, and he has added to it dramatic power and narrative movement. He has not lost touch either with the natural world of tree and rock and bird or with the human community to which he as man and as philosophic mind has been committed. His poetry has gained in depth and density, and it has lost only in the constriction which set patterns of thought have impressed upon it. It would appear certain that Warren's career as a poet is not complete in the mid-fifties.[2]

2. *Editor's note*: A fact perhaps now too obvious to comment on, e.g., *You, Emperors and Others* (1960), *Selected Poems: New and Old, 1923–1966* (1966), *Incarnations: Poems 1966–1968* (1968), *Audubon: A Vision* (1969), *Or Else: Poem/Poems, 1968–1974* (1974), *Selected Poems 1923–1975* (1976), *Now and Then: Poems 1976–1978* (1978), *Being Here: Poetry, 1977–1980* (1980), and *Rumor Verified: Poems 1979–1980* (1981).

The Function of the Pasiphaë Myth in *Brother to Dragons*

George Palmer Garrett

Early in Robert Penn Warren's tale in verse and voices, *Brother to Dragons*, Thomas Jefferson alludes to the myth of Pasiphaë to illustrate the brute reality of inner evil in man. There he presents a vivid picture of Pasiphaë's coupling with the bull, after which Jefferson invokes her memory: "We have not loved you less, poor Pasiphaë." She is seen by Jefferson as the mother of this inner evil; for her son, the minotaur, is "Our brother, our darling brother." It is, of course, entirely within the decorum of the poem to have Jefferson take his figure from classical mythology, and it is a startling contrast to that other aspect of the classical world which Jefferson loved in the form of the *Maison Quarrée* at Nîmes. But to the reader the allusion to Pasiphaë offers much more. Some of the psychological complexity of this allusion in its relation to the chief characters of the poem has been suggested by Frederick P. W. McDowell in his study of the poem.[1] One value of the story and its aftermath, the birth of the minotaur and the creation of the Labyrinth, is justly seen by McDowell as "a symbol which dominates the poem in vividly suggesting the lurking evil in the dark heart of man." However, the myth has at once a deeper and a more immediate function in the poem, and a glance at the meaning of the Pasiphaë myth will show how aptly chosen it is for Warren's purposes.

    Robert Graves' compilation of the Greek myths is readily accessible to readers and contains, as well as the usual variants of the story, some of the anthropological speculation on the myth.[2] There are three

"The Function of the Pasiphaë Myth in *Brother to Dragons*" by George Palmer Garrett. From *Modern Language Notes*, LXXIV (April, 1959), 311–13. Copyright © 1959 by the Johns Hopkins University Press, Baltimore, Md. Reprinted by permission.
1. Frederick P. W. McDowell, "Psychology and Theme in *Brother to Dragons*," *PMLA*, LXX (September, 1955), 565–86 [q.v., p. 46].
2. Robert Graves, *The Greek Myths* (2 vols.; Baltimore: Johns Hopkins University Press, 1955), I, 298–308.

versions of the source of Pasiphaë's lust. Two involve Minos, her husband, and his breaking of an oath to Poseidon. The other involves Pasiphaë herself, telling that she "failed for several years to propitiate Aphrodite, who now punished her with this monstrous lust." These are not incompatible; for all deal with the failure to perform required services to the gods. The lust of Pasiphaë was, therefore, a punishment for disobedience. It represents a kind of original sin. It is the lack of awareness of original sin which is presented by Warren as the basic flaw in Jefferson's vision, his dream for mankind. The result of Pasiphaë's action was concealment. "Minos spent the rest of his life in the inextricable maze called the Labyrinth, at the very heart of which he concealed Pasiphaë and the Minotaur."[3] The myth can be seen, too, as a fine figure for our modern psychological concept of the concealed *id* at the heart of the *psyche*. Daedalus, who has come through Joyce to be our figure for the artist, has a curious function in the Pasiphaë story. It is he who creates the wooden cow wherein Pasiphaë receives the bull. Similarly, he is the creator of the Labyrinth. It seems not unlikely that Warren has here an ironic comment on his own function as the creator of the poem and as the character "R. P. W." in the poem. It is his quest and his curiosity which call up old ghosts and create a structure for the reenactment of old crimes. He is responsible, too, to the extent of creating the artifice whereby the brute ugliness of human evil can be demonstrated. Thus Warren includes himself in the general guilt.

There is another way in which the evocation of the Cretan mythology is singularly exact in Warren's design. The Cretan myths and their cult of the bull are seen by classical scholars as mystic in character. Of their religious practice W. K. C. Guthrie writes:

> It is the essence of a mystery cult, that by means of such stimulants as Strabo describes, the worshipper felt the god enter into his own being and could, while the ecstasy lasted, call himself, the follower, by the name of the god he worshipped. The culminating point of the rite was often the eating of a newly slain animal who was thought to embody the god. By imbibing the fresh life-blood, the visible, physical form or symbol of deity, the worshipper believed himself to acquire the spirit, strength, holiness or whatever of the divine characteristics was most desired.[4]

3. *Ibid.*, 294.
4. W. K. C. Guthrie, *The Greeks and Their Gods* (Boston: Houghton Mifflin Company, 1955), 45.

It will be remembered by the readers of the poem that Lilburn Lewis, in the first distress of his mother's death, is sickened by the fact that he had been breast-fed by an old Negro mammy, Aunt Cat. Later as madness begins to possess him, he equates the blackness of the Negroes with the blackness of his own soul, with the kind of absolute blackness of evil. When rage finally possesses Lilburn completely, he kills his slave, George, in a kind of ritual murder in the meat house in view of a circle of squatting slaves, and the flesh of the murdered man is thrown on a fire and cooked, though not eaten. The Pasiphaë myth as a part of the ecstatic Cretan religion serves as a symbolic background for Lilburn's specific crime, and it is the disregard of this fact, the terrible potential of mankind for irrational ecstasy, good or evil, which Warren sees as the fatal defect in Jefferson's vision. Pasiphaë is invoked as the proper muse for *Brother to Dragons*.

Theme and Metaphor in *Brother to Dragons*

Victor Strandberg

When *Brother to Dragons* came out ten years ago, its reviewers were inclined to show deep admiration. "An event, a great one," was Randall Jarrell's opinion, as he sought to substantiate his judgment that "this is Robert Penn Warren's best book."[1] Another of Warren's fellow poets, Delmore Schwartz, likewise evinced high enthusiasm, calling *Brother to Dragons* "a work which is most remarkable as a sustained whole," a work having "perfect proportion throughout."[2] Both these reviewers, furthermore, placed Warren in some very distinguished company on the basis of this work, Jarrell by finding echoes of Milton, Shakespeare, and Eliot, and Schwartz by observing "Warren's resemblance to Melville."

In the wake of high praise such as this, one might have expected serious, full-length studies to appear soon after. Curiously, such was not to happen. In these ten years, only one really significant, comprehensive study of the poem has come forward, that being Frederick McDowell's "Psychology and Theme in *Brother to Dragons*." This very perceptive article, by discussing the theme in terms of character analysis (or character psychoanalysis), helps us to understand *Brother to Dragons* as a drama, or play, and as such has been indeed useful. But *Brother to Dragons* is not only a play. It is a poem—a "dramatic poem," its author tells us—and so it requires poetic as well as dramatic analysis.

In viewing *Brother to Dragons* as a dramatic poem, rather than a poetic drama, we find the structure of the work depending not so much on characterization as on a finely wrought pattern of images,

"Theme and Metaphor in *Brother to Dragons*" by Victor H. Strandberg. From *PMLA*, LXXIX (September, 1964), 498–508. Copyright © 1964 by the Modern Language Association of America. Reprinted by permission of the Modern Language Association of America.

1. Randall Jarrell, "On the Underside of the Stone," *New York Times Book Review*, August 23, 1953, p. 6 [q.v., p. 160].
2. Delmore Schwartz, "The Dragon of Guilt," *New Republic*, September 14, 1953, p. 17.

images calculated to transmit Warren's theme to the reader in a subtle but convincing way. Unfortunately, this imagery appears to have been a bit too subtle for many readers: although it permits Warren to avoid mere didacticism, so distasteful to the modern temper, this framework of images carries a high risk of leakage of meaning in so long and complex a work. I propose to reduce that leakage. In this paper I shall trace out the poem's master metaphor—the beast image—and its two major subsidiary metaphors, the Lewis house (the house of the psyche) and the twice-recurring winter setting (the winter of philosophic naturalism). These dominant and interrelating image patterns bear the major burden of Warren's theme, and I should like to consider each in its turn.

* I *

It may at first surprise the reader, since Warren nowhere tells the source of his title allusion, to find that the title of his most celebrated poetic achievement comes from the most ancient book of the Bible, The Book of Job (30:29): "I am a brother to dragons and a companion to owls." On second glance, however, this reference is not so surprising. The occasion of Job's complaint is his feeling of resentment towards his Maker for bringing intolerable humiliation upon him. The loss of wealth and family and even his physical torment he could possibly abide, but the humiliation is another matter: "But now they that are younger than I have me in derision, whose fathers I would have disdained to set with the dogs of my flock" (Job 30).

It is most revealing to observe that Warren's attention is focused not on Job's suffering and loss and endurance but upon the one thing he could not endure, his loss of pride. Being a brother to dragons and a companion to owls, after all, is a fate singularly undeserved for a man who had always (like Thomas Jefferson) walked "upright and perfect . . . and eschewed evil." "Did I not"—Job puts the question bitterly—"Did I not weep for him that was in trouble? was not my soul grieved for the poor?" (30:25). And all Job gets for a lifetime of high-minded service, tendered in absolute innocence, is ridicule at the hands of "base men . . . viler than the earth":

> They were children of fools, yea, children of base men:
> they were viler than the earth.
> And now I am their song, yea, I am their byword.
>
> (Job 30:8–9)

Job's bitterness at finding himself a "brother to dragons" (a condition he actually refuses to admit until the very end of The Book of Job) provides a most satisfactory analogy to the attitude of Warren's Thomas Jefferson. Both men lacked, in Warren's estimation, the sense of limitation which is essential to the religious attitude. Both thought themselves freed, by dint of an absolute virtue, from the common human contamination. Even Divinity must surely recognize their triumph, their disentanglement from the influence of the Fall, they would contend. Surely God, if He be just and true, could not fail to distinguish the righteous from "base men . . . viler than the earth."

But, of course, Warren does not grant such a distinction. Humanity's black collective shadow, the acknowledgment of which formed the crux of Eleven Poems on the Same Theme, belongs as much to a Job or a Thomas Jefferson, for all their innocence and virtue, as to all the rest of mankind. Warren's answer to Job's complaint of injustice, then, is to fling Job's own protest back at him shorn of its original sarcasm: You are indeed a brother to dragons, Brother Job (and Brother Jefferson). And so we have the poem's master metaphor, its dominant and most recurrent image.

The exact meaning of this master metaphor has not, I feel, been completely or properly understood. Critics have been inclined to lean too heavily on one recurrence of this beast-image, while ignoring others. Such an approach would be useful if the beast-image meant the same thing each time it appears, but it does not: like Melville's whale, Warren's beast has a different meaning for each of his characters. Thus I believe that George Palmer Garrett and Frederick McDowell err when they agree in viewing "the birth of the minotaur and the creation of the Labyrinth" as "a symbol which dominates the poem."[3] This is actually only Thomas Jefferson's view of the beast within the self, and it is a view badly distorted by an excess of outrage and revulsion. For this reason, the minotaur image, though in itself a masterpiece of poetic brilliance and power, is only briefly handled. After the first few pages, it gives way to something more akin to the title image, "dragons." Here I refer to the serpent seen by R. P. W. with startled fright, but without outrage or revulsion.

Because R. P. W. lacks Jefferson's outrage and revulsion—because, that is, R. P. W. has (like Melville's Ishmael) the most compre-

---

3. Mr. Garrett quotes this passage from McDowell as the starting point for his "The Function of the Pasiphaë Myth in Brother to Dragons," Modern Language Notes, LXXIV (April, 1959), 311–13 [q.v., p. 77].

hensive and objective perspective of anyone in the story—we must consider his vision of the beast-image to be the most accurate and crucial of them all. The actual dominant symbol of the poem, then—to which the minotaur image is related but subordinate—initally appears as R. P. W. describes his first visit, in the heat of summer, to the ruined home site on the hill:

> I went up close to view the ruin, and then
> It happened. . . .
>
> In some black aperture among the stones
> I saw the eyes, their glitter in that dark,
> And suddenly the head thrust forth, and the fat, black
> Body molten flowed, as though those stones
> Bled forth earth's inner darkness to the day.[4]

We have seen this fellow before somewhere. To be specific, he first appeared in *Eleven Poems on the Same Theme*, where in such poems as "Crime" and "Original Sin" he lay toad-like in the "hutch and hole" of the "cellar-dark," and was later repudiated altogether by the conscious mind and locked out of the mind's metaphorical house. He reappears here in *Brother to Dragons*, however, in truly awesome magnitude, for in this tale of subconscious depravity he can no longer be locked out by even so high-minded a consciousness as Jefferson's. His existence, as this tale (drawn from actual history) proves, is real; the "fat, black" serpent rising from "earth's inner darkness" represents the unconscious self, which "haunts beneath earth's primal, soldered sill, / And in its slow and merciless ease, sleepless, lolls / Below that threshold where the prime waters sleep" (33).

Because of its central importance in the poem, Warren devotes several pages to this first encounter of R. P. W. and the serpent. The poet's highest powers of imagination go into this attempt to describe the emergence of the inner self from "earth's inner darkness to the day." Transmuted by the viewer's imagination, this perfectly natural serpent ("just a snake") attains a mythical superstature appropriate to its symbolizing of the unconscious self:

> Thus it flowed forth, and the scaled belly of abomination
> Rustled on stone, rose, rose up . . .
> I saw it rise, saw the soiled white of the belly bulge,
> And in that muscular distension I saw the black side scales

---

4. Robert Penn Warren, *Brother to Dragons* (New York: Random House, 1953), 32–33. Hereafter the page references to this edition are parenthetical within the essay.

> Show their faint flange and tracery of white,
> And so it rose and climbed the paralyzed light.
> On those heaped stones it was taller than I, taller
> Than any man, and the swollen head hung
> Haloed and high in light. (33)

"Taller than any man," R. P. W. called it, as his "natural tremor of fatigue converted to the metaphysical chill" and his "soul sat in [his] hand and could not move." But being a representative of modern man, R. P. W. quickly assures himself that "after all, the manifestation was only natural." This was not, surely, the serpent whose archetype appears throughout the history of religion in various civilizations: "Not Apophis that Egypt feared . . . Nor that Nidhogg whose cumbrous coils and cold dung chill / The root of the world's tree, nor even / Eve's interlocutor by Eden's bough." It was not even a "Freudian principle": "Nor symbol of that black lust all men fear and long for / Rising from earth to shake the summer sky." (Warren specifically rejects the "Freudian principle," I am sure, in an effort to discourage those critics who insist on reading all literature as sexual allegory.)

But if the snake is neither a traditional religious image nor a Freudian principle of sexuality, neither is he (despite R. P. W.'s scientific classifications) "just a snake." His rising "taller than any man" evokes too many parallels in other parts of the poem for us to be able to dismiss his appearance so easily. The first such parallel, the beast-image rising "taller than any man," appears in connection with Jefferson's minotaur image at the poem's beginning. At that time, however, the image of man's unconscious self seemed to Jefferson, rapt in his folly of joy, not a beast but an angel:

> I was nothing, nothing but joy,
> And my heart cried out, "Oh, this is Man!"
> And thus my minotaur. There at the blind
> Blank labyrinthine turn of my personal time,
> I met the beast. . . .
>   . . . But no beast then: the towering
> Definition, angelic, arrogant, abstract,
> Greaved in glory, thewed with light, the bright
> Brow tall as dawn. (9)

As we shall see, Jefferson will have plenty of time to correct his mistaken impression of the nature of man's innermost self. This revision, in fact, will constitute the main substance of Jefferson's commentary until his final speech of the poem, where he finally accepts the beast within the self as neither minotaur nor angel but deeply human.

The third major occurrence of this beast-image in *Brother to Dragons* arises in connection with the third major character, Lilburn. The first two occurrences, noted above, represent the beast-image as seen by the other two of the poem's three main characters, R. P. W. and Thomas Jefferson. What distinguishes Lilburn's version of the beast "taller than any man" is that Lilburn does not *see* the horrendous inner self; he *is* that darksome entity. I do not mean to oversimplify Lilburn's position in the poem, for Warren takes great pains to emphasize throughout the work that Lilburn is not *merely* the monster-self which Jefferson tries so hard to exorcize. Lilburn is, as R. P. W.'s consistent sympathy with him ("poor Lilburn") is intended to show, a real, recognizable, commonplace human being, motivated by an understandable though horribly perverted love for his mother. It is clear, however, that Lilburn does embody personally that dimension of unconscious evil which the serpent symbolizes and which is present, whether acknowledged or not, whether active or latent, in every man. Our authority for this identification of Lilburn with R. P. W.'s serpent and Jefferson's minotaur is the hapless Laetitia, seer and (aware or unaware) exponent of truth in the poem.

The occasion of Laetitia's vision is the scene where Lilburn persuades her to describe in words, and wickedly to relish such telling, the "awful thing"—something unspeakably carnal—he had done to her the previous night. ("Then he did it. And it was an awful thing / I didn't know the name of, or heard tell"—75.) After she finally "said the words," and Lilburn answered, "Now didn't you like it some, and even to tell me?," this is what she saw:

> And sudden rose up from my side,
> And stood up tall like he would fill the room,
> And fill the house maybe, and split the walls,
> And nighttime would come pouring in like flood,
> And he was big all sudden, and no man
> Was ever big like that, and way up there
> His face was terrible and in its dark . . .
> His eyes were shining, but they shone so dark. (79)

Like the serpent "taller than any man," Lilburn assumes a symbolic superstature ("no man / Was ever big like that") that identifies him with the monster-self in the subconscious and foreshadows the greater "awful thing" around which the story is woven, the incident in the meat house.

In addition to the above passages, the image of the beast within the self recurs at least a dozen separate times within the poem, the recurrence in each case being colored by the speaker's individual perspective. Jefferson always speaks of it in bitterness and sarcasm, his voice filled with loathing for both the conscious self, aspiring futilely for sainthood or heroism, and the monster-self within that thwarts such aspiration:

> And as for the heroes, every one, . . .
> The saints and angels, too, who tread, yes, every
> And single one, but plays the sad child's play
> And old charade where man puts down the bad and then feels
>   good.
> It is the sadistic farce by which the world is cleansed.
> And is not cleansed, for in the deep
> Hovel of the heart that Thing lies
> That will never unkennel himself to the contemptible steel,
> Nor needs to venture forth ever, for all sustenance
> Comes in to him, the world comes in, and is his,
> And supine years for the defilement of his slavering fang. (41–42)

(Jefferson's description of the beast within as "that Thing," we may note in passing, probably ties in with the "awful thing"—again undefined—which Lilburn did to Laetitia and which subsequently gave rise to her vision of Lilburn standing "tall like he would fill the room . . . and house, maybe, and split the walls.") On one very important point, Jefferson is wrong about the nature of "that Thing" within the "Hovel of the heart." He claims it will "never unkennel himself" to the "contemptible steel," but the truth is that the monster-self continually unkennels itself (as its prototype did in "Original Sin" and others of *Eleven Poems*), even at the risk of repudiation and destruction (and both befall Lilburn), in the hope of attaining acknowledgment and definition. It is only Jefferson's excess of revulsion which blinds him, until the poem's resolution, to the more redemptive possibilities of the deeper self.

Another recurrence of this master metaphor comes into view with the appearance of Meriwether Lewis, whose bitter accusations against his uncle finally bring Jefferson to an awareness of his own part in the universal complicity, and thus to an acceptance of Lilburn.

Meriwether's recollection of having slain a wolf and a bear, both rather extraordinary creatures (*"This day a yellow wolf was slain,"* and "We slew the great bear, / The horrible one"), seems to tie in with the theme of the beast within the self, though the correlation is not explicitly indicated (179, 180). The connection, if there is one, would be ironic, since, as Meriwether finds out upon his return to civilization, no amount of dragon-slaying will avail against the dragon in the human heart. It is interesting to note, in this connection, the similarity between Bates's and Jefferson's description of the minotaur, who "hulked . . . hock-deep in ordure, its beard / And shag foul-scabbed, and when the hoof-heaves— / Listen! the foulness sucks like mire" (7). Bates's heart, "ordure" and all, is a suitable home for this creature: "And treachery gleamed like green slime in the back-water.— / That Bates, whose hell-heart is a sink and a bog / Of ordure—that Bates, he smiled. He stank in sunshine" (182).

By far the most frequent and most significant references to the beast-image, the master metaphor, come from the tongue of R. P. W., the spokesman for modern man and the chief advocate of reconciliation in the poem. In his desire to effect a re-unification of the divided self, conscious self and unconscious (Jefferson and Lilburn), R. P. W. always speaks in a temperate voice, urging understanding, acknowledgment, and acceptance, even though he clearly identifies the inner self with the monstrous collective guilt of mankind which theologians call "original sin":

> And there's always and forever
> Enough of guilt to rise and coil like miasma
> From the fat sump and cess of common consciousness
> To make any particular hour seem most appropriate
> For Gabriel's big tootle. (64)

Probably the most obscure and complex, though a very significant, version of the "beast within" metaphor is that of the catfish with "the face of the last torturer" underneath the Mississippi ice:

> The ice is a foot thick, and beneath, the water slides black like a
>   dream,
> And in the interior of that unpulsing blackness and thrilled zero
> The big channel-cat sleeps with eye lidless, and the brute face
> Is the face of the last torturer, and the white belly
> Brushes the delicious and icy blackness of mud. (94)

We have frequently seen Warren use water imagery—in "Billie Potts," for example—as an archetype for time flowing into the sea of eternity, but here the meaning of the river is, I think, quite different. Although the movement of time may be related to this usage, the primary meaning of the River is that which the metaphysical poets were so fond of exploring in their comparisons of macrocosm to microcosm. John Donne comments in "Meditation Four" that "the whole world hath nothing, to which something in man doth not answer," and in filling out the details of this comparison Donne makes, in passing, the exact analogy which Warren is driving at above: "If all the Veines in our bodies, were extended to Rivers."

In the "catfish" passage, Warren does extend the collective "Veines" of mankind into a River (and the Father of Waters at that), at the bottom of which is the familiar face of our collective unconscious, the bestial, never-sleeping ("with eye lidless") inner man wantonly delighting in the "delicious" muck and ooze of the channel-bottom. The "unpulsing blackness" where he makes his home, far beneath the star-lit world of the conscious mind above the ice (the "pulsing" world of time), should remind us of the "blind dark" wherein dwelt Jefferson's minotaur and of the "earth's inner darkness" out of which R. P. W.'s serpent appeared.

The distinctive feature of the catfish image, that which elevates its significance above most recurrences of the master metaphor, is its extension from the psychological realm into the theological. In its perfect adjustment to its environs, primeval as they are, the unconscious self has attained absolute identity and, thereby, oneness with God:

> But there is no sensation. How can there be
> Sensation when there is perfect adjustment? The blood
> Of the creature is but the temperature of the sustaining flow:
> The catfish is in the Mississippi and
> The Mississippi is in the catfish and
> Under the ice both are at one with God.
> Would that we were! (94)

Repugnant as it appears, the inner self has something which the conscious self hasn't, and wants desperately. Its being "at one with God" ("Would that we were!") pretty well obviates its lack of respectability, in the end. In this synthesis of psychology and theism we are reminded of C. G. Jung's contention that "the unconscious [is] the only

accessible source of religious experience."[5] The way to God is not onward and upward, but the way back and the way down, until the conscious self besmirches its sanctity in the primeval slime, "the delicious
and icy blackness of mud" where our catfish brother awaits "with lidless eye" our brotherly embrace. There, incredibly, unreasonably, may
be found oneness with God, that state in which the unified self finds
at last its absolute identity, which is all the surface self has ever longed
for.

*   **II**   *

I have withheld up to now the major point that needs to be clarified
about the master metaphor. That point concerns the relationship between the conscious and the unconscious self, a relationship that was
the central subject of *Eleven Poems on the Same Theme* (1942) and which
continues to be the central theme in *Brother to Dragons*, where the
drift of events hangs about the efforts of Lucy Lewis and R. P. W. to
reconcile Jefferson to Lilburn.[6] Up until the very end, Jefferson stoutly
maintains his individual sanctity, for after all, *he* hadn't wielded any
meat-axe:

> JEFFERSON: But I know this, I'll have no part, no matter
> What responsibility you yourself wish.
> LUCY: I do not wish it. But how can I flee what is nearer
> Than hands or feet, and more inward than my breath? (188)

Even up to three pages before his exit from the poem, Jefferson
can recoil in indignation at the suggestion that he take Lilburn's hand
("take it, and the blood slick on it?"—191), but he breaks down at last
and begins to see the truth as Lucy and R. P. W. see it. This final vision of universal complicity, a vision espousing Warren's characteristic tragic view of the human condition, sees all human good not as
"given," in the manner presumed by the Romantic utopians, but as
earned out of the general human "wrath" and "guilt" and suffering
"in the midst of our coiling darkness":

5. Carl Gustav Jung, *The Undiscovered Self* (New York: Mentor Books, 1959), 101.
6. In his study of archetypes, Joseph Campbell, like Warren, follows Jung's lead in
declaring the cleavage within the self to be modern man's most serious problem. In *The
Hero with a Thousand Faces* (New York: Pantheon Books, 1953), 388, Campbell writes:
"The lines of communication between the conscious and unconscious zones of the human psyche have all been cut, and we have been split in two."

We must strike the steel of wrath on the stone of guilt,
And hope to provoke, thus, in the midst of our coiling darkness
The incandescence of the heart's great flare.
And in that illumination I should hope to see
How all creation validates itself. (195)

"Nothing . . . / Is lost," Jefferson goes on to say, and follows that fundamental Warren premise with another: "All is redeemed, / In knowledge." That such knowledge includes acknowledgment of the monster-self within, the catfish in the general human bloodstream, is clear enough, for Jefferson goes on to say that "knowledge . . . is the bitter bread." But bitter or not, Jefferson partakes at last of that communion symbol—"I have eaten the bitter bread"—and so earns, in his last speech of the poem, access to lasting joy: "In joy, I would end" (195, 196). This joy, which stands in contrast to the delusory jubilation when Jefferson thought man an angel (see above, p. 84), comes from his two-part reconciliation, involving, on one hand, an acceptance by the conscious self of the darker self, the beast in the labyrinth (Lilburn), and on the other hand, a return of the awakened, self-knowing individual to the group.

This reconciliation of Jefferson to his darker self within paves the way for R. P. W.'s lengthy synthesis which ends the poem. Here the serpent self, his recognition accomplished at last, sinks back into "earth's dark inwardness" again, imperturbable (like the catfish) in his timeless dark:

Down in the rocks . . . looped and snug
And dark as dark: in dark the white belly glows,
And deep behind the hog-snout, in that blunt head,
The ganglia glow with what cold dream is congenial
To fat old *obsoleta*, winter-long. (208)

(The serpent's scientific name, we may note in passing, is particularly useful to Warren's purpose in an ironic way, for the whole scheme of the poem is calculated to show that "old *obsoleta*," as a symbol of something innate in human nature, is not really "obsolete" after all, even in an age which has repudiated the notion of original sin, the alleged brotherhood with mythical dragons.) Here, too, in his concluding synthesis, R. P. W. specifically identifies himself and his age with Lilburn's crime ("We have lifted the meat-axe in the elation of love and justice"—213), and he later apprehends, as did Jefferson, something redemptive in such painful awareness of guilt: "The recog-

16171819

nition of complicity is the beginning of innocence" (214). "And our innocence needs, perhaps, new definition," Warren had said at the end of "The Ballad of Billie Potts"; here, at the end of *Brother to Dragons*, our innocence has achieved that "new definition," and has achieved it, paradoxically, through a descent to the ooze at the River's bottom, through an acceptance of guilt and complicity, through reconnecting the lines of communication between the conscious self, aspiring toward sanctity, and unconscious self, polluted, bestial dweller in darkness.

This matter of communication between the conscious self and the unconscious is, as I have said, the crucial issue in *Brother to Dragons* as in much of Warren's earlier verse. As in Warren's earlier verse, also, and with particular reference to *Eleven Poems on the Same Theme*, the initial overtures are made by the deeper self, the beast in the labyrinth, the serpent-self which the conscious mind tries so hard to repudiate. In contrast to the surface self, aloof in its pride and sanctity, the deeper self appears not so monstrous after all. Instead, it comes forward in shy, sad humility, begging and giving forgiveness simultaneously, asking only to be reunited with its brother self, the conscious identity. Unlike Jefferson, R. P. W. had seen this redemptive aspect of the deeper self in his first encounter with the serpent:

> . . . he reared
> Up high, and scared me, for a fact. But then
> The bloat head sagged an inch, the tongue withdrew,
> And on the top of that strong stalk the head
> Wagged slow, benevolent and sad and sage,
> As though it understood our human pitifulness
> And forgave all, and asked forgiveness, too. (35)

This remarkable passage may well be the most important key to the poem, for it anticipates the moral and thematic resolution of the tale. All that remains after this vision, this "moment of possibility" (as Warren was to call it in "Gull's Cry," in *Promises*), is to get Jefferson and all he stands for in the modern world to see it too, and thus to restore the broken lines of communication. The deeper self, "benevolent and sad and sage" under its brute countenance, patiently awaits the necessary, redeeming embrace throughout the remainder of the poem. Because of this redemptive humility and need, the monster-self transcends its loathsomeness in the end. The "sad and sage" head sagging in the above passage thereby takes its place alongside the similar brute faces we have seen in Warren's earlier verse, the "sad head lifting to the long return / Through brumal deeps" at the end of "The Ballad of Billie Potts," and the even sadder face in "Original Sin: A Short Story" (in *Eleven Poems*), the face that "whimpers and is gone" in the fashion of "the old hound that used to snuffle your door and moan."

Of the remaining recurrences of the master metaphor, two in particular deserve mention. The first of these shows that Jefferson's darker self, Lilburn, has his own inner self as well, and that both Jefferson and Lilburn are guilty of the same butchery in the end, though Jefferson's act of mutilation is spiritual, Lilburn's physical. It is Lucy Lewis who calls her brother's attention to the damaging analogy:

> He saw poor George as but his darkest self
> And all the possibility of the dark that he feared,
> And so he struck, and struck down that darkest self. . . .
> And . . . in your rejection you repeat the crime.
> Over and over, and more monstrous still,
> For what poor Lilburn did in exaltation of madness
> You do in vanity.(189)

The other reference to the monster-self, and the last I shall consider, is the face whose "red eye" glares in spontaneous hatred at R. P. W. on the highway (15). The occasion of this apparition, it is worth noting, is the ironic contrast Warren sets up between Jefferson's idyllic vision of the Promised Land, his West, and the actual waste land on which, amid flies, R. P. W. urinates (making appropriate answer to Eliot's prayer, "If there were only water"). Jefferson's vision of the West, "great Canaan's grander counterfeit," was originally paradisaical:

> . . . like the Israelite,
> From some high pass or crazy crag of mind . . .
> I saw all,
> Swale and savannah and the tulip-tree
> Immortally blossoming to May,
> Hawthorn and haw,
> Valleys extended and prairies idle and the land's
> Long westward languor lifting toward the flaming escarpment at the
>   end of day. (11)

Through the handiwork of Jefferson's protegé, the Common Man, the Promised Land has devolved into a waste land by the time R. P. W.

comes ripping over the highway a century and a half later, there to encounter the unforgiving red eye of New Canaan's present inhabitant:

> We ripped the July dazzle on the slab—
> July of '46—ripped through the sun-bit land:
> Blunt hills eroded red, stunt-oak, scrag-plum,
> The ruined coal-tipple and the blistered town,
> And farther on, from the shade of a shack flung down
> Amid the sage-grass by the blasted field,
> A face fixed at us and the red eye glared
> Without forgiveness, and will not forgive. (15)

The ferocity of hatred in this red glare, casual, anonymous, and impersonal as the hatred is, carries forward the beast-image into the realm of time present, I should say, and into a permanent time present, moreover—into the "any time" Warren speaks of in his headnote. And though R. P. W. says, "But touch the accelerator and quick you're gone / Beyond forgiveness, pity, hope, hate, love," he knows very well that he can't really escape the red eye's pitiful malediction. As a matter of fact, R. P. W. himself helps to perpetuate the general cursedness of things when, the accelerator being abandoned by reason of a natural compulsion, he spatters the parched earth with hot urine, while the sunlight screams and a million July-flies voice their "simultaneous outrage" at what he has done:

> So we ripped on, but later when the road
> Was empty, stopped just once to void the bladder,
> And in that stunning silence after the tire's song
> The July-fly screamed like a nerve gone wild,
> Screamed like a dentist's drill, and then a million
> Took up the job, and in that simultaneous outrage
> The sunlight screamed, while urine spattered the parched soil. (15)

There are those who take exception to passages such as the one above, which are not unusual in Warren's poetry, on the grounds that such coarseness and crudity is offensive and unnecessary. With respect to such responses, I would like to conclude this part of my discussion by rendering a personal opinion. Most of the time Warren's humor, whether coarse or delicate, is absolutely functional; the passage above, as I have read it, is a case in point. But even aside from its organic function in any particular context, Warren's humor and irony deserve nothing but our deepest gratitude, it seems to me. In an age of carefully self-protective and self-conscious poets, Robert Penn Warren has written poetry with a broad, generous, manly irony that gives his work a refreshing, almost unique quality, by comparison with which even the work of so great an ironist as T. S. Eliot seems frequently lacking. Warren's irony, unlike Eliot's, is never petty, cruel, or superior. More than that, it is never (except in his very early poems) self-pitying. For all his involvement with the Puritan Mind, which is especially evident in his concern with "original sin," it is clear that Warren does not commit the fundamental Puritan error of taking himself (so far as his conscious identity is concerned) too seriously. His poetry is enriched, surely, by such unstinting, straightforward giving of himself to his art.

* III *

Up to now, I have considered the master metaphor, the motif of the beast within the self, pretty much on its own terms, exploring its inner meanings and implications in this and earlier poems. I think this has been the proper approach to the poem, for it is a work that deals primarily with the inner darkness of man, that sense of debasement which led Job to complain about being a "brother to dragons." The title allusion clearly indicates that Warren's central concern is what we might describe as the inner dimension of the dark night of the soul: a sense of moral anxiety. Here as in previous poems, the search for identity begins with a journey inward and downward through fearsome pollution and darkness.

It is important to note, however, that Warren places this central theme within a larger perspective—within, ultimately, the largest possible perspective. That largest perspective would relate to the external dimension of darkness, that part of the dark night of the soul which considers the individual man in relation to final reality—an immensity of time and cosmos leading finite, transient man to despair of his own significance. This perspective is the main substance of R. P. W.'s lengthy concluding statement, which takes place after the poem's main issue has been satisfactorily resolved, Jefferson having acknowledged his darker self and the serpent having withdrawn into his primal, subterranean drowse.

Warren begins to develop this larger perspective quite early in the poem. R. P. W.'s first long speech, in fact, places the events of the story in the vast, minimizing perspective of time. Speaking of the long-vanished Ohio boatmen, who represent the generations of man on the river of time, Warren recapitulates the time perspective we saw in "The Ballad of Billie Potts." The narrator is particularly moved here by the hearty strength with which those vanished forefathers of ours undertook their one-way river journey:

> Haired hand on the sweep, and the haired lip lifts for song,
> And the leathery heart foreknows the end and knows it will not be
>   long,
> For a journey is only a journey and only Time is long,
> And a river is only water. Time only will always flow.
> . . . .
> The last keel passes, it is drawing night. (16–17)

We shall see this river image several times again in the poem. One instance, which I have already touched upon, is the passage about the catfish in the Mississippi mud. Another is R. P. W.'s vision of "All men, a flood upon the flood," as the poem ends (210). Still a different variation of this motif is the glimpse R. P. W. has, near the end of his first long speech, of a "lost clan feasting" at nightfall by the sea of eternity. This image parallels T. S. Eliot's vision of his ancestors' merriment in "East Coker." Whereas Eliot saw "Feet rising and falling. Eating and drinking. Dung and death," Warren sees "a lost clan feasting while their single fire / Flared red and green with sea-salt, and the night fell— / Shellfish and artifact, blacked bone and shard, / Left on the sea-lapped shore, and the sea was Time" (21).

In addition to these images suggesting the immensity of time, there are also a number of passages in *Brother to Dragons* bespeaking the vastness of space, the purpose here also being to place "the human project," as Warren later calls it, in its proper perspective. Jefferson begins this motif when he says, "I was born in the shadow of a great forest" (37). Although this dark forest may have Biblical allusions, most likely to the myth of Adam and Eve being cast out of Eden because of Original Sin, it is likely also that this "great forest" has naturalistic connotations suggesting, in a manner reminiscent of Faulkner's "The Bear," the vast unconquerable wilderness of nature against which the encroachments of human civilization seem negligible. R. P. W. takes up this motif a few pages later when, commenting on "the massive darkness of forest," he observes that "for forest reaches / A thousand miles in darkness beyond the frail human project" (45).

This sense of nature's all-encompassing vastness reaches its consummation towards the middle of the poem when R. P. W. describes the coming of winter in the *annus mirabilis*. The lyric power of this passage and its breadth of imagination make it one of the most mov-

ing reading experiences in the book. Even the great forest, whose
vastness swallows up the "human project," appears small and sub-
missive under the onslaught of "the unleashed and unhoused force
of Nature, / Mindless, irreconcilable, absolute; / The swing of the
year, the thrust of Time, the wind." Primal forces of nature move in
over the planet as "far north the great conifers darkly bend." Whereas
the summer journey to the site of the Lewis house (the summer
bespeaking the high noon of human life and energy) had afforded
R. P. W. a glimpse into man's inner darkness (the serpent metaphor),
the winter setting here and at the end of the poem serves to dramatize man's relationship to the outer darkness, the black abyss of nature. In the "glittering infinitude of night" the arctic stars' "gleam
comes earthward down uncounted light-years of disdain" as the wide
empty land lies waste and frigid in a scene deathsome and static as
eternity: "in radius of more than a thousand miles the continent / Glit-
ters whitely in starlight like a great dead eye of ice" (95).

The fullest expression of this mood, this sense of time—space immensity, comes significantly at the end of the poem, when R. P. W.
makes his winter visit (December 1951) to the Lewis home site. Here,
as R. P. W. stands near "the shrunken ruin," watching the "last light
of December's, and the day's, declension" and thinking "of the many
dead and the places where they lay," he sees how "winter makes
things small. All things draw in" (215). Underscoring this feeling of
diminishment, as R. P. W. looks at the pathetic decay and rubble of
what was once a "human project," are the vast "emptiness of light,"
or "cold indifferency of light," and the great, vacant hush of afternoon
in which the sounds of living creatures ("Some far voice speaking, or
a dog's bark") are thin and faint, waning into nothingness. Even the
river of time has a "cold gleam" in this perspective. Thinking how
"the grave of my father's father is lost in the woods" and "how our
hither-coming never knows the hence-going," R. P. W. sees that river
for the last time as "that broad flood" on which men move, and are
moved, together: "The good, the bad, the strong, the weak, all men
. . . All men, a flood upon the flood" (204, 209).

Taken together, these images suggesting the immensity of time
and space, images that seem to dwarf the "frail human project,"
effectively culminate the "naturalistic considerations" that R. P. W.
mentioned early in the poem (29). When first mentioned, these "naturalistic considerations" applied to the inner darkness of man, the
psychological theory of determinism which, if accepted, would ren-

der virtue meaningless and non-existent, and which, consequently, R. P. W. rejects, though he has seen man's inner darkness: "But still, despite all naturalistic considerations, / Or in the end because of naturalistic considerations, / We must believe in virtue" (29).

This qualification of the "naturalistic considerations" applying to man's inner darkness has, as we might expect, a counterpart with respect to the naturalistic darkness exterior to man. Though he has seen both the inner and outer darkness, Warren does not accept the premises of naturalism as the final truth of existence. Just as "we must believe in virtue," despite naturalistic considerations ("considerations" implies something less than dogmatic acceptance), so, too, Warren would say, we must believe in an ultimate meaning to our existence despite the all-enveloping oppressiveness of external darkness.

Warren's answer to the problem of cosmic darkness is, in a Jungian sense, theological. Since the inner darkness is his main concern in this poem, the theological implications are not very profuse in number or obvious in meaning, but clearly they do exist. There is, first of all, the concept of being "at one with God" already discussed. In ascribing deific connections to the catfish, Warren is restating his intuition—first stated in his essay on *The Ancient Mariner* and first illustrated in "Billie Potts"—that "Nature participates in God." As an embodiment of this conception, the catfish denotes a kind of immortality not available to the conscious psyche.

The most significant theological content of the poem, and that which most closely approximates religious orthodoxy, is the series of Christian paradoxes that form the thematic resolution of the work. Both the style and the content of these lines resemble the resolution of *Four Quartets*, but the ideas are much older than Eliot or anything in the modern period. These paradoxes were a favorite theme of the metaphysical poets and preachers, such as John Donne and Lancelot Andrewes, and their ultimate source goes all the way back to the sayings of Jesus. The inner and outer darkness come together here, as Warren considers virtue and a permanent identity ("the beginning of selfhood") ultimately interrelated:

> Fulfillment is only in the degree of recognition
> Of the common lot of our kind. And that is the death of vanity,
> And that is the beginning of virtue.

> The recognition of complicity is the beginning of innocence.
> The recognition of necessity is the beginning of freedom.

The recognition of the direction of fulfillment is the death of the self,
And the death of the self is the beginning of selfhood. (214–15)

We may note in passing, by way of explaining the abstract, prosaic
style of this passage (poetry of statement, one might call it), that all
these ideas were implicit in "The Ballad of Billie Potts"—there was the
"recognition of complicity" and of "necessity" and the "fulfillment"
through the "death of the self"—but critical understanding of that
poem was very scant. For this reason, I believe, Warren undertook in
Brother to Dragons to restate these fundamental premises of his art in
explicit, prosaic terms, since subtler modes of communication had apparently failed in his earlier poetry.

*   **IV**   *

Having now discussed both the inner and the outer darkness in *Brother
to Dragons*, I would like to conclude with a comment about the relationship between those dual dimensions of the dark night of the soul.
The relationship between the inner and outer darkness, or between
the beast-metaphor and the "naturalistic considerations" of the great
forest and the "glittering infinitude of night," is rendered, as I see
it, by means of an intermediary image—the "house" of the human
psyche. We saw this image elaborately worked out in "Crime," one of
the *Eleven Poems*, where the conscious self sat in the attic amid rub-
bish suggesting temporal identity ("the letter names over your name")
while the deeper self lay buried (only to be humiliatingly resurrected)
in the "hutch and hole" of the "cellar-dark." It may be fanciful to at-
tach similar connotations to Lilburn's house, but there is some evidence that Warren intended such a meaning.

Jefferson first broaches this use of the "house" image when he
speaks of "that sweet quarter of the heart where once . . . faith / Her
fairest mansion held" (24). The lines following this one, where Jefferson tells Lucy, "Sister, we are betrayed, and always in the house!"
would strongly imply the concept of the house of the psyche, I would
think. R. P. W.'s subsequent comment, "If you refer to the house
Charles Lewis built . . . [it's] nothing but rubble," could be taken both
literally and metaphorically. If taken both ways, it ties together the
motifs of inner and outer darkness, for Lilburn and Nature between
them have indeed reduced a nation's proudest household to "rubble,"
morally and physically.

If we assume that the Lewis house is indeed the house of the psyche—and every such house does in fact have its own meat house, Warren would insist—then R. P. W.'s first look at the ruins, in his July visit, has some very interesting, though not immediately apparent, overtones. First of all, there is the contrast between the "huddled stones of ruin," which is all that remains of the surface self, and the underground burrow where the serpent-self still endures (32). This contrast is repeated in R. P. W.'s second visit—his December trip at the end of the poem—where we picture the serpent "looped and snug" underground, safely beyond the reach of naturalism's winter. The image of the catfish, perfectly adjusted to its utterly dark, frigid surroundings under the ice, also reinforces this contrast between the conscious self and the unconscious. What these images add up to, we may surmise, is Warren's concept of individual immortality: the conscious self, that part of the psyche represented by the "huddled stones of ruin" dies away in time, leaving the human hope for survival to reside in the collective human unconscious, the inscrutable bedrock identity which renders us "all one Flesh, at last" in *Promises* (see Lyric 3 of "Ballad of a Sweet Dream of Peace").

A number of obscurities come clear, I think, as a result of this reading. It explains, for example, the urgent, repetitious insistence on accepting the inner self that we have seen as the central theme in much of Warren's poetry. Only the deeper, unknown self can hope to transcend time's decay; the conscious, temporal self is doomed to naturalistic oblivion. And such oblivion is hardly hope-inspiring, if we may rightly infer that Warren's description of the ruined house extends to the house of the psyche:

> And there it was: the huddled stones of ruin,
> Just the foundation and the tumbled chimneys,
> To say the human had been here and gone,
> And never would come back, though the bright stars
> Shall weary not in their appointed watch . . . (32)

The concept of the house as an extension of human identity appears elsewhere in the poem with similar implications of ruin. R. P. W. evokes his lyrical depiction of winter in the middle of the poem for the specific purpose, he says, of escaping the human house, dominated now by the dark psyche of Lilburn:

> . . . we also feel a need to leave that house
> On the dark headland, and lift up our eyes

> To whatever liberating perspective,
> Icy and pure, the wild heart may command,
> To escape the house, escape the tightening coil . . . . (95)

The perishable self is again identified with the house in the scene, late in the poem, where R. P. W. thinks of his vanished ancestors of only one or two generations ago. Riding with his father under the "lemon light" of December, R. P. W. looks out over "the land where once stood the house of his [father's] first light," and observes, "No remnant remains. The plow point has passed where the sill lay" (204). The conscious, temporal identity, it appears, has disappeared into nothingness—"I do not know what hope or haplessness there / Inhabited once"—and so R. P. W. concludes that "the house is a fiction of human possibility past." Warren's feeling that "nothing is ever lost," an idea that Jefferson affirmed after his conversion ("It would be terrible to think that truth is lost"—194) is tenable, I think, only because of the potentiality of the deeper, undiscovered self, the serpent serenely "looped and snug" under the ruins of the house above ground. This mysterious, undefinable self, our collective unconscious, is the sole repository of all experience, and our sole hope, against "naturalistic considerations," of transcending temporal limitations. This is the final significance of the beast-metaphor: there is not only shame but hope in acknowledging oneself a brother to dragons.

The Persona R. P. W. in Warren's
Brother to Dragons

Dennis M. Dooley

It is something of a literary curiosity when an author includes himself among the characters of one of his works, as does Robert Penn Warren with the persona R. P. W. in his dramatic poem *Brother to Dragons*. And yet, in the only lengthy studies to date on this poem, Victor Strandberg is content to pass over this curiosity by simply noting that R. P. W. is "the spokesman for modern man and the chief advocate of reconciliation in the poem"[1] while Frederick McDowell relegates R. P. W. to the role of "commentator on the action."[2] While R. P. W. certainly does function as commentator, the question needs to be raised as to the right of R. P. W. to comment. In short, is his superior wisdom justified within the context of the poem? Furthermore, if R. P. W. is to function solely as commentator, what is the purpose of his three long, personal digressions in the poem? The answer to the second question reveals the answer to the first. Through the three digressions, Warren gives us the spiritual history of R. P. W., a spiritual history which parallels in many respects the spiritual history of Jefferson, the central concern of the poem, and which justifies the superior wisdom of R. P. W. the commentator.

Before discussing the three digressions, it might be helpful to summarize the psychological conflicts of Jefferson and his nephew, Lilburn Lewis. Lilburn had organized life around his love for his mother, Lucy. Upon her death, for which he was, to a large extent, responsible, the respect and love of the other members of the Lewis

"The Persona R. P. W. in Warren's *Brother to Dragons*" by Dennis M. Dooley. From *Mississippi Quarterly*, XXV (Winter, 1971), 19–30. Copyright © 1971 by Mississippi State University, State College, Miss. Reprinted by permission.
1.   Victor Strandberg, *A Colder Fire: The Poetry of Robert Penn Warren* (Lexington: University of Kentucky Press, 1965), 149.
2.   Frederick P. W. McDowell, "Psychology and Theme in *Brother to Dragons*," *PMLA*, LXX (September, 1955), 572 [q.v., p. 57].

household for Lucy seemed to diminish so that it appeared to Lilburn that the one principle of definition and order in his life would wither to non-existence. Thus he sought to make his love for his mother the one absolute principle of life. Such an irrational devotion blinded Lilburn to the necessity of other emotional commitments and to the fearful complexity of reality. Such an assertion of will in the face of reality led to ultimate degradation in the form of butchering the slave George for accidentally breaking Lucy's pitcher.

His nephew's butchering of the slave proves to be a traumatic experience for Jefferson. Prior to this event, Jefferson saw man as standing between beast and God and aspiring to the divine. Evil was merely the blot of centuries of oppression, which could be erased within the context of the American Eden. In this context, man's basic nobility, goodness, and innocence would assert themselves and man would fulfill his God-like potential. The slaying of George is such a traumatic experience for Jefferson that he reverses his philosophic position and denies that man is capable of any good. This is the Jefferson we encounter at the opening of the poem. Ironically, both Jefferson and Lilburn display the same flaws: both proudly cling to simplistic views of life which cannot bear the weight of reality. Neither possesses the humility to accept the complexity of reality and the complicity of each in that reality.

R. P. W.'s three digressions center around his two visits to the ruins of the Lewis home, Rocky Hill, near Smithland, Kentucky. The visits occur in July, 1946, and December, 1951, and, while the main movement of the poem takes place at "Any Time,"[3] the visits are at least experientially past for R. P. W. Each digression represents a stage in the spiritual development of R. P. W., and the action of each digression is dominated by one or more key images which establish the mood and tone.

The first visit to Rocky Hill is recounted in two digressions, the first of which centers on the town of Smithland (14–21) and the second on Rocky Hill itself (24–35). The image which predominates in the Smithland section is that of the Wasteland. The area approaching Smithland is "the sun-bit land: Blunt hills eroded red, stunt-oak, scrag-plum, / The ruined coal-tipple and the blistered town" (15).

---

3. Robert Penn Warren, *Brother to Dragons* (New York: Random House, 1953). All quotations will be taken from this source and will be cited in parentheses in the text.

Smithland itself, where the Cumberland "pours / All its own wash and wastage up from Tennessee" into the Ohio (17), "never came to much" (15) for it ". . . had nothing, canebrake and gray clay, / And hoot owls aren't a poultry highly prized, / And even now no locomotive scares those owls" (17). Indeed, except for the Dixie Theater and the filling stations, Smithland's glory, "It looks the sort of town Sam Clemens might / Grow up in now and not be much worse off" (18). Yet, despite being a hundred years behind the times, Smithland is the Universal City, containing "all the pitiful confusion of life" (21):

> The pillow bitten in the midnight pain
> Of love disprized or lust exacerbated,
> Ambition burked and the ego oozing like
> The secret sore and the suppuration smells,
> Time's slow contraction on the most hopeful heart,
> And all the moil and human jar, and every
> Malice and stratagem and cankered dream. (18)

While the Universal City of the Wasteland was not "the vision and vainglory the man / Named Smith . . . had / in mind" (15), R. P. W. speculated that perhaps this is all that could come from a dream fostered

> In that heyday of hope and heart's extravagance
> When Grab was watchword and earth spread her legs
> Wide as she could, like any jolly trollop
> Or bouncing girl back in the bushes after
> The preaching or the husking bee, and said,
> "Come git it, boy, hit's yourn, but git it deep."
>
> And every dawn sang, "Glory, glory be!"
> Sang, "Glory be to Grab, come git it, boy!"
> Sang, "Git it, boy, hit's yourn, but git it deep!" (16)

For even in the modern Smithland, man continues his search for glory, if only in "the careful cultivation of cirrhosis, / For drink's a kind of glory too" (20).

This initial view of Smithland is R. P. W.'s or, more correctly, the R. P. W.'s of July, 1946. As such, it reveals the attitude or spiritual state of R. P. W. at that point in his development. The tone is bitter and somewhat cynical. Smithland "never came to much" and human glory has been reduced to a "jolly trollop" and alcoholism. This attitude parallels the attitude of the Jefferson we see as the poem opens.

Lilburn Lewis, in butchering the slave George, has destroyed Jefferson's vision of the essential nobility, goodness and innocence of man. As a result, Jefferson has vacillated to the other extreme, where he sees man as incapable of any selfless good and as mired in the bestiality of his nature. Certainly this is similar to R. P. W.'s attitude in the first digression. This dark vision of reality and the consequent cynicism which it breeds awakens in R. P. W., as it does in Jefferson, the need to dissociate himself somehow from that reality, to stand off somehow from it. Thus, when, as R. P. W. is driving through the Wasteland, "A face fixed at us and the red eye glared / Beyond forgiveness, pity, hope, hate, love" (15). And yet he cannot escape complicity in Smithland for it is like his "own hometown" (19). To the Wasteland's call for water, the bitter R. P. W. can only respond with "urine splattered [on] the parched soil" (15).

The second digression (24–35) is concerned with the actual visit to Rocky Hill itself. The tone of this section and thus the attitude of R. P. W. is rather different from that of the initial digression. The bitterness and cynicism have been modified to a neutral, searching tone. The man who climbs Rocky Hill is

> A fellow of forty, a stranger, and a fool,
> Red-headed, freckled, lean, a little stooped,
> Who yearned to be understood, to make communication,
> To touch the ironic immensity of afternoon with meaning,
> To find and know my name and make it heard. (26–27)

The man who touched the accelerator to escape the glare of the red eye was a stranger to his fellow man, in the sense that his aloofness and alienation isolated him from the rest of man. But, while this man who climbs Rocky Hill is also a stranger, he is also one who "yearned to be understood, to make communication," to find meaning and identity.

Two images dominate the Rocky Hill digression: the image of R. P. W.'s father and the image of the snake. In going to climb the mountain, R. P. W. left his father sleeping in the car, for he was nearly eighty years old.

> No truth on mountains any more for him,
> No marvel in the bush that burns and yet is not consumed,
> Nor on the exposed height terror in the astonishing tonality of thunder.
> For he had climbed his mountains long ago,

And met what face—ah, who can tell?
He will not, who has filled the tract of Time
With rectitude and natural sympathy. (27)

The old man had climbed a mountain long ago and found a "face," "truth," meaning, identity, which has brought him to some sort of spiritual maturity and endowed him with "rectitude and natural sympathy." The son, searching for understanding, meaning and identity, is about to climb a mountain. Furthermore, the mountain imagery suggests at least two incidents in Exodus. The burning bush recalls God's summoning of Moses, then alienated from his people, to deliver the children of Israel from the bondage of the Pharaoh to the glory of the Promised Land (Exodus 4). The terror at the thunder recalls Moses' reception of the Commandments, which at once remind man of the dark side of his nature and at the same time hold out the promise of spiritual glory (Exodus 19:20). The two incidents touch on both degradation (the Egyptian bondage, sin) and glory (the Promised Land,[4] spiritual reward). If the images are to be extended to R. P. W.'s father, then, apparently, by climbing his metaphorical mountain, he too has achieved some sort of balance or reconciliation between the extremes of human nature. The failure to achieve such a balance or reconciliation is the basic failure of Lilburn and Jefferson. Lilburn, in his perverted idealism, embraces degradation to the exclusion of all else while Jefferson can see at first only good and then only evil. This same sort of extremism is reflected in the unrelieved cynicism and bitterness of R. P. W.'s first digression, although the cause is left unstated.

R. P. W. recalls that once he had come "to that most happy and difficult conclusion: / To be reconciled to the father's own reconciliation" (28). It was the "most happy" conclusion, for to be reconciled to one's father would be "to find and know my name" (27), to touch life with meaning. Yet, it is the most difficult because it "Costs the acceptance of failure," not just the failure of the father, but the knowledge that "the failures of our fathers are the failures we shall make, / Their triumphs the triumphs we shall never have" (28). Thus, the reconciliation is difficult because it "Signifies the purification of vanity" (28). It requires the humility to admit one's part in the Wasteland and

4. *Editor's note:* See Sister M. Bernetta Quinn's "Robert Penn Warren's Promised Land," p. 18 herein.

the courage to face the difficult and lonely ascent to virtue. Yet, despite the difficulty, in the end,

> We must believe in virtue. There is no
> Escape. No inland path around that rocky
> And spume-nagged promontory. (29)

Everyman, ultimately, must climb his own Rocky Hill.

At the summit of Rocky Hill, amidst the ruins of the Lewis house, Warren introduces what is probably the most important image of the poem, the "fat, black" snake, rising from "earth's inner darkness to the day."

> Thus it flowed forth, and the scaled belly of abomination
> Rustled on stone, rose, rose up
> And reared in regal indolence and sway.
> I saw it rise, saw the soiled white of the belly bulge,
> And in that muscular distension I saw the black side scales
> Show their faint flange and tracery of white.
> And so it rose and climbed the paralyzed light.
> On those heaped stones it was taller than I, taller
> Than any man, and the swollen head hung
> Haloed and high in light . . . . (33)

"Taller / Than any man," the snake takes on an almost mythical stature, befitting its relation to Jefferson's image of the minotaur as the symbol of man's dark nature, while, when Job calls himself a brother to dragons and a companion to owls (Job, 30:29), he is commenting on the degree of his degradation. Furthermore, the description of the snake looks forward to Laetitia's vision of Lilburn when he persuades her to describe "the awful thing"—some sort of sexual perversion—which he had done to her on the previous night.

> And sudden rose up from my side,
> And stood up tall like he would fill the room,
> And fill the house maybe, and split the walls,
> And nighttime would come pouring in like flood,
> And he was big all sudden, and no man
> Was ever big like that, and way up there
> His face was terrible and in its dark,
> Like 'twas the darkness of an awful sky,
> His eyes were shining, but they shone so dark. (79)

Thus, while R. P. W. would deny the traditional religious and Freudian implications of the snake ("just a snake" [34]), the pattern of imagery within the poem itself associates the snake with the dark aspect of human nature. And it is this aspect which Lilburn embraces, which blinds Jefferson, and which gives rise to R. P. W.'s bitterness at the Wasteland.

Moreover, acceptance of this aspect of human nature is the price of reconciliation to the father and the subsequent spiritual maturity which reconciliation brings. But such acceptance demands humility, "the purification of vanity," a virtue which each of the three lonely egotists lacks. And yet, when the snake rises to its full height,

> The bloat head sagged an inch, the tongue withdrew,
> And on the top of that strong stalk the head
> Wagged slow, benevolent and sad and sage,
> As though it understood our human pitifulness
> And forgave all, and asked forgiveness, too. (35)

In the first digression, the red eye glared at R. P. W. "Without forgiveness, and will not forgive." In his bitterness, R. P. W. could only "touch the accelerator" and flee. At the beginning of this second digression, he is at least aware that reconciliation to the father is a means to spiritual maturity and that each man must climb his own mountain. Having climbed Rocky Hill, the "rocky / And spume-nagged promontory" of virtue, R. P. W. receives his vision, his burning bush, his truth: the necessity of understanding "our human pitifulness," to forgive and to ask forgiveness. In short, what is needed is the humility to accept one's humanity and, thus, the humanity of all men. In this humble acceptance lies the discovery and knowledge of one's own name and reconciliation to the father. And in reconciliation one gains spiritual maturity. Thus, the snake, at once associated with the dark aspect of human nature, at the same time comes to symbolize the human moral ideal.

Having received the vision of truth, R. P. W. is now capable of spiritual maturity, and the spiritually mature R. P. W. is the subject of the final digression, the second visit to Rocky Hill (203–16). This second visit takes place in December, 1951, just prior to Christmas (203, 206). Significantly, R. P. W. must travel from east to west to reach Rocky Hill ("Up Highway 109 from Hopkinsville, / To Dawson Springs, then west on 62, / Across Kentucky at the narrow neck" [15]). Like the magi, R. P. W. must make a westerly winter journey, at the end of which he experiences a great epiphany.

Again the tone of the digression changes from a neutral, searching tone to one of subdued hope. Smithland, the Universal City of the Wasteland of the opening digression, has become "No, not Sam Clemens' town now, after all."

> A traffic signal jangles red and green,
> And paint is on the houses, and new stores,
> And gas pumps are a rash that's worse than measles.
> And Ford and Plymouth vie to make you happy,
> And money jingles in the local jeans. (206)

This new image of Smithland by no means negates the first image of Smithland, as R. P. W. is well aware. For there is a correlation between the new Smithland and "the dark audit of blood / In some Korean bunker" (206). The difference between the two images of Smithland is not one of kind, but of degree. In the first digression, R. P. W. could see only the darkness of the Wasteland. Here, in the final digression, he has attained the maturity and wisdom to accept that every entry on the ledger of history is "a scrawl of blood." In the "paleness of the lemon light" of December, "The heart of earth drew inward, and was still" (203), for "winter makes things small" (208). Having seen the vision of the snake and realized the necessity of humility, R. P. W. can now come to possess the spiritual maturity which reconciles the disparities of human experience and gives some sort of perspective to the problem of evil.

Only in this psychological stage can R. P. W. receive his father's anecdote about percoon. The old man recalls that it was about that time of year that his father used to make a medicine for his sons out of yellow percoon, "bark of prickly ash" and a gallon of whiskey.

> "It's old-folks talk, but then they held it true,
> How in the spring you had to thin the blood.
> My father said how winter thicked boys' blood
> And made 'em fit for devilment, and mean.
> And he'd sure fix it, whisky and percoon.
> Percoon was bitter. It would wry your tongue." (205)

Lilburn, Jefferson and, perhaps in a more limited degree, R. P. W., through their rejection of their links with humanity and through their consequent isolation, commit evil. Jefferson, through Lucy and R. P. W., and R. P. W., through the vision of the snake, learn that it is only through the acceptance of one's humanity, through the taking of the bitter percoon, that one can attain the humility to avoid such sins of pride as Lilburn's. And yet, such is the paradoxical nature of human reality, that, only through being a "stranger at the breaking of bread," do we share

> . . . the most common
> Human experience, which makes all mankind one,
> For isolation is the common lot,
> And paradoxically, it is only by
> That isolation that we come to know how to name
> The human bond and thus define the self. (205–206)

Thus, R. P. W. can climb Rocky Hill, which now "doesn't look so high," and be "prepared for what I find up yonder" (208).

What R. P. W. finds, or rather sees, on the bluff is the river, but no longer just the river which "pours / All its own wash and wastage up from Tennessee." Rather, now, R. P. W. sees

> . . . how men had moved on that broad flood,
> The good, the bad, the strong, the weak, all men
> The drawn, the driven, the fortunate, the feckless,
> All men, a flood upon the flood. . . . (209–10)

Thus, he can apostrophize the river:

> "I take you now as image and confirmation
> Of all that deep flood that is our history,
> Of that deep flood that makes each new day possible
> And bears us westward to the new land.
> I take you as the image and confirmation
> Of some faith past our consistent failure, and the filth we strew."
>   (210)

Immediately, however, R. P. W. realizes that the river can no more be the confirmation of his vision than the West could be a confirmation of Jefferson's vision of innocence. Earlier R. P. W. had learned that there was "No inland path around that rocky / And spume-nagged promontory" (29), that each man in isolation had to climb his own mountain. As a result, he now realizes that the river can only serve as a "Mirror to the human heart's steadfast and central illumination. / If there is glory, the burden, then, is ours. / If there is virtue, the burden, then, is ours" (211).

Ultimately, the spiritual truth which R. P. W. and, later, Jefferson come to grasp is very similar to the Christian paradox of life through

death. We have all sought to identify with human glory and, in the
process, sought to define adequately that glory. But, R. P. W. argues,
"To make that definition would be, in itself, / Of the nature of glory"
(214). To make that definition requires the humility to admit and to
understand the bestial as well as the angelic nature of man. Moreover, it requires the courage to admit and to understand that man has
not two natures but one, with the result that often we have "named
the bad thing good and the good thing bad." Indeed, until one has
acquired such humility and courage, there can be no glory. Ultimately,

> In so far as man has the simplest vanity of self,
> There is no escape from the movement toward fulfillment.
> And since all kind but fulfills its own kind,
> Fulfillment is only in the degree of recognition
> Of the common lot of our kind. And that is the death of vanity,
> And that is the beginning of virtue.
>
> The recognition of complicity is the beginning of innocence.
> The recognition of necessity is the beginning of freedom.
> The recognition of the direction of fulfillment is the death of the self,
> And the death of the self is the beginning of selfhood.
> All else is surrogate of hope and destitution of spirit. (214–15)

As he is about to go down the mountain, "from an undifferenti-
ated impulse," R. P. W. picks up several acorns (215). This action recalls the image of the oak which R. P. W. used in describing a winter
storm after the death of Lucy Lewis. "The oak is Jacob, and all night
in anguish wrestles the incessant / And pitiless angel of air" (95). An-
chored in the earth with its boughs reaching skyward, the oak, like
the snake, becomes a symbol of the spiritual anguish and the moral
glory of man. With the symbolic acorns and the knowledge attained
at Rocky Hill, R. P. W. can now descend "into the world of action and
liability" (215). To his father's query whether " 'You finished what you
climbed up there for, Son?'" R. P. W. can now reply, " 'Yes, I've finished. Let's go home'" (216).

The three digressions in *Brother to Dragons*, then, can be seen to
mark the three stages of spiritual growth of the persona R. P. W. In
the first digression, he is disillusioned, bitter and alienated. In his ascent of Rocky Hill, the second digression, R. P. W. receives the truths
necessary for spiritual growth from the image of his father, the mountain and the snake. The third digression marks the assimilation of

these truths, which assimilation permits R. P. W. to be reconciled to his father and to enter "the world of action and liability." The events within the digressions are all experientially prior to the "Any Time" reality of the central action of the poem and thus vindicate the mature spiritual wisdom which R. P. W. displays in confronting Jefferson.

Furthermore, R. P. W.'s spiritual progress parallels the spiritual progress of Jefferson. The Jefferson who opens the poem has been shattered by the violence which his nephew had perpetrated. Like R. P. W. of the first digression, he is bitter, disillusioned and alienated. The rest of the poem, after the initial presentation of the psychological state of Jefferson's mind, concerns the efforts principally of Lucy and R. P. W. to present the truth of spiritual reality to Jefferson (the second digression) and Jefferson's acceptance and assimilation of that truth (the final digression).

Finally, the digressions serve two other functions. First, the R. P. W. episode functions as the traditional Warren device of the story within the story. In much the same manner as the Willie Proudfit episode in *Night Rider*, the "Statement of Ashby Wyndham" in *At Heaven's Gate*, and Cass Mastern episode in *All the King's Men*, and the Munn Short episode in *World Enough and Time*, the R. P. W. episode in *Brother to Dragons* provides a miniature working out of the ethical ideal of the main narrative action. Here the episode works more as a frame than a contained exemplum. After Jefferson has been introduced, R. P. W. gives us his first digression. The second digression follows almost immediately while the third digression takes the final seventeen pages of the poem. Given the second digression, the third follows logically and organically. In the vast gap between the second and third digressions, Jefferson's confrontation and assimilation of spiritual reality take place. Thus, the main action of the poem, Jefferson's conversion, is framed by R. P. W.'s conversion. This frame works in a second way. Warren says in his introduction that the main issue with which *Brother to Dragons* is concerned is a "human constant." By having Jefferson's spiritual progress also acted out by R. P. W., the issue of the poem ceases to be simply an issue of the nineteenth century. By enclosing the past within the frame of the present, Warren is able to transcend mere past and present and to create his poetic "Any Time."

Voices of Community: The Function of Colloquy in Robert Penn Warren's *Brother to Dragons*

Neil Nakadate

At the end of *All the King's Men* (1946), when Jack Burden goes "out of history into history and the awful responsibility of Time," he is inspired by an author whose own stance toward the material of his fictions has shifted considerably from that of his earlier years. From this point on, neither Burden nor Robert Penn Warren will be as distanced from the world of liability and fact as he was before confronting the awesome presence of Willie Stark. In the case of Burden, inertia and illusion, sarcasm and disdain have given way to action and accountability in the world of men. In the case of Warren, where (in *Night Rider*, for example) the distance was more aesthetic than ethical, the implied stance of the invisible author gives way to the acknowledged presence of the writer in his work, both rhetorically and philosophically. There is much of Warren in the narrator-historian of *World Enough and Time* (1950), for example; and in *Promises: Poems 1954–1956* (1957), the voice of the poet-father could hardly be more poignant or clear. In *Brother to Dragons: A Tale in Verse and Voices* (1953), the foreshortening of narrative distance and the surfacing of direct philosophical statement result in a compelling colloquy unique in Warren's *oeuvre*.

The crux of the tale and subject of the colloquy is the murder, dismemberment, and cremation of a Negro slave by Lilburn and Isham Lewis—a shocking, even repulsive event. (Next to this, the barn-burning of *Night Rider*, the assassinations of *All the King's Men*, and the passion and murder of *World Enough and Time* seem easy enough to comprehend—and acknowledge.) The incident is so repulsive, in

"Voices of Community: The Function of Colloquy in Robert Penn Warren's *Brother to Dragons*" by Neil Nakadate. From *Tennessee Studies in Literature*, XXI (1976), 114–24. Copyright © 1976 by University of Tennessee Press, Knoxville, Tenn. Reprinted by permission of the University of Tennessee Press.

fact, as to resist assessment; even as homicide, the crime seems particularly wanton and inexplicable. We could reject it as "inhuman." It is typical of Warren, however, that he insists on explicating the issues raised and develops a viable form for doing so. The issues emerge for him because the killers in his case were nephews of Thomas Jefferson: "The philosopher of our liberties and the architect of our country and the prophet of human perfectibility had this in the family blood."[1] Warren is interested in what Enlightenment man might say when informed of his darkest potentialities, reflected in the actions of countrymen and kin: he is eager to examine the incongruity between our elusive ideals and immediate reality, and the self-deception and error to which this often leads. As D. H. Lawrence once observed, "You can't idealize the essential brute blood-activity, the brute blood desires, the basic, sardonic blood-knowledge."[2] The verse colloquium, the form of the poem, emerges in order to make such "blood-knowledge" possible. "Violence is a component of our experience," Warren tells us. "It is a component of ourselves. Therefore, we are involved in the tale of violence." But it is crucial, he adds, "to know the nature of our involvement—discover bit by bit—the context of our involvement. And . . . the effective thing is when you begin to sense the context . . . the thing that's there, mirroring your own possibilities."[3] The tale of *Brother to Dragons* is such that while one voice is sufficient to cite the facts, several are needed to frame their context and reveal their implications—and ultimately to accept the knowledge they offer. As his historical "Notes" remind us, and as is often the case in Warren, it is a confrontation with the past which gives rise to this book (the murder occurred in 1811): but in the end Warren's

1. Robert Penn Warren, "The Way It Was Written," *New York Times Book Review*, August 23, 1953, p. 6.
2. D. H. Lawrence, *Studies in Classic American Literature* (New York: Viking, 1964), 105. We might also recall that elsewhere (62) Lawrence describes "the esssential American soul" as "hard, isolate, stoic, and a killer."
3. Robert Penn Warren, in "Violence in Literature" [A Symposium, with William Styron, Robert Coles, and Theodore Solotaroff], *American Scholar*, XXXVII (Summer, 1968), 490. Later in this discussion Warren observes that it is a specific brand of violence which has long preoccupied his imagination. "I equated long ago with a world where violence was quite common, was always intensely personal, was based on a personal grievance, a personal thwarting of some kind; but it had to do with the ego, or as they called it in sociology in those days, 'status homicide'—as opposed to homicide for gain" (493).

primary concern in *Brother to Dragons* is with the meaning of the tale
and the manner of discovering that meaning. Here, as in *World
Enough and Time* and *All the King's Men*, his impulse is philosophical
and his mode is inquisition. As always in Warren's work, at the heart
of the discussion are human sin and suffering and the need to seek
redemption through knowledge: suffering must be understood so
that wisdom might be possible.[4]

It is only through trial and error that Warren arrives at a form
which will enable him to articulate his interest in the tale. He starts
and rejects novelistic and dramatic versions, and then begins a narrative poem, in the manner of his "Ballad of Billie Potts" (1944). But the
"folk simplicity" of this form will not do,

> For the beauty of such simplicity is only
> That the action is always and perfectly self-contained,
> And is an image that comes as its own perfect explanation
> In shock or sweetness to the innocent heart.

The ballad treatment is tempting but inadequate, for the action of
Lilburn's story can only be explained

> by our most murderous
> Complicities, and our sad virtue, too.

> No, the action is not self-contained, but contains
> Us too, and is contained by us, and is
> Only an image of the issue of our most distressful self-definition.[5]

The explanation, the self-definition, lies in man, not the long-dead
figures of the historical past; the appropriate form must contain "us."
Warren finally decides to construct a verse colloquium, "a dialogue of
all the characters, including Jefferson, at some unspecified place and
time—really 'no place' and 'no time.' This would allow me, I hoped,
to get out of the box of mere chronology, and of incidental circumstantiality."[6] He summons what Jeremiah Beaumont, the confused idealist

4.   Readers of both Faulkner and Warren should recognize interesting similarities between *Absalom, Absalom!* and *Brother to Dragons*. The relentless R. P. W. recalls Shreve
McCannon, for example, and the pained Jefferson shares much with Quentin Comp-
son. Both books are, of course, colloquies with a historical focus.
5.   Robert Penn Warren, *Brother to Dragons: A Tale in Verse and Voices* (New York: Random, 1953), 43. Subsequent page references will be incorporated into the text.
6.   Warren, "The Way It Was Written," 6. Cf. the complementary remarks of John L.
Stewart, *The Burden of Time: The Fugitives and Agrarians* (Princeton: Princeton University
Press, 1965), 510–12.

of *World Enough and Time*, would call "a great chorus of truth in many voices" in order to affirm the brotherhood of democrat and dragon, suicide and slave, and of these several with the poet.

The colloquium structure allows Warren to escape the troublesome flatness of the very documents which inspired the poem, and it enables him, as the "R. P. W." of the poem, to ask questions, forge definitions, and influence intellectual direction. He becomes a participant in a discussion in which he has more than an academic investment and more than token control, and his overt willingness to give up authorial omniscience is a subterfuge both calculated and humane; it is the enabling tactic in the creation of a dialogue. At the same time, the Jefferson to whom Warren addresses himself has lost the self-possession which once enabled him to create. Having witnessed the outrages of American as well as family history, he is disillusioned and alienated. Like the Adam Stanton who refuses to take charge of Willie Stark's hospital, he now rejects in disdain that which he would earlier have embraced. " 'It is because he is a romantic, and has a picture of the world in his head,' " says Jack Burden of Adam, " 'and when the world doesn't conform in any respect to the picture, he wants to throw the world away. Even if that means throwing out the baby with the bath.' "[7] Jefferson's definition of man, his "picture," like his description of the *Maison Quarrée* at Nîmes, was based on precision, proportion, and harmony; "the Square House spoke to my heart of some fair time / Beyond the Roman tax-squeeze, and the imperial / Licentiousness, and the Gothic Dark" (41). Like his French contemporary, Condorcet, he voiced a deep faith in the progress of the human spirit; he lived, however, in "a pride past pride, / In my identity with the definition of man" (6). His definition was incomplete, and hence his faith; he did not perceive the doubleness of the promise, the complexity of potential, the irony of experience. "And thus my minotaur," Jefferson declares:

> better, indeed,
> Had it been the manifest beast and the circumstantial
> Avatar of destruction. But no beast then: the towering
> Definition, angelic, arrogant, abstract,
> Greaved in glory, thewed with light, the bright

---

7. Robert Penn Warren, *All the King's Men* (New York: Harcourt Brace, 1946), 262. Frederick P. W. McDowell provides a useful summary of Jefferson's case in "Psychology and Theme in *Brother to Dragons*," *PMLA*, LXX (September, 1955), 577–78.

> Brow tall as dawn. I could not see the eyes.
> ....
> I did not know its eyes were blind. (9–10)

Rather than discipline and design, Jefferson has seen disproportion, chaos, and the grotesque contortions of the meathouse murder. The "Shade of the Gothic night" (39) can eclipse "the law of Rome and the eternal / Light of just proportion and the heart's harmony" (40). Overwhelming the firm assertions and measured phrases of the Declaration is the time-transcending scream of the murdered slave.

Outraged and disgusted by his nephews' crime, Jefferson has plunged from self-confident prophecy to self-indulgent hindsight. He can only repudiate as meaningless gestures in a metaphysical swamp his own humanitarian efforts and those of others—"Marmosets in mantles, beasts in boots, parrots in pantaloons" (6)—to define the glory of human effort. He would acknowledge only the possibility of animality, corruption, and terror:

> beyond some groped-at corner, hulked
> In the blind dark, hock-deep in ordure, its beard
> And shag foul-scabbed, and when the hoof heaves—
> Listen!—the foulness sucks like mire.
>
> The beast waits. He is the infamy of Crete.
> He is the midnight's enormity. He is
> Our brother, our darling brother. (7)

And Jefferson would admit of only one reality: "Pain, and from that inexhaustible superflux / We may give other pain as our prime definition—" (132). At this point Jefferson comprehends the brotherhood of man with Minotaur and dragon; he does not understand the significance of the kinship or the nature of filial responsibility.

Warren, however, refuses to take Jefferson as seriously in his self-indulgence as Jefferson takes himself. It is the poet who senses the incompleteness of the President's vision and the selfishness of his repudiations. And it will be the poet who, by means of the colloquy, calls the President back from his heresy of despair. Quick, tough, ironic, and totally aware of the perverse appeal of quiet desperation, R. P. W. establishes his intense, inquisitive stance and then goes on to voice the central paradox of the poem:

> . . . Despite all naturalistic considerations,
> Or in the end because of naturalistic considerations,

> We must believe in virtue. There is no
> Escape.

In the end, "virtue is / Only the irremediable logic of all the anguish / Your cunning could invent or heart devise" (29, 30). Of course Jefferson would like to believe that naturalistic forces prevail, for if "philosophic resignation" can be equated with the fatigue of the "relaxed nerve," then catfish can be likened to hog snake and both to Lilburn Lewis, and all can be exorcised from the President's mind. "There's no forgiveness for our being human," says Jefferson; "it is the inexpugnable error" (24). And later:

> Nothing would change nothing!
> For Lilburn is an absolute of our essential
> Condition, and as such, would ingurgitate
> All, and all you'd give, all hope, all heart,
> Would only be disbursed down that rat hole of the ultimate horror.
>
> Nothing would change. (93)

Clearly Lilburn *is* disgusting—in committing the axe-murder itself, in the sadism he practices on brother (Isham), wife (Laetitia), surrogate mother (Aunt Cat), and dog, and later in his solipsistic sorrow when "He craves the sight of the wounded earth" (103)—and it is this which at first makes it easy on Jefferson, R. P. W., and us. But as Warren repeatedly reminds us, both here and elsewhere, if alteration of our humanness is impossible, then the search for or offering of "forgiveness" for this condition is a source of "obscene gratification," a cheap catharsis. The rhetoric of "forgiveness" distracts us from the fact that where error is a condition of existence, innocence and guilt are relative terms. If we know anything of the mystery of the heart, it is that all actions are a matter of will, of decision and choice—both Lilburn's and ours.

> . . . the accomplished was once the unaccomplished
> And the existing was once the non-existing,
> And that transition was the agony of will
> And anguish of option—or such it seems
> To any man who has striven in the hot day and glare of contingency
> Or who has heard the breath of darkness stop
> At the moment of revelation. (111)

The question is whether one is to exploit "the agony of will / And anguish of option" in the interest of good (as does R. P. W.) or ignore it to the benefit of evil (Lilburn and, in his own way, Jefferson).

A proper stance toward agony and anguish is achieved through perspective, and here it is the perspective of the poet which clarifies for us virtue's "irremediable logic." The grotesque murder was "Just an episode in the long drift of the human / Narrative," Warren tells Laetitia Lewis:

> . . . there's always and forever
> Enough of guilt to rise and coil like miasma
> From the fat sump and cess of common consciousness
> To make any particular hour seem most appropriate
> For Gabriel's big tootle. (64)

As Jefferson later learns through Laetitia herself, human experience contains myriad unnamed anxieties and acts (they need not, like Lilburn's Oedipal drive, be dramatized), but chaos and despair should not hold sway simply because we do not understand them. Warren will neither wallow in Lilburn's corruption nor join in Jefferson's lament. He waits for Jefferson to accept knowledge with his pain. In the meantime the poet warns his complacent reader to refrain from judging and rejecting Jefferson for his error. It is the voice of self-irony which asks in speaking of Lilburn, "Why does he suffer and understand nothing? / Were we in his place, we should surely understand. / For we are instructed in the mystery of the heart . . ." (103). The self-irony must apply when we speak of Jefferson, too. Warren the teacher knows that instruction does not always lead to understanding, or understanding to knowledge, and that at best modern man is open to both the advantages and the temptations of historical hindsight. He asks us if tales like this are intriguing only because their melodramatic cast excuses us from all responsibility for guilt; he asks if we relish the search for the scapegoat-killer only because this means that we ourselves will never be accused. He asks how might we, the heirs to Jefferson's dream, also be brothers to the dragon, Lilburn Lewis. If we are to rejoice in the benevolent possibilities of will, then we must also acknowledge its darkest needs. "We have to want to kill King Duncan," Warren remarks elsewhere, "to enjoy *Macbeth*."[8] It is possible, R. P. W. allows, "That George himself was quite responsible" (138), that the slave was a self-styled victim and in a

8. Warren, "Violence in Literature," 490.

sense victimized Lilburn; however, he reminds Jefferson, this is only "A way to say we're all each other's victim. / Potentially, at least" (140).

But by now Jefferson has withdrawn from the world of men, and it is not until the arrival of Meriwether Lewis, his nephew and spiritual son, that he is forced to respond (though not yet constructively) to the challenge of the colloquy.[9] Apparently a victim of his own despairing hand somewhere in the Natchez Trace, Meriwether comes to accuse his kinsman: "I am the man you did give the bullet to. / I am the man you killed." And he adds: "It was your lie that sent me forth, in hope" (176–77). It was Meriwether who co-led the great expedition to wilderness and "Shining Mountains," unknown beasts and rigorous seasons. Pacific vision (*"O Ocian in view! O! the joy!"*), and the return. And it was Meriwether, once more in the company of "civil" men, and serving as governor of the Territory he had explored, who became a victim of his own naïveté and others' evil. Having been falsely accused of embezzlement and mismanagement, and having taken his own life because of it, Meriwether now rejects as a lie Jefferson's claim "that men are capable / Of the brotherhood of justice" (182).

> Had I not loved, and lived, your lie, then I
> Had not been sent unbuckled and unbraced
> To find the end—oh, the wilderness was easy!—
> But to find, in the end, the tracklessness of the human heart. (184)

If the black slave George was the victim of Lilburn's love, then Meriwether is the victim of Jefferson's virtue and vanity. The accusation is direct and unequivocal, but Jefferson responds by denying responsibility, just as he has already rejected Lilburn.

It is Lucy Lewis, speaking out of her love for both Lilburn (her son) and Jefferson (her brother), who finally makes the accusation stick:

> We had hoped to escape complicity,
> You and I, dear Brother. But we have seen the unfolding
> Of time and complicity, and I, even in my love,
> And in the milk of my breast, was in guilty involvement,

---

9. And, according to Stewart, it is not until this point that Warren comes to fullest terms with the writing of the poem itself. "Meriwether's accusation, for Warren, was the turning point of the poem. He had the shape of his meaning," *The Burden of Time*, 512.

> And my son died. And you, even in your aspiration,
> Could prime the charge for our poor Meriwether.
> And this is why in our best gifts we could give
> Only the worst. It is because my love and your aspiration
> Could not help but carry some burden of ourselves,
> And to be innocent of that burden, at last,
> You must take his hand, and recognize, at last,
> That his face is only a mirror of your possibilities,
> And recognize that you
> Have deeper need of him than he of you,
> For whatever hope we have is not by denial,
> But in confronting the terror of our condition.
> All else is a lie. (191–92)

Any abstract ideal ("my love and your aspiration") is insufficient in itself, for exposed to the uncertain world of men ("the unfolding / Of Time and complicity") it is open to distortion, misuse, and betrayal— in short, to destruction and failure. Articulation of an ideal does not guarantee non-involvement and innocence, and at its worst (e.g., as in Jefferson here) it simply betrays an urge toward willful ignorance of culpability and choice. It is not true that, as Jefferson argues, once having given a project his blessing, he need not be concerned with its practical effects; the argument is as bankrupt for him as it is for such other Warren protagonists as John Brown, Perse Munn, Willie Stark, and Jeremiah Beaumont. Lucy suggests that it is only by acknowledging his own worst possibilities in the disgusting figure of Lilburn ("You must take his hand") can he define the dream to suit men's needs.

Confronted by R. P. W. as interrogator and Lucy and Meriwether as witnesses, Jefferson's bitterness gives way to weariness and confusion; he fumbles for the phrase with which to voice his sadness.

> Yes, Meriwether said I lied,
> But long since I had lost the strength for that lie,
> But cannot yet find the strength to endure without it,
> But can affirm my need only in the curse and rejection
> Of him who had robbed me of the comfort of the lie.
> I am tired. (192)

But Lucy, like R. P. W., would have him cast off his resignation; she strengthens him with a reassertion. "We are human," she says, "and must work / In the shade of our human condition. The dream remains" (193), she adds, but only in that context. At last Jefferson, recalling an old letter to John Adams, acknowledges "That the dream of the future is not / Better than the fact of the past, no matter how terrible. / For without the fact of the past we cannot dream the future" (193). (The narrator of *All the King's Men* had said, "If you would not accept the past and its burden there was no future.") Finally Jefferson acknowledges that "we are condemned to reach yet for a reason" for our anguish and guilt. "We are condemned to some hope" (194). The emphasis here is on the word "yet," for creation is not a finite act, but an ongoing gesture which characterizes the vitality of the human condition. The declaration of possibility must be remade and revitalized, for

> if there is to be reason, we must
> Create the possibility
> Of reason, and we can create it only
> From the circumstances of our most evil despair.
> We must strike the steel of wrath on the stone of guilt,
> And hope to provide, thus, in the midst of our coiling darkness
> The incandescence of the heart's great flare,
> And in that illumination I should hope to see
> How all creation validates itself,
> For whatever you create, you create yourself by it,
> And in creating yourself you will create
> The whole wide world and gleaming West anew. (194–95)

Like Jeremiah Beaumont and Jack Burden, Jefferson revises his conception of human potential and responsibility, and in doing so, redefines himself. Knowledge is the seed of creation, and re-creation itself is the definitive act. In *Brother to Dragons*, Jefferson engages, haltingly but in the end successfully, in the fundamental New World impulse to transform and redefine the self.

At the end the poem is more Warren's than Jefferson's, a matter of reconciliation of man in the present rather than re-creation of men of the past. The last dozen pages of *Brother to Dragons* concern the man earlier described as "A fellow of forty, a stranger, and a fool, / Redheaded, freckled, lean, a little stooped, / Who yearned to be understood, to make communication . . ." (26). And it is Warren, scholar and teacher, who claims along with Jefferson that

> nothing we had,
> Nothing we were,

Is lost.
All is redeemed,
In knowledge. (195)

Now, having reconciled Jefferson to Lilburn, the poet must reconcile himself to Jefferson: "that most happy and difficult conclusion," he had called it, "To be reconciled to the father's own reconciliation" (28). For to be reconciled metaphysically to the forefather is to be reconciled to his own father's father, whose now-vanished house and whatever "hope or haplessness" it once held is itself "a fiction of human / Possibility past" (204). Revisiting the site of the Lewis house, this time in the dead of winter, the poet reinforces at his own expense (not Lilburn's now, not Jefferson's) our awareness that creation and fabrication are often confused and that the imposing images of the mind's eye, whether of President or poet, are often only the products of our expectations and need. He recalls his first visit, in an earlier July, and how he "damned the heat and briar, / Saw-vine, love-vine, and rose" and

              clambered through
The tall, hot gloom of oak and ironwood,
Where grapevine, big as boas, had shagged and looped
Jungle convolvement and visceral delight. (207)

Yet he sees that in reality the thicket is meager and "scraggly—thin," and the "piddling" trees scattered and bare. Of course "winter makes things small. All things draw in"; but even granting this, he confesses, "I had plain misremembered. / Or dreamed a world appropriate for the tale" (208). Even now Warren, again like Jefferson, must guard against offering his own sweeping vision "'as the image and confirmation / Of some faith past our consistent failure, and the filth we strew'" (210). He must, in other words, resist the temptation to see radiance in the grandeur of nature and the nature of words, rather than in man himself, for

         whatever the gleam of massive magnificence or glimmer of
         shy joy
May be, it can only resemble the moon
And is but mirror to the human heart's steadfast and central
         illumination.

Magnificence is ours, Warren asserts, and also responsibility:

If there is glory, the burden, then, is ours.
If there is virtue, the burden, then, is ours. (211)

We cannot escape our burden of guilt, he has told us: the tale of kinsman and dragon compels us to acknowledge that, like Lewis and
Jefferson, "We have lifted the meat-axe in the elation of love and justice" (213). Now he also accepts a redeeming burden, our obligation to
"argue the necessity of virtue" (214). It is the burden he has per-
suaded Jefferson to bear.

Finally R. P. W.'s rigorous treatment of Jefferson is another way of
demanding much of himself, his invocation of Lilburn, Meriwether,
and the rest a voicing of his need (better: obligation) to know himself.
For finally it is the obligation of the separate self to acknowledge separateness and struggle with the texture of experience—past and present and past-in-present—in order to come to terms with it. "Isolation
is the common lot," he asserts, "And paradoxically, it is only by / That
isolation that we know how to name / The human bond and thus define the self" (205–206).[10] In *Brother to Dragons* Warren elicits the con-
firmatory testimony (alienation, disillusionment, despair) of men like
Lilburn, Jefferson, and Meriwether as witness to his (and our) own
separateness; he elicits Lucy's demanding spirit of responsibility and
love in order to strengthen his own. In their respective combinations
of confusion, illusion, and hope they confirm what is common to the
lot of man. Finally acknowledgment of our common involvement is
made possible by a community of voices—a community of voices
makes possible a community of man. "Whatever you create," Jefferson had finally realized, "you can create yourself by it."

The form of a work of literature, Warren tells us, "the organic relation among all the elements of the work," is a vision of our experience too. In *Brother to Dragons*, it is by invoking a chorus of voices
from a century and a half ago, and making the voices render the
meaning of their history, that Warren fully realizes his image of man.
"The form is a vision of experience, but of experience fulfilled and redeemed in knowledge, the ugly with the beautiful, the slayer with
the slain, what was known as shape now known as time, what was

10.   In his early poem "Revelation" Warren had said: "In separateness only does love
learn definition." Here the context is different, but the conviction is sustained. For a
discussion of "The Persona of R. P. W. in Warren's *Brother to Dragons*," see Dennis M.
Dooley, *Mississippi Quarterly*, XXV (Winter, 1971), 19–30 [q.v., p. 101].

known in time now known as shape, a new knowledge. It is not a thing detached from the world but a thing springing from the deep engagement of spirit with the world."[11] In his "tale in verse and voices" Warren achieves "identification / With the glory of the human effort" (213) and a revelation of complicity, necessity, and the direction of fulfillment. The achievement enables Jefferson, Warren, and the reader "to go into the world of action and liability" (215), to confront the world of men.

11.   Robert Penn Warren, "Knowledge and the Image of Man," *Sewanee Review*, LXII (Spring, 1955), 191–92.

Brother to Dragons: The Fact of Violence vs. the Possibility of Love

Richard G. Law

> *"We are but shadows—we are not endowed with real life, and all that seems most real about us is but the thinnest substance of a dream—till the heart be touched. That touch creates us—then we begin to be—thereby we are beings of reality, and inheritors of eternity."*—Letter of Nathaniel Hawthorne to Sophia Peabody

Now that we have in Warren's *Selected Poems, 1923–1975* the artist's own sense of the shape of his career as a poet, the importance of *Brother to Dragons* as a turning point in his development emerges in sharp perspective. The publication in 1953 of Warren's *Tale in Verse and Voices* marked his rediscovery of the possibilities of the poem, a form which he had abandoned for nearly a decade, while it introduced the new and more personal voice which the artist was to exploit successfully from *Promises* to the present. The transitional nature of *Brother to Dragons* has been suggested over the years by the writer's several brief accounts of the genesis of the work, of his struggle to find the appropriate form for his material.[1] The early Warren is best remembered for his prose, especially *All the King's Men*, for which he received the Pulitzer Prize in 1946, a handful of short stories collected

"*Brother to Dragons*: The Fact of Violence vs. the Possibility of Love" by Richard G. Law. From *American Literature*, XLIX (January, 1978), 560–79. Copyright © 1978 by Duke University Press, Durham, N.C. Reprinted by permission.
1. The story may be pieced together from fragmentary accounts, beginning with "The Way It Was Written," *New York Times Book Review*, August 23, 1953, p. 6, and the *Paris Review* interview with Ralph Ellison and Eugene Walter, "The Art of Fiction XVIII: Robert Penn Warren," reprinted in John L. Longley, Jr. (ed.), *Robert Penn Warren: A Collection of Critical Essays* (New York: New York University Press, 1965), 18–45, and continuing through Richard B. Sale, "An Interview in New Haven with Robert Penn Warren," *Studies in the Novel*, II (Fall, 1970), 340–41, and Jean Crawford, "A Conversation with Robert Penn Warren," *Vanderbilt Alumnus*, LV (March–April, 1970), 21. The author's nine-year effort is alluded to briefly in the work itself on pp. 42–44.

and republished in 1948, and three or four critical essays, the best of which appeared before 1951. In his later career, although his historical and journalistic essays are widely respected, Warren's laurels have come chiefly through his poetry. *Promises*, the most personal and affirmative of his later works, won the Pulitzer Prize for poetry in 1957. Following and confirming this pattern, *Brother to Dragons* began in the late forties as a novel and was transformed in the process of composition into a "dialogue in verse." Warren considered and abandoned fictional and dramatic and ballad forms (all of which he had used previously) before he created this new "hybrid genre,"[2] a free-flowing dialogue which combines the qualities of both prose and verse, lyric and drama. *Brother to Dragons* was no casual experiment, however, but the result of a prolonged reassessment on Warren's part of the relation of his art to his own life.[3]

Brother to Dragons is, critics agree, an act of moral accounting, an attempt to balance the books on two hundred years of American experience since the Declaration. In it Warren examines a crime committed by the nephew of Thomas Jefferson as an image of the tragic core of American history, thus renewing the large, uncomfortable questions which arose in all his more youthful work. In fact, Warren's exploration of this nightmare of the American past treats of so many themes from his early development that the extent to which it also breaks with that previous work has seldom been recognized and never fully explored.[4] Though the newness is partly elusive, it may be

2. Warren's phrase in an interview, "Some Important Fall Authors Speak for Themselves," *New York Herald Tribune Book Review*, October 11, 1953, p. 11.
3. Warren has mentioned this period of change and reassessment in several places, but his discussion with Richard B. Sale (*Studies in the Novel*, 340–41) is probably the fullest account. In the *Paris Review* interview, Warren mentioned in passing that ". . . in the last ten years or a little more the personal relation to my writing changed. I never bothered to define the change. I quit writing poems for [ten] years. . . . I didn't finish one for several years, they felt false. Then I got back at it, and that is the bulk of what I've done since" (28–29).
4. Although without suggesting the underlying causes, George P. Garrett has vigorously asserted the significance of *Brother to Dragons* as a watershed in Warren's career: "More than anything else, this work managed to bring together the concerns and themes which had separately haunted his poetry and his prose. For any study of his whole work it is crucial. For a consideration of Warren as poet, it marks a turning point. . . . In a sense, then, after *Brother to Dragons*, Warren was liberated, free to turn to something new if he chose to, equally free to carry along with him whatever he wished from his poetic experience."—"The Recent Poetry of Robert Penn Warren," in Longley,

sensed immediately in the lifting, at the end of the poem, of the gloom pervasive in his earlier work. The stoical acceptance of *At Heaven's Gate* and *All the King's Men* now gives way to joyous affirmation; even the darkness of *Night Rider* and *World Enough and Time* appears to be dispelled. Far more significant, however, is the writer's invitation to read this work autobiographically. The artist, identified simply as "R. P. W.: the writer of this poem,"[5] has become a character in the work; and what the action finally dramatizes is a profound change in him—the change, one assumes, which led to the work itself. As his first self-portrait, the character "R. P. W." represents more than a culmination of the gradual movement away from T. S. Eliot's conception of the artist as an impersonal, invisible "catalyst" and Warren's arrival at an open, confessional stance from which the writer speaks undisguisedly in his own voice. It represents a wholly new dimension in Warren's work, a new willingness to take the direct risks of self-involvement in the issues he raises. It announces that events in the author's own life—specifically, his discovery in a new relationship of the nature of love—have become, in a sense, the source and the subject of the poem.

*   I   *

Seen in the context of this change in the writer, it seems appropriate that *Brother to Dragons* be as much an inquiry into the nature of love as a reconstruction of an ax murder. In spite of its nearly overwhelming impact, the slaying serves not as the center of the action but as an occasion for a wide-ranging dialogue between the protagonists, R. P. W. and Thomas Jefferson. Lilburn Lewis's crime functions largely to image one of the "constants" of human experience; it stands for the ineradicable worst at which the two men must look. The act of

---

p. 227. Monroe K. Spears has also noted the change and remarked that while it occurred at a time when many other poets were beginning to write more "open" or "confessional" poetry, "it is equally plain that the change was the end product of an internal development."—"The Latest Poetry of Robert Penn Warren," *Sewanee Review*, LXXVIII (Spring, 1970), 348. See also George Core, "In the Heart's Ambiguity: Robert Penn Warren as Poet," *Mississippi Quarterly*, XXII (Fall, 1969), 314–15.

5.   Robert Penn Warren, *Brother to Dragons: A Tale in Verse and Voices* (New York: Random House, 1953), 2. Subsequent references to this text will be by page number in the body of the text.

violence is balanced throughout the action, however, by a consideration of what love is or what it might be. In Warren's depiction of the
slaying, love is the murderer's dominant motive; love, or the need for
love, pervades every recess of the dark interior world which Lilburn
inhabits. Whatever understanding of the nature of love is to be possible in the drama, it must, consequently, accommodate and subsume
the form it takes in him; it must "tally" with the fact of murder.

The meaning of this violent fact, however (and the facts, as
always in Warren, appear to bear a number of constructions), becomes the issue between Jefferson and R. P. W. Though Jefferson and
R. P. W. represent antithetical character types with opposing points
of view, stubbornly adhered to, the points of view of neither character
remain static; both change as they move toward a common ground of
understanding.[6] Initially, Jefferson appears in the throes of a profound "moral shock . . . caused by the discovery of what his own
blood was capable of" (p. xi). Knowledge of his nephew's brutality
has turned his optimism at the human prospect to gall and driven
him into a sour misanthropy. Jefferson represents one of the familiar
"idealist" figures in Warren's work who are wedded to some abstract
conception which proves eventually destructive to themselves and
others.[7] In this case Jefferson's belief in human perfectibility is also
one of the most cherished and, according to Warren, dangerous and
superficial of our national myths. Jefferson's moral revulsion at his
nephew's crime is presented as the other face of his Enlightenment
optimism, and both are projections of his self-pride.

Warren's characterization of himself is subtler and more interesting. He portrays himself as a combined historian and detective, visiting the site, sifting through the old court records, and pondering the
motives which led to the slaying. While Jefferson is presented as a disillusioned idealist, R. P. W. appears as a cynical realist, devoid of op-

6.   In the only article to focus specifically on the role of "R. P. W." in the work, Dennis M. Dooley asserts that "R. P. W.'s spiritual progress *parallels* the spiritual progress
of Jefferson"—"The Persona R. P. W. in Warren's *Brother to Dragons*," *Mississippi Quarterly*, XXV (Winter, 1971), 19–30 [q.v., p. 101]—italics added. My own position here
is only slightly at odds with Dooley's; I think his account of the change in character
of R. P. W. substantially correct and a significant contribution to the critical debate on
the work.
7.   The role of Jefferson has been described perceptively by Frederick P. W. McDowell
in the first lengthy study of the work, "Psychology and Theme in *Brother to Dragons*,"
PMLA, LXX (September, 1955), 565–86 [q.v., p. 46].

timistic illusions. Lacking both Jefferson's intellectual and emotional range, he is neither taken in nor even attracted by utopian visions. He has instead a dogged, nagging determination to test every conclusion, to measure every generalization of Jefferson's against all the facts at his disposal. But his worrying of every question from all possible sides seems to reflect a deep strain of anxiety as well as skepticism. If R. P. W. is "afflicted with logic" as with a disease, it is perhaps because his compulsion to analyze indicates a tacit, not wholly conscious acceptance of "naturalism," a view of the world as meaningless mechanism. How far his preoccupation with causation brings him toward this form of nihilism is not clear. His assertion at one point in the dialogue, however, that power, "power empty and abstract," is ". . . still, in the last analysis, the only / Thing worth the struggle" (92), is certainly symptomatic of that typically modern malaise. On another level R. P. W.'s interest in the sordid seems almost a parody of the preoccupations of some self-styled literary "naturalists," who shared R. P. W.'s conclusion (or his fear) that the "facts" were necessarily ugly.

In any event, Warren's characterization of himself seems hardly intended as a model of sanity or all-encompassing wisdom.[8] On the contrary, that laconic, fact-ridden, alternately shrill and mundane voice belongs to a man who stands as much in need of "redemption" as Jefferson. In the two of them, in fact, Warren has personified the two chief heresies of modernism: a too facile optimism about progress and human perfectibility; the nihilism which comes from staring too long into the abyss. The excesses of R. P. W.'s rhetoric—a "Seneca in the meat-house," according to Leslie Fiedler[9]—resemble, particularly in the early speeches, the excesses of Jack Burden in *All the King's Men*. The rhetorical styles of both serve a similar function: to indicate stress and their half-successful, half-foolish attempts to control it. The R. P. W. who first visits the site of the murder, for instance, moves through a landscape alive with terrifying visceral and sexual images.

8.   Victor Strandberg argues on the contrary that R. P. W. has "the most comprehensive and objective perspective of anyone in the story," and sees him as "the spokesman for modern man"; R. P. W., he insists, "always speaks in a temperate voice, urging understanding, acknowledgment, and acceptance." In *A Colder Fire: The Poetry of Robert Penn Warren* (Lexington: University Press of Kentucky, 1965), 143, 149, *et passim*.
9.   Leslie A. Fiedler, review of Robert Penn Warren's *Brother to Dragons*, in *Partisan Review*, XXI (March–April, 1954), 208–12.

Both the landscape and his encounter with the blacksnake in the ruins of the old Lewis mansion provide perfect correlatives for his state of mind. The irrational terror which the snake evokes is fear of himself, of his own as well as the world's "intolerable inwardness":

> In some black aperture among the stones
> I saw the eyes, their glitter in that dark,
> And suddenly the head thrust forth, and the fat, black
> Body molten flowed, as though those stones
> Bled forth earth's inner darkness to the day,
> As though the bung had broke on that intolerable inwardness,
> And now divulged, thus focused and compacted,
> What haunts beneath earth's primal, soldered sill,
> And in its slow and merciless ease, sleepless, lolls
> Below that threshold where the prime waters sleep.
> Thus it flowed forth, and the scaled belly of abomination
> Rustled on stone, rose, rose up
> And reared in regal indolence and swag.
> I saw it rise, saw the soiled white of the belly bulge,
> And in that muscular distension I saw the black side scales
> Show their faint flange and tracery of white.
> And so it rose and climbed the paralyzed light.
> On those heaped stones it was taller than I, taller
> Than any man . . . . (33)

The imagery of the scene associates the snake with primal evil and that "darker self" which manifested itself in Lilburn in the meat-house but is also present in every man, in R. P. W. himself. Here that specter of the writer's own potential is manifest in a terrifying, almost supernatural dimension: ". . . it was taller than I, taller / Than any man." To regain his composure the writer has to name over to himself, as if reciting a charm, the familiar and scientific names which designate this apparition as mere snake, as *Elaphe obsoleta obsoleta*. In thus attempting to exorcise the symbolic dimensions of the encounter, he substitutes a naturalistic view for the metaphysical one which terrifies him. The scene thus raises one of the main issues in the work: whether evil is a reality of (the pun is perfect) an "obsolete" conception. At the same time the scene reveals a split in the psyche of the character: the rough, garrulous exterior of a man who believes in nothing and is surprised at nothing barely conceals a deep-seated, almost hysterical revulsion at what he suspects to be his true nature.

There must consequently be a double movement towards a re-

demptive vision of life in *Brother to Dragons*. Jefferson and R. P. W.,
originally the poles of a dialectic dramatic structure, end in reconciliation and affirmation. The ax murder by the nephew of Thomas Jefferson which is the subject of their dialogue is, paradoxically, both the
means by which reconciliation comes about and the thing to which
they must be reconciled. To confront the horror is to dispel it, and in
this sense, as Victor Strandberg has pointed out, the action has strong
Jungian parallels.[10] The language of their debate frequently evokes the
image of a "labyrinthian" descent into the unconscious self, though
the purpose of that descent is not to slay the Minotaur, but to drag the
monster to light. This confrontation involves the discovery by both
Jefferson and R. P. W. of themselves in Lilburn; each eventually acknowledges Lilburn's act as a fulfillment of qualities latent in himself.
Once he accepts responsibility for the disillusionment and suicide of
his own "near son," Meriwether Lewis, Jefferson can see Lilburn's self-
justification as an extension of his own.[11] Similarly, R. P. W. comes to
recognize as his own the murderer's compulsion to strike at any cost
through the fog of uncertainty to "Truth" and the peace of some single definition.

   Initially the "facts" of the reconstructed slaying seem to bear out
Jefferson's contention that a perverse moral duplicity pervades all. All
acts, he believes, stem (like Lilburn's crime) from a blind, devouring
egotism where murderer and victim alike conspire together to satisfy
their deepest needs, where even George, who returns to "wreak his
merciless frailty on Lilburn" (139), may be a party to the crime. In
Jefferson's disillusioned view, human nature is worse than bestial; it is
monstrous. It is ruled by a disguised and acknowledged Minotaur
that lurks somewhere in the Labyrinth of self:

> . . . and in that dark no thread,
> Airy as breath by Ariadne's fingers forged.
> No thread, and beyond some groped-at corner, hulked
> In the blind dark, hock-deep in ordure, its beard
> And shag foul-scabbed, and when the hoof heaves—
> Listen!—the foulness sucks like mire.

10.   Strandberg, *A Colder Fire*, 151.
11.   The best brief account of these changes in Jefferson's character is still Charles H.
Bohner's in *Robert Penn Warren* (New York: Twayne, 1964), 118–24. According to John L.
Stewart, Warren himself intended that Jefferson's confrontation with Meriwether Lewis
be the turning point of the poem—*The Burden of Time: The Fugitives and Agrarians*
(Princeton, N.J.: Princeton University Press, 1965), 512.

The beast waits. He is the infamy of Crete.
He is the midnight's enormity. He is
Our brother, our darling brother. (7)

Or, more precisely, he is Jefferson's nephew. Jefferson sees Lilburn as an embodiment of that monster, a waking, daylight manifestation of the nightmare lurking in every self. And in that composite image Jefferson discerns (so he thinks) the underlying truth, the real nature of things. Thus, to Jefferson, as to Faulkner's Addie Bundren, words are a disguise, a mask of rationalization. The actuality, the "doing," is the brutal service of the beast's needs. Lilburn's fatal ax had been lifted in vindication of his "love"—actually an unacknowledged incestuous yearning for his mother. "Love," then, is the most insidious form of self-deception in a world in which everything is a charade, everything is flatteringly disguised as its moral opposite. In Jefferson's horrified definition,

. . . all love, all kinds, descriptions, and shapes,
Is but a mask to hide the brute face of fact,
And that fact is the immitigable ferocity of self,
And once you find it in your blood, and find even
That the face of love beneath your face at the first
Budding of the definitive delight—
That every face, even that one, is but a mirror
For your own ferocity, a mirror blurred
And breathed upon and slicked and slimed with love,
And through the interstices and gouts of that
Hypocritical moisture, the cold eyes spy out
From the mirror's cold heart, and thus self spies on self
In that unsummerable arctic of the human alienation. (47)

Love is a weapon, meekness is betrayal, forgiveness is "desire / Gone craven with placation, / . . . the self's final ferocity / Whetted in sweetness as a blade in oil" (49). Tirelessly through this charade, the conscious self plays out its self-deceptive, self-vindicating roles as it serves the monster-self within. Ultimately, Jefferson concludes, only the pain is real:

. . . So let us name the truth, like men.
We are born to joy that joy may become pain.
We are born to hope that hope may become pain.
We are born to love that love may become pain.
We are born to pain that pain may become more

> Pain, and from that inexhaustible superflux
> We may give others pain as our prime definition— (131–32)

The pain which Lilburn inflicts on George is therefore the absolute authentication of his own existence at the same time it is (to Jefferson) the concrete image and indictment of *all* existence.

* II *

However dark Jefferson's view of experience, it is clear that he speaks from a point of view which is moral, even though inverted. In the cruel charade he describes, evil masquerades as good. R. P. W.'s pessimism is subtler. His analysis of the possible sources of the slaying in the psychology of the participants tends, in its cumulative effect, to reduce the significance of Lilburn's act to zero, to another datum in an infinite series of pathetic, meaningless human acts. And just as Lilburn's story seems initially to confirm Jefferson's disillusionment but eventually transcends his views of it, the story also *appears* initially to confirm R. P. W.'s nihilism, his view of man as helpless automaton. R. P. W. discovers (or invents) in the background of the slaying all the elements of a psychological case study: an unhappy, loveless marriage in which the mother seeks companionship in her son, the Oedipal rivalry in her two sons, the nursemaid who competes with the mother for the son's love, and the son's wife who is unwittingly a surrogate for his mother. In addition, Lilburn's path is strewn with all the tragic mischances and coincidences necessary to disaster. Insofar as this chain of cause and effect appears adequate to explain the tragedy, it must follow that Lilburn "had" to do what he did. And having had no choice in the matter, he (and, ultimately, mankind in general) must be absolved from guilt. The same logic, however, "absolves" his action, or any action, from significance. This has been Warren's underlying objection to naturalism throughout his career and the reason for his stubborn defense of "contingency" as opposed to determinism. The attraction of naturalism, he acknowledges, lies not only in the "absolution" it confers but in the convenient distance which it puts between us and our actions:

> We feel that the force now driving Lilburn on
> Is but part of the unleashed and unhoused force of Nature,
> Mindless, irreconcilable, absolute:

The swing of the year, the thrust of Time, the wind.
But we also feel a need to leave that house
On the dark headland, and lift up our eyes
To whatever liberating perspective,
Icy and pure, the wild heart may command,
To escape the house, escape the tightening coil
And mathematical constriction: and so the glimmering night scene
    and storm under
The incalculable and distant disdain of starlight, serve, therefore,
As an image of lethal purity, the incessant
And whirling dream of desperate innocence,
The infatuate glitter of the land of Platonic ice.
It is an image to free us from the human trauma,
And the wind drives unremitting, and the oak will bend. (95–96)

As the action makes clear, however, there is no escape from the "human trauma," no sufficiently "liberating perspective." Here and in the lines just preceding the quotation, Warren images the seeming helplessness of Lilburn in the oak bending before the pressure of the "wind," one of his favorite metaphors for the blind forces of nature: "The wind is unceasing, and the stars likewise" (95). These images of immense cold and infinite space evoke a powerful sense of the bleakness of the nonhuman universe, devoid of both sentience and value.[12] Only the intrusion by the poet of what is ostentatiously a "pathetic fallacy," an allusion to Jacob's anguish and an *illusion*, purposely not sustained, of sentient, purposeful behavior on the part of the elements (the "pitiless angel of air"), reminds us of the human perspective, which is practically synonymous here with the capacity for anguish. The passage delineates sharply the boundary between the human and the "natural," implying at the same time that to dissolve Lilburn wholly into the natural (as a deterministic view would do), to merge him wholly with the image of the unconscious and "lifeless" oak acted upon by the "wind," would be a falsification, an error as obvious as the attribution of pitilessness to the wind or disdain to the stars.

The fact of consciousness itself, that capacity for anguish and self-

---

12. Strandberg discusses these same images and the "naturalistic considerations" to which they give rise, but concludes that "Warren's answer to the problem of cosmic darkness is, in the end, theological."—*A Colder Fire*, 160–62. This position seems to me to beg the question.

delusion, remains to be accounted for, both in the passage and in the events leading up to the murder. To be aware of the mechanisms of nature without being free of them appears to be the anomalous human burden. Because of it, there can be no "perfect adjustment" of conscious mind with unconscious nature; the gulf between them, Warren implies, is absolute. In one of the most quoted passages in the book, the artist imagines an existence in the flow of time in which being and sustaining environment *are* in perfect harmony:

> A thousand miles and the fabulous river is ice in the starlight.
> The ice is a foot thick, and beneath, the water slides black like a
>   dream,
> And the interior of that unpulsing blackness and thrilled zero
> The big channel-cat sleeps with eye lidless, and the brute face
> Is the face of the last torturer, and the white belly
> Brushes the delicious and icy blackness of mud.
> But there is no sensation. How can there be
> Sensation when there is perfect adjustment? The blood
> Of the creature is but the temperature of the sustaining flow:
> The catfish is in the Mississippi and
> The Mississippi is in the catfish and
> Under the ice both are at one with God.
> Would that we were! (94)

This image of *un*conscious being is the antithesis of human existence, the essense of which is not "perfect adjustment" but "sensation"—or, as Jefferson insists, pain.

From this inexplicable but stubborn fact of consciousness comes, Warren has always maintained, the human need to wrest significance out of pain, to find sanctions, to bestow value on the "unpulsing blackness" which encompasses man. In addition to the endurance of pain, then, the essence of consciousness involves the perception of— or rather the creation of—values, the making of a context for "virtue." That is to say, man necessarily creates a frame of reference in which his actions may acquire meaning. To be conscious is to live by discriminations, to judge, and to require therefore a definition of "good" as well as of "self." Hence, the paradox (which R. P. W. affirms) of value existing within a naturalistic world: ". . . despite all naturalistic considerations, / Or in the end because of naturalistic considerations, / We must believe in virtue" (29). Elsewhere, Warren has explained more fully the nature of these "values." "Against all reason," he has

argued, "man insists . . . on creating and trying to live by certain values. These values are . . . 'illusions,' but the last wisdom is for man to
realize that though his values are illusions, the illusion is necessary, is
infinitely precious, and is . . . his only truth."[13] The fragility of such
values is self-evident: self and self-concept, the world and one's vision
of it, can never perfectly coincide. But yet, in some manner, "all life
lifts and longs toward its own name, / And toward fulfillment in the
singlenesss of definition" (121).

Ultimately Lilburn's story confirms that yearning. Longing for
some transcendent moment of what Warren calls "glory," a moment
of intensity great enough to stand for meaning and force all the objects of his interior world to coalesce into meaning, Lilburn—in part,
and in some sense of the word—*chooses* the moment in the meat-
house. The seductive promise of a single, defining act to redeem him
from the "anguish of complication" is the real motive for his crime:
". . . any act, / Any act at all, the bad, the good, affords, / Or seems to
afford, the dear redemption of simplicity: / The dear redemption in
the mere fact of achieved definition, / Be what that may" (56).[14]

The universality of this struggle to wrest coherence out of chaos is
suggested throughout the work in many ways. Charles Lewis, the father of the murderer and in some ways the source of the family problems, describes his own actions in similar terms:

> I built the house, left Albermarle and ease,
> Took wife and sons, slaves, chattels, beasts, and goods,
> Potions and pills, picked-lint, and scalpel, all
> My marks of rank and occupation, all
> *Those things, intangible and tangible, that men*
> *Clutch round them like a cloak against the time*
> *The wind will shift*, and sit sudden in the dire
> Airt, and the cold creep.
> *I took those things, for they are like*
> *The shell the shellfish spins from the slick slime*
> *The deliquescence of itself to fend*
> *That self, and its poor palpitation, boxed in dark.*
>
> (12–13, italics added)

13.   Robert Penn Warren, "Conrad and *Nostromo*," in *Selected Essays* (New York: Random House, 1958), 45.
14.   For a useful gloss of this idea, see McDowell, "Psychology and Theme," p. 61 in
this volume.

Similarly, the deep need of all the characters to be purified and freed by projecting their guilt elsewhere (as in the ancient Hebrew ritual of the scapegoat) illustrates, however pitifully, the necessity of constructing a "moral universe" around oneself. It is as if all the main characters unconsciously assume the existence of a retributive moral order to which they are personally accountable and a savage god which they must propitiate. The god, of course, is within, and perhaps but another version of the blind beast of egotism. The charade which Jefferson describes appears to be performed for its benefit; all of experience is bent to accommodate it:

> . . . yes, every one,
> The saints and angels, too, who tread, yes, every
> And single one, but plays the sad child's play
> And old charade where man puts down the bad and then feels
>   good.
> It is the sadistic farce by which the world is cleansed.
> And is not cleansed, for in the deep
> Hovel of the heart that Thing lies
> That will never unkennel himself to the contemptible steel,
> Nor needs to venture forth ever, for all sustenance
> Comes in to him, the world comes in, and is his. (42)

While Lilburn may realize at some level that *he* is the betrayer, he suppresses that knowledge and invents the treacherous and conspiratorial servants who try to obliterate his mother. Jefferson's revulsion at Lilburn is a similar evasion by projection, a way of denying the existence of the same potential in himself. This convenient externalization of evil and the projection of it onto others takes myriad forms; it may, as in the case of R. P. W., emerge as an image of a monster-self which is really *other*-than-the-self, a demon alien for whom one is not really responsible.

This false exorcising of one's own evil seems a kind of mental game, a set of moral gymnastics universally indulged in. If it were the whole story, Jefferson's darkest utterance about man's nature would be understatement. But the very fact of this charade, the universal necessity to rationalize sadism and lust into virtues, implies that lust and sadism are not all: ". . . Lilburn's heart-deep need / To name his evil good is the final evidence / For the existence of good" (144). Lilburn's sordid act, then, cannot stand as a definitive image of human nature; it must stand instead as a tragic possibility, ever present, of the perversion of good.

Lucy Lewis, the mother of the killer and a kind of catalyst in the process of R. P. W. and Jefferson's enlightenment, becomes the means through which this idea is explored. Of all the characters in the drama who struggle toward some self-vindicating definition of good, she is the only one who does not blind herself through some secret (and unreal) dream of self, or turn experience into alibi. "The human curse," she discovers, "is simply to love and sometimes to love well, / But never well enough" (123), and she resists, successfully, the temptation to deny the evil consequences of her love for her son. "I accept," she says:

> . . . the responsibility of my love,
> And know, somehow, that my love was infected with failure.
> No, I must maintain that my love in some part,
> Some part at least, was love. Else how had I lived?
> But even my love had infected my son's heart. (187–88)

That one's best gifts may kill or corrupt is a bitter but crucial recognition which frees her from the self-deceptions that limit the understandings of the others. It is Lucy (the bearer of light) who loves unstintingly and sees, therefore, what Jefferson cannot, that in Lilburn's brutal act were mingled his best as well as worst qualities: "He saw poor George as but his darkest self / And all the possibility of the dark that he feared, / And so he struck, and struck down that darkest self . . ." (189). Even in his moment of sadistic self-gratification, then, Lilburn affirms in some twisted way that he is more than brute. He kills for the highest value he is capable of recognizing, performs his evil deed in the name of good. If he thus participates in the charade which Jefferson described, so do they all. To reject Lilburn as a monster, then, is to compound his crime and to repeat it in its essence.

*   **III**   *

The universality of the need to wrest meaning out of experience is suggested in yet one other way, in an analogy implicit between the process of individual self-definition and an artist's act of creation. The individual's creation of a moral universe in which to act and the artist's shaping of his materials into form manifest the same deep, imaginative process. Out of both come the fragile human artifacts: order, meaning, and value. In Warren's characterization of himself in *Brother to Dragons* we observe that *process* as well as its results. We see the artist assembling the sources and records of his story, pondering the motives of the participants, groping for a *form* adequate to its complexity, and inventing at one point where the records are silent the necessary and ironical engine of Lilburn's destruction, the faithful hound who betrays him. And if we miss the import of that spectacle there remains the conversation in which R. P. W. broaches the subject of artistic form to his own creation, Jefferson. To the artist's comments on the inadequacy of certain genres, Jefferson replies:

> . . . There is no form to hold
> Reality and its insufferable intransigence.
> I know. I know, for I once tried to contrive
> A form I thought fit to hold the purity of man's hope.
> But I did not understand the nature of things. (44)

Form in art and the "myth" which one makes of experience are thus nearly interchangeable terms; both impose meaning and pattern on essentially inert materials. They are equally attempts to make comprehensible an intractable "universe" of experience. As Warren remarks in the introduction to the book, ". . . if poetry is the little myth we make, history is the big myth we live, and in our living, constantly remake" (xii).

Lilburn, of course, understands the "nature of things" even less than Jefferson. The moral universe he has created around himself is patently false and self-vindicating, and he cannot see past it to the actual world. He sees only the roles in which he has cast the inhabitants of his imagination, roles which, of course, the people around him fail to play. Lilburn's error—perhaps the "type" of all error—is solipsism. His fate suggests that the process of "justifying" may just as easily destroy as redeem, may as easily distort and hide as reveal and clarify. But if consciousness may as readily be trapped in a solipsistic circle of illusion as freed to act in the "real" world, how, then, may one find a set of values or definition of self which is not a cleverly disguised deadfall? How may one "find sanctions" without committing an elaborate form of suicide?

Warren has always answered this question rather cryptically with the single word "knowledge." In *Brother to Dragons* R. P. W. explicitly rejects the usual sense of the word in favor of "some new and better definition," at the nature of which he only hints:

> . . . knowing is,
> Maybe, a kind of being, and if you know,
> Can really know, a thing in all its fullness,
> Then you are different, and if you are different,
> Then everything is different, somehow, too. (127–28)

It is evident here that Warren means a special kind of knowledge which extinguishes self and transcends the simplistic gestalt of ordinary perception, a knowledge which brings contact with the actual other, not with one's own projected symbol-world. His images for such an experience have nearly always been drawn from religion: Moses on the mountain, Saul on the road to Damascus, or backwoods Southern Protestants violently struck down by grace. In *Brother to Dragons*, however, that kind of knowledge seems to be synonymous with the final sense of the word "love" and is implied when Warren (through Lucy Lewis) equates "love" with (successful) "definition":

> . . . [love] is all you have.
> It is all you can bring with you to the inhabited silence.
> For if love's anything, it is the thing
> That, once existing, may not be denied,
> *For it is definition*, and denial
> Is death, but is
> That death in which you may not ever lie down.
>
> (174, italics added)

Like Lilburn's sadistic self-indulgence, then, love may provide that moment of "glory" or "Pentecostal intuition" through which the value of all things becomes known. If sheer intensity of feeling may stand for meaning—or bestow meaning—then "love" creates the very possibility of "knowing" (in the special sense in which it must be taken in the work). And if more is possible, if solipsism can be broken, love may be the bridge, even the contact itself, which provides the sense of the "thing in all its fullness." The New Critical vocabulary of aesthetic experience seems relevant here: love bestows what the New Critics claimed that art provides, a "concrete" sense of the "world's body." To *know* requires a putting aside of our ordinary and essentially solipsistic games, our symbolic role-playing and projections, in a transcendent moment of *appreciation* (in the root sense of the word) of some part of the Not-me, of the actual other. Such self-transcending glimpses of the world provide the certitude or "reality" which the mind craves, and thus they provide a new definition of self.

To love means, therefore, to create a private moral universe which is not mere illusion but accommodates, at one end of the scale, the sources of our "guilt" and "despair"—the experience of pain. Such a vision must account for and yet transcend that common denominator and only certitude of experience. Love is consequently a revelation, an excruciating "searing" of the self which creates both world and self anew. Jack Burden touches very briefly on the idea of love's transforming power in one of his less successful philosophical flights in *All the King's Men*: ". . . in the act of loving somebody, [you] become real, cease to be a part of the uncreated clay and get the breath of life in you and rise up."[15] But the idea is dramatized, forcefully, for the first time by Warren in *Brother to Dragons*.

The profound transformation which occurs in R. P. W. accounts for (and is dramatized by) the contrast between his first visit to the site of the Lewis tragedy and the second, the episode with which the book closes. In the first visit, which ends with the terrifying encounter with the snake, the scene is colored by an agitation and confused yearning which are different in degree but not in kind from Lilburn's:

> . . . A fellow of forty, a stranger, and a fool,
> Red-headed, freckled, lean, a little stooped,
> Who yearned to be understood, to make communication,
> To touch the ironic immensity of afternoon with meaning,
> To find and know my name and make it heard,
> While the sun insanely screamed out all it knew,
> Its one wild word:
> *Light, light, light!*
> And all identity tottered to that remorseless vibration. (26–27)

While this assessment is attributed to the farmer who owns the old Lewis place, the judgment is also R. P. W.'s and an ironic echo of Lilburn's only speech a few pages earlier—an anguished cry at the extinction of all "light" in his life (23–24).

On the second visit the scene is completely altered, its objects shrunken and unterrifying: the "jungle convolvement and visceral

15. Robert Penn Warren, *All the King's Men* (New York: Harcourt, Brace, 1946), 299.

delight" have vanished, and the landscape no longer throbs with menace like the forest in *Heart of Darkness*. "For that's the way I had remembered it," R. P. W. comments; "But no, it's not like that. At least, not now, / And never was, I guess, but in my head" (207). The change, then, is not merely seasonal (it being winter on this second occasion), but a reflection of changes in the observer. Inexplicably, all the previously threatening aspects of the scene have been transformed into a vision of peace and normality. The Black Snake is present again in the imagination of the poet, but in its natural dimensions, and snug underground in winter hibernation. That specter of what the unconscious may hold has, in short, been reduced to "natural," unmetaphysical proportions. All the terror it held for him has been dissipated.[16]

The implicit explanation for this transformation, of course, lies in the structure of the work, in everything that has transpired earlier in the action. The whole process of coming to terms with Lilburn's crime has involved the acknowledgment of the monster *as self* and not as terrifying alien. The scene is therefore the culmination, dramatically, of a process of understanding and acceptance. But in the subsequent lines Warren uncharacteristically adduces as a second explanation a cause essentially *outside* the structure of the work. He moves abruptly to a description of another winter scene in his own life—a first kiss and the belated discovery of love:

>   . . . I stand
> Amid the brown leaves and snow. I lift up my eyes
> Beyond the bluff and the flat land farther
> To where the river gleams. Its gleam is cold.
> And I think of another bluff and another river.
> I think of another year and another winter.
> I think of snow on the brown leaves, and below
> That other bluff, how cold and far was light on that northern river.
> I think how her mouth and mine together
> Were cold on the first kiss. (208–209)

This event becomes, through this sudden retrospective glance, the center of the work, the mysterious redeeming event which the action both explores and dramatizes: the phoenix-like renewal of self. In

---

16. For a discussion of the functional nature of the two "digressions" describing the author's visits to Rocky Hill, see Dooley, "The Persona R. P. W.," p. 101 herein.

Jefferson's parallel "redemption," his change and the causes of it are spelled out more fully: in the "incandescence of the heart's great flare," Jefferson asserts, ". . . all creation validates itself, / For whatever you create, you create yourself by it, / And in creating yourself you will create / The whole wide world and gleaming West anew" (195). But Warren's summary of his own transformation penetrates without elaboration to the heart of the mystery: "Since then," he says simply, "I have made new acquaintance with the nature of joy" (209).

"Canaan's Grander Counterfeit": Jefferson and America in *Brother to Dragons*

William Bedford Clark

Throughout the Bicentennial year, Americans were invited time and again to observe the pieties of the Past, to contemplate those images, more mythic now than simply historical, that figure forth this nation's genesis, and no doubt chief among the celebrants were those elderly Virginia vestals who tend the flame of Thomas Jefferson's memory at Monticello, his functionally elegant home outside Charlottesville. There the visitor finds one of Jefferson's ingenious devices for counting the passing of the hours—profound testimony to his faith in a clockwork universe. There also one finds zoological trophies forwarded to Jefferson by Lewis and Clark—mute prophecies of a despoiled continent. The ladies in charge of the tour, serenely gracious and genteel, point out a music stand of Mr. Jefferson's design, a practical mechanism for duplicating letters as they are written, Mr. Jefferson's waistcoat and ewer, and an underground passageway through which Mr. Jefferson's chamber pot could be carried out of the house and emptied. The ladies generally fail to mention who it was who carried out the chamberpot; nor are they likely to stress the fact that Monticello was completed only after Jefferson took out a mortgage on his most readily convertible property, his human chattel, his Black slaves.

To focus thus upon the irony of Jefferson's paradoxical career as prototypal American liberal and as slaveholding planter is nothing new. Indeed, the troubling gap between Jeffersonian theory and practice was belabored, however ineffectively, by Jefferson's Federalist enemies in his own lifetime. Yet the irony remains a suggestive factor in the *mythos* of America, for it stands as a persistent reminder of the disparity between American dreams and American realities as well as

"'Canaan's Grander Counterfeit': Jefferson and America in *Brother to Dragons*" by William Bedford Clark. From *Renascence,* XXX (1978), 171–78. Copyright © 1978 by *Renascence*. Reprinted by permission.

of certain central contradictions within the personality of Jefferson himself, a personality that seems to represent so much of what is commonly regarded as our national character. The study of history can provide us with such ironies, but a fuller exploration of their implications often requires an exercise of the literary imagination. Fortunately, in the case of Jefferson, we can turn to Robert Penn Warren's *Brother to Dragons* for insight not only into the character and thought of the third President of the United States, but into significance of the American experience as a whole.

At one point in his book-length "Tale in Verse and Voices"—the setting of which is an imaginary realm of "any time" and "no place"— Warren's persona, R. P. W., confronts the literal *spirit* of Thomas Jefferson with the fact that the building of his beloved Monticello "demanded / A certain amount of black sweat."[1] Jefferson responds: "I lived in the world. / Say that. But say, too, that I tried to envisage / The human possibility" (109). His response is facile and not altogether satisfactory, but moments before Jefferson has revealed unwittingly the real reasons for his accommodation to a social system that denied the principles set forth as "self-evident" absolutes in his *Declaration of Independence*. These reasons grow out of a strange amalgam of guilt and fear. Speaking of the dark presence of slaves, Jefferson notes with an obvious touch of paranoia:

> . . . they spy from the shadow.
> They spy from the darkest corner of the hall,
> They serve you the dish and stand with face blandly
> Averted, but sidewise that picklock gaze has triggered
> The tender mechanism of your destructive secret.
> Oh, they've surprised you
> At meat, at stool, at concupiscence, and with sardonic detachment
> Have even inspected your face while you turned inward
> To the most soul-searching meditation. And when
> You turn inward, at the heart's darkest angle you meet
> The sly accusation and the shuttered gleam
> Of that sidelong eye. (108–109)

From Jefferson's own writings, both public and private, we can see that these sentiments attributed to him by Warren have at least a psy-

---

1. Robert Penn Warren, *Brother to Dragons* (New York: Random House, 1953), 109. All subsequent references to the text of this poem are taken from this edition and appear parenthetically in my essay.

chological validity. Since slavery, as Jefferson perceived it, was a tyran-
nical evil, it bred inevitable guilt, and that guilt, in turn, bred a fear of
retribution that argued paradoxically against emancipation without a
workable plan for colonizing a potentially vengeful black population.
It is not my intention here, however, to dwell upon the historical accuracy of Warren's portrayal of Jefferson in *Brother to Dragons*, although Warren is, in certain respects, the most self-consciously historical of leading American writers. Rather, it is to interpret Warren's
characterization of Jefferson in accordance with his prefatory remark
that "history is the big myth we live."[2] In the final analysis, the Jefferson of *Brother to Dragons*, however convincing and well-drawn he may
be, is less important as an individual reconstructed from the past than
as a symbol embodying Warren's critique of America's history and his
hopes for America's future. The extent to which the reader can come
to share in a sense of the validity of such a vision is, as Warren knows,
the author's "ultimate gamble."[3]

   Warren's portrayal of Jefferson is hardly marked by a reverential
deference, as we have already seen, and this has been a disturbing
factor for some who approach *Brother to Dragons*. Warren's lifelong
friend, Cleanth Brooks, to whom, along with Mrs. Brooks, the work
is dedicated, writes that "For a great many Americans, Jefferson
comes close to being a sacred figure, and to dare to portray a Jefferson
troubled and in doubt, a Jefferson embittered and cynical" is tanta-
mount to laying "profane hands upon the idol."[4] Indeed, Jefferson is
"embittered and cynical" at the work's outset, and he traces his despair to a single act of seemingly pointless violence—the brutal butchering of a slave boy by Lilburn Lewis, the ex-President's nephew. The
horror of this crime is intensified by virtue of the fact that the slave's
offense was ostensibly a trivial one; he broke a pitcher prized by
Lilburn's late mother, Jefferson's sister Lucy. The effect of the crime is
to assure Jefferson that all his celebrated faith in man and mankind's
glorious destiny is vanity and error, that man is not merely a fallen
creature, but a "master-monster" in comparison with which "all hip-
pogrifs and dragons, Grendel and Grendel's dam" are innocent (41).

   While Jefferson caustically renounces his rationalist's libertarian

2. *Ibid.*, xii.
3. *Ibid.*
4. Cleanth Brooks, *The Hidden God: Studies in Hemingway, Faulkner, Yeats, Eliot, and Warren* (New Haven: Yale University Press, 1963), 100 [q.v., p. 15].

dream, he still speaks longingly of its loss. In Philadelphia when he feverishly drafted the *Declaration*, Jefferson had merged himself with an idea so powerful that, as he tells R. P. W., ". . . I was nothing, nothing but joy, / And my heart cried out, 'Oh, this is Man!'" (9). Jefferson's total surrender of selfhood to this single-minded image of human possibility is, as he recognizes, a paradoxical "pride past pride," and it bears a clear resemblance to the egocentric absolutism of the "higher law" men whose position Warren attacks in a later book, *The Legacy of the Civil War*. Jefferson found a formal representation for his democratic ideal in the classical simplicity of the *Maison Quarrée* at Nîmes, which he sees as lit with "the eternal / Light of just proportion and heart's harmony" reflecting "the correctness of our human aspiration" (40). For Jefferson, the *Maison Quarrée* is a promise of a world realized along the lines of the Enlightenment vision of reason and order, a world peopled by men unfettered by ignorance and brute instinct.

In sharp contrast to this vision is that materialized in the Gothic cathedrals of Europe which Jefferson regards with distaste as "abominable relics" (39), gargoyle-ridden products of "the nightmare of a sick child who screamed in the dark" (39). What Jefferson does not realize, however, is that Gothic architecture has its own order, an order following organic rather than geometric imperatives. It too represents a world-view, but one in which the fact of evil has its place alongside the good. Only when, near the narrative's conclusion, Jefferson can come to subscribe to such an inclusive vision of the world and man's place in it, does he find the basis for a renewal of faith.

In the meantime, he despairs and indulges in the luxury of misanthropic rhetoric. Even those who shared his dream in Philadelphia, the Founding Fathers, appear to him as "Marmosets in mantles, beasts in boots, parrots in pantaloons. / That is to say, men" (6). "There's no forgiveness," he tells his sister, "for our being human. / It is the inexpugnable error" (24). Yet, if there is more than a touch of pride in Jefferson's original optimism, his despair is at bottom based, ironically enough, on an even more virulent *hybris*, and here too, Jefferson's psychology parallels that of the "higher law" advocates in *The Legacy of the Civil War*. While he posits his murderous nephew, Lilburn, as "an absolute of our essential / Condition" (93), he never really acts as if he partakes of that condition himself. In effect, he hates and blames Lilburn less for the agony he inflicts upon the slave than for the fact that "The death of that black boy was the death / Of all my hope . . ." (132). Jefferson, like any reformer, was not blind to violence and human suffering even prior to the horror at Rocky Hill, but that shock of that example of inhumanity wounds him precisely because it is perpetrated by his sister's son, his *own* flesh and blood. In assuming the cloak of self-righteous wrath, he can forget his earlier insistence that it is the slayer of the monster, and not the monster himself, who lacks innocence. It would have been better, Jefferson suggests, to have thrown the infant Lilburn "Out where the hogs come to the holler, out with the swill" (61). To this suggestion, he adds another for the benefit of Lilburn's mother, who reminds him that Lilburn was once her helpless baby:

> . . . I'll say what I should have done then.
> Listen, the Indian, when some poor frontier mother, a captive, lags
> By the trail to feed her brat, he'll snatch its heels
> And snap the head against a tree trunk, like a whip.
> Just so, and the head pops like an egg. Well,
> There wasn't any tree, it being indoors, but the brickwork
> Of the chimney in your room would have been perfectly
>   adequate. (63)

Lilburn's own barbarism springs from precisely such a distempered imagination, and the simple fact is, as Frederick McDowell has shown, that Lilburn and Jefferson both suffer from the same kind of absolutist mentality.[5] Lilburn seeks only to destroy his own darker self by striking out at the slave, George, and his crime is ultimately a pathetic effort to defend the purity of his devotion to the memory of his mother. If there is madness behind his act, madness in *Brother to Dragons* is, in the words of old Charles Lewis, Lilburn's father, ". . . but the cancer of truth, the arrogance / Of truth gone wild and swollen in the blood" (12). In turn, Lilburn serves as a symbol of Thomas Jefferson's darker self, the demon Jefferson seeks to exorcize

---

5.   Frederick P. W. McDowell, "Psychology and Theme in *Brother to Dragons*" in John Lewis Longley, Jr. (ed.), *Robert Penn Warren: A Collection of Critical Essays* (New York: New York University Press, 1965), 204 [q.v., p. 52]. I also owe a general debt in the present essay to the discussion of *Brother to Dragons* in Victor H. Strandberg, *A Colder Fire: The Poetry of Robert Penn Warren* (Lexington: University Press of Kentucky, 1965), and to Dennis Dooley's essay, "The Persona of R. P. W. in Warren's *Brother to Dragons*," *Mississippi Quarterly*, XXV (Winter, 1971), 19–30.

in order to reassert his own sense of preeminent virtue. Jefferson can focus his personal bitterness and self-doubts on Lilburn, and, in reviling his nephew, draw upon what Warren elsewhere calls the "Treasury of Virtue," the conviction of moral superiority that lies behind the ethical myopia of much of our national experience.[6] It is important here to remember that the Jefferson of *Brother to Dragons* represents, on one level, what Everett Carter identifies as the "prototypal American consciousness,"[7] and while Warren's poem is no simple allegory, one of its central concerns is with the problem of our history as Warren envisions it.

Accordingly, it is significant that the Great American West, that geographical emblem of all the hope and dreams of American life, plays a vital part in shaping Jefferson's final reconciliation with Lilburn, mankind, and, most importantly, himself. Historically, Jefferson was the first great champion of westward expansion, a course of collective action he made possible through the Louisiana Purchase. Quite fittingly, he commissioned yet another of his Lewis kinsmen, Meriwether, along with Captain Clark to explore this vast tract of western land on the Day of Independence, July 4, 1803. This same Meriwether Lewis, whose despair drove him to eventual suicide, appears toward the end of *Brother to Dragons* to turn the tables on Jefferson by blaming him for his death. Meriwether had immersed himself in Jefferson's vision of the redemptive promise of the West, only to regard it finally as a destructive "lie," a "lie" that made life for him, as for the disillusioned Jefferson, an unbearable travesty. Jefferson initially regarded the West as a corollary to man's future perfection, the setting for the physical realization of his democratic scheme for a republic of yeoman farmers:

> . . . it was my West, the West I bought and gave and never
> Saw, or but like the Israelite,
> From some high pass or crazy crag of mind, saw—
> I saw all,
> Swale and savannah and the tulip-tree
> Immortally blossoming in May,
> Hawthorn and haw,

6.   Robert Penn Warren, *The Legacy of the Civil War: Meditations on the Centennial* (New York: Random House, 1961), 59–66.
7.   Everett Carter, "The 'Little Myth' of Robert Penn Warren," *Modern Fiction Studies*, VI (Spring, 1960), 4.

> Valleys extended and prairies idle and the land's
> Long westward languor lifting toward the flaming escarpment at the
>   end of day.
> Saw the sad bison lick the outstretched hand,
> And on the western rock, wracked in the clang and smother,
> The black seal barks, and loves us, knowing we will come.
> For wind is steady, and the moon rides gold,
> Suns execute their arrogant precessional
> Of deep delight, and the illimitable glitter
> Of distance dazzles to our human fulfillment.
> It was great Canaan's grander counterfeit.
> Bold Louisiana,
> It was the landfall of my soul. (11)

Jefferson's ecstatic vision of the West presents it as the familiar Garden of the World but his reference to the bison and the seal, inevitable victims of America's westering, points toward the withering of both the Garden and the Jeffersonian dream, for Jefferson had failed to anticipate the rape of the West borne of human greed.

The sardonic, and at times cynical, R. P. W. knows full well that there were inducements for westering considerably less pristine than those espoused by the visionary Jefferson—those of the founder of Smithland, Kentucky, for instance:

> He had a right to hope, that fellow Smith,
> In that heyday of hope and heart's extravagance
> When Grab was watchword and earth spread her legs
> Wide as she could, like any jolly trollop
> Or bouncing girl back in the bushes after
> The preaching or the Husking bee, and said,
> "Come git it, boy, hit's yourn, but git it deep."
> And every dawn sang, "Glory, glory be!"
> Sang, "Glory be to Grab, come git it, boy!"
> Sang, "Git it, boy, hit's yourn, but git it deep!" (16)

Smithland's prosperity is soon preempted by that of Louisville and Paducah (although it finally comes to enjoy a minor boom thanks to the Korean War); still, its gas station, Dixie Theater, and town drunk are the ironic culmination of its founder's materialistic ambition, and they stand as burlesques of Jefferson's sense of national destiny. This wide disparity between dream and reality prompts the downfall of Meriwether Lewis. It is the "Grab" and rapacious greed of western speculators and corrupt politicians directed against him that convinces him that Jefferson's aspirations for the West are only a vicious lie, and this conviction drives him over the brink of self-destruction. Thus it is that, in accordance with the ruthless dialectic of *Brother to Dragons*, Jefferson's idealism inadvertently destroys the man he regarded as a kind of son in much the same way that Lilburn's obsession with the purity of his love for his mother finds fruition in atrocity. Ironically, it is Jefferson's sister Lucy, portrayed as confused and ineffectual throughout most of the narrative, who first hits upon this key to the reconciliation of Jefferson with the fact of evil within his blood and within himself. She speaks the sobering truth that frees him at last from the twin burdens of despair and pride.

Lucy puts Jefferson's original dream of man's future in its proper perspective:

> If there was vanity, fear, and deceit, in its condition,
> What of that? For we are human, and must work
> In the shade of our human condition. The dream remains. (193)

But, she continues, there is "a nobler [dream] yet to dream," a future based on a recognition of mankind's potential for evil as well as for good, a future achieved through an awareness of human limitations. Jefferson can once again surrender to a vision of promise renewed; the West, and by extension the American nation itself, is reborn to a new set of possibilities:

> Dance back the buffalo, the shining land!
> Our grander Ghost Dance dance now, and shake the feather.
> Dance back the morning and the eagle's cry.
> Dance back the Shining Mountain, let them shine!
> Dance into morning and the lifted eye.
> Dance into morning past the morning star,
> And dance the heart by which we have lived and died.
> My Louisiana, I would dance you, though afar! (195)

It is significant that in this paean to the promise of America Jefferson adopts the language of the American Indian, whom he had earlier dismissed as a savage, and it is also significant that by the end of *Brother to Dragons* he can come to address the slave boy, George, as "my son" in recognition of their common human dilemma. Warren's Jefferson, unlike Hawthorne's Young Goodman Brown, does not shrink from the communion of his race. Instead, he embraces it, realizing that if it is characterized by suffering and imperfection, it also has its glory.

What does all this mean on a national level? Warren has put it succinctly and well in *Democracy and Poetry*, appropriately enough, the text of the Jefferson Lectures he delivered in 1974:

> Perhaps we are, indeed, the Chosen People—and I should like to think that we are. But it is hard work to stay "chosen," and it is harder to scrutinize any situation and ourselves when our chosenness seems to wear a little thin. And hard to realize that there may be no more automatic solutions, even for us. This is not pessimism. It is, rather, optimism—in the sense that it implies confidence in our will to be, not victims, but makers, of our history. But that optimism implies, too, that we are not free from the hazards of selfhood, nor of time.[8]

Warren's advice to the nation, as he presents it with dramatic force in *Brother to Dragons*, is, it would appear, an outgrowth of his peculiarly Southern identity. The historian C. Vann Woodward, a close friend of Warren, has pointed out that the South, unlike the rest of the nation, has experienced defeat and frustration and despair.[9] That fact makes it possible for a Southern man of letters like Warren to see through the potentially dangerous hollowness of the perennial American myths of ever-beneficent progress, military invincibility, and unqualified national virtue. Warren preaches optimism, but it is, as we have seen, an optimism chastened by an awareness and acceptance of the realities of human history and our own shortcomings. By comparison, the optimism of another distinguished American poet, Archibald MacLeish, as expressed in his explicitly Bicentennial drama, *The Great American Fourth of July Parade* (in which the figure of Jefferson also plays a vital role), seems facile indeed.

8. Robert Penn Warren, *Democracy and Poetry* (Cambridge, Mass.: Harvard University Press, 1975), 4.
9. C. Vann Woodward, *The Burden of Southern History* (Baton Rouge: Louisiana State University Press, 1968), 187–211.

Reviews

Babette Deutsch

New York Herald Tribune Book Review, August 23, 1953

Every man who reads this page is brother to dragons. And the millions who will never read it, the living and the dead. But this is 1953. The stories of saints and of psychoanalysts, as of those archaic creatures, the poets, may be haunted by dragons. Such monsters are old hat to atomic physicists, to people working with supersonic weapons, to the children who play they are "space-men." With their dog tags swinging like scapulars. What can the phrase mean: "brother to dragons"? The meaning is, of course, the substance and significance of Robert Penn Warren's poem. This savagely dramatic piece was originally planned as a novel, and at one time as a ballad, but the theme proved too intimate, too complex, to fit either form. Yet here is the novelist's gift for exhibiting character in action and in speech, and some times the sad mellifluousness, if not the simplification of balladry. The work also shows throughout the philosopher's concern with definition. If it were not a poem, it might be an exercise in moral semantics. Fortunately, it remains a poem, and a resonant one.

The search for definitions is plain from the start. The author, a native of Kentucky, was for years mulling over the meaning of a crime committed by one of its earlier inhabitants: Lilburn Lewis, the elder son of Thomas Jefferson's sister Lucy. She died soon after her husband, Dr. Charles Lewis, had taken her away from Virginia, along with their two grown sons, Lilburn and Isham, and his slaves, to live near a frontier settlement overlooking the Ohio. "On the night of Dec. 15, 1811—the night when the New Madrid earthquake first struck the Mississippi Valley—Lilburn, with the assistance of Isham and in the presence of his Negroes, butchered a slave named George, whose offense had been to break a pitcher prized by the dead mother, Lucy Lewis." Thus the foreword, which relates further how, following the discovery of the murder, the brothers agreed to shoot each other across their mother's grave, but Lilburn alone fell. Isham fled and is reported to have been killed in the Battle of New Orleans. We are told that Jefferson appears never to have referred to "the tragic end of his family in Kentucky." But he is one of those who speaks here, as does another young kinsman who came to a tragic end: Meriwether Lewis, the leader of the Lewis and Clark expedition. The other speakers are the men and women, whites and Negroes, who were involved in the crime, physically or morally, directly or indirectly. Among them is the poet, the narrator. He tells how he first visited the scene, in the fierce blaze of a July day, directed up the mountain by a local farmer, who stared at him: "A fellow of forty, a stranger, and a fool, / Red-headed, freckled, lean, a little stooped, / Who yearned to be understood, to make communication, / To touch the ironic immensity of afternoon with meaning." The story of the murder is set between this confession and an account of his final effort, after a second and wintry visit to "the shrunken ruin," to arrive at an understanding of the condition of man. The poem as a whole is an attempt to define it.

But it must be emphasized that this is a poem, not an essay on morals. The dramatic interest is exploited fully. With one important exception, the speakers reveal themselves in dialogue as various as their natures. A remarkably different quality of tenderness and penetration is expressed by the white woman, Lucy Lewis, the mother of Lilburn, and the Negro Mammy who gave him suck, mother to the boy he hacked to death in the meat house, and again by that poor girl, Laetitia, whom he named in his will as his "beloved but cruel wife." A different sort of animal blindness finds utterance in the voice of Lilburn and of his brother Isham, of Laetitia and of her brother, and of Lilburn's Negro body servant and victim.

Everywhere the poet shows his mastery of his craft in the physical actualizing of the mean detail and the superb prospect, the private intake of sensation, feeling and belief, the nonhuman landscape, lonely or inhabited, under the changes of weather and of season. There is a description of an encounter with a snake as actual as Lawrence's, and more symbolic than the poet admits. Whatever literary references occur, and they range from St. Augustine to Spender and beyond, they have been so thoroughly assimilated and are so integral to the text that they will delight the initiate and leave the uninstructed undisturbed.

The form of the poem is an extremely flexible blank verse; except for two passages veined with song, the rhymes that the poet permits himself are rare and unobtrusive. It is the language, whether exalted or racily colloquial, delicate as Herrick's or harsh as one of Lear's diatribes, that makes for the poetry. Indeed, the interplay of vulgarity and nobility in the language is as it should be, the outward and audible sign of the poem's meaning.

The only failure of appropriateness is in some speeches given to Jefferson. He, not his nephew, the brutal, half-incestuous murderer, is the villain of the piece. He is the damned author of our failure, Warren insists, because he ignored the darkness of the heart of man, apparent both in the hideous act of his nephew Lilburn and in the moral desolation of his young cousin, Meriwether Lewis. When he moves onto the scene, the hands may be the hands of Jefferson but the voice is singularly like the voice of Robert Penn Warren. This is especially noticeable in the passages referring to some ugly incidents in more recent American history, such as the judicial murder of Sacco and Vanzetti.

It is not the absence of eighteenth-century locutions that one misses but the twentieth-century bluntness that sounds off key. Pondering the poem, one comes to believe that the poet's agonized rage is directed not at the hopeful Virginian who promulgated "the great lie that men are capable / Of the brotherhood of justice . . . that man at last is man's friend." To denounce that lie (is it a lie or only a half-truth?) with such ferocity, Warren must himself have cherished it. This notion is encouraged by his final pronouncement, couched in abstractions from which the body of the poem is relatively free:

> We have yearned in the heart for some identification
> With the glory of the human effort, and have yearned
> For an adequate definition of that glory.
> To make that definition would be, in itself,
> Of the nature of glory. This is not paradox.
> It is not paradox, but the best hope.

These words might have been spoken not by the poet but by Jefferson. As a man of the twentieth century Warren has an even deeper intimacy with "the wilderness of the human heart" than was possible to Lilburn's uncle. Nevertheless, he repeatedly attests to "the glory of the human effort." Sometimes he does so in one of the apothegms with which the work is studded. The sensitive, skillfully placed portraits of his father point toward a faith, not so different from Jefferson's, in human grace and dignity.

Early in the poem he declares that the single lesson worth learning "is that the only / Thing in life is glory." One might ask, as Alice asked Humpty Dumpty, what he means by it. He does not tell you, and of the yearning for identification with "the glory of the human effort" he does not speak until the very end. But first he must draw the motives of his characters from the stinking filth in which they tangle, make you hear the scream when Lilburn, "in affirming love lifts high the meat-axe" to bring it down on the Negro boy's bound, huddled body. First he must offer, speaking for himself or through the mouths of gentle Lucy Jefferson Lewis and of her brother Thomas, contradictory reflections on love.

When the tragedy has been recounted, Jefferson, assenting to his complicity, states his sorrowful conviction that "We shall be forged / Beneath the hammer of truth on the anvil of anguish," adding: "It would be terrible to think that truth is lost. / It would be worse to think that anguish is lost, ever." He puts his hope in knowledge, "It is bitter bread. / I have eaten that bitter bread," he says, finally, "In joy I would end." But the poet, for whom this work may represent an effort to redeem a small part of the anguish, answers: "We must consider those who could not end in joy." Let us indeed consider them. They are beyond counting. But then let us ask why they are so many. Was Jefferson the architect of the meat-house where, on Dec. 15, 1811, the murder was committed? Was he the architect, as the poet implies, of the modern prison camps in Europe and Asia, and of this industrialized, mechanized, war-geared slum of a world? As much as he was able to foresee of it, he recognized it for what it was, and he warned his countrymen against letting it develop. Could he have implemented that warning? His mistake was to believe that because man is a reasoning animal, he is also a reasonable one. Paradoxically, judgment has joined with experience to teach us that reason is not enough. "What is any knowledge," asks the poet, "without the instrinsic mediation of the heart?" And yet how shall we adequately define "the glory of the human effort" unless the heart is guided by reason's uncertain light?

The poem raises these questions. It is an index to its contemporaneity that it should seem rather to raise than to answer them, in spite of the rather didactic pronouncements on virtue just before the end. The close is not didactic. Like the better part of the book—in both senses of that adjective—it is poetry: words that simply and precisely show a landscape with figures, words that give the particular atmosphere of the place and the quality of the persons who are passing through it, words that remind us of the sharp joy and the grief and the endurance that belong to those who, if they are brothers to dragons, are also men.

Randall Jarrell

New York Times Book Review, August 23, 1953

This is Robert Penn Warren's best book. It is the story of a peculiarly atrocious murder that took place in the family of Charles and Lucy Lewis, the brother-in-law and sister of Thomas Jefferson. The murderers were their sons, Lilburn and Isham; the murdered man was their slave. These people, Jefferson, Lilburn's wife Laetitia, Lilburn's Negro mammy Aunt Cat, Lilburn's (and Jefferson's) cousin Meriwether Lewis, Laetitia's brother, and Warren himself speak the poem. They say what people do not say, but would say if they could. When they are through we know them, and what they have done, very thoroughly, and we give a long marveling sigh.

About Laetitia and Ishey-Boy, two of the most touching creations in American literature; about Aunt Cat, whose concluding lullaby Schubert and Mahler and Wolf together couldn't have done justice to; about that brother, about Lilburn, about the moth that lights on Lilburn's hand, even, our disbelief is suspended forever. We *were* Laetitia and Isham and Lilburn: so they are clubs we can beat Jefferson and Charles and Lucy and Meriwether Lewis and—but only half the time—Warren over the head with, when these seem to us more rhetorical and moralizing than life.

Warren's florid, massive, rather oratorical rhetoric, with its cold surprises, its accustomed accomplished continuations, its conscious echoes of Milton and Shakespeare, its unconscious echoes of Eliot and Arnold and Warren, is sometimes miraculous, often effective, and sometimes too noticeable to bear. Warren's impressive verbal gifts are less overwhelming than his dramatic gifts, one is tempted to say; but then one remembers Laetitia and the others—and the first speeches of Adam and Eve and the animals were hardly fresher, hardly more natural, hardly more unexpected, than the best of the speeches of these descendants of theirs.

Warren moralizes for effect and out of necessity: man is the animal that moralizes. Man is also the animal that complains about being one, and says that there is an animal, a beast inside him—that he is brother to dragons. (He is certainly a brother to wolves, and to pandas too, but he is father to dragons, not brother: they, like many gods and devils, are inventions of his.) The character in *Brother to Dragons* most loathingly obsessed with man's dragonish heart is a part of Warren which he calls Thomas Jefferson. The live Jefferson spoke and believed that Noble Lie of man's innocence and perfectibility which, Meriwether Lewis is made to say, "was my death."

The live Jefferson had not prepared Lewis for the ignoble truth of man's depravity; the dead Jefferson hammers it home with ignoble avidity. The dead Jefferson looks at the obscene underside of the stone and—he can do no other—licks his lips: he knows, now. Most of us know, now, that Rousseau was wrong: that man, when you knock his chains off, sets up the death camps. Soon we shall know everything the eighteenth century didn't know, and nothing it did, and [it] will be hard to live with us.

Brother to Dragons is written out of an awful time, about an awful, a traumatic subject: sin, Original Sin, without any Savior. The time is the subject; but the poem is a net, wide enough, high enough, deep enough, to have caught most of the world inside it—and if happiness, "a butterfly and not a gloomy bird of prey," has flown through its iron interstices as if they weren't there, it wasn't happiness Warren was in pursuit of, but the knowledge of Good and Evil.

Cruel sometimes, crude sometimes, obsessed sometimes, the book is always extraordinary: it does know, and knows sadly and tenderly, even. It is, in short, an event, a great one. There is a wonderful amount of life in it, of living beings who are free of Warren's rhetoric and moralizing, and of ours—are freed by their share in that reality or power or knowledge or glory which, as Warren says contradictorily and very humanly, is the one thing man lives by.

Robert Lowell

Kenyon Review, XV (Autumn, 1953), 619–25.

In spite of its Plutarchan decor, *Brother to Dragons* is a brutal, perverse melodrama that makes the flesh crawl. On a chopping block in a meat house in West Kentucky, "on the night of December 15, 1811—the night when the New Madrid earthquake first struck the Mississippi Valley—" Lilburn and Isham Lewis, nephews of Thomas Jefferson, in the presence of their Negroes, "butchered a slave named George, whose offense had been to break a pitcher prized by their dead mother, Lucy Lewis." Coming upon this preface, the reader is warned that he will not find Monticello and Jefferson with his letters from John Adams, his barometers and portable music stands, but Lizzie Borden braining the family portraits with her axe. This incongruity, which dislocates nearly everyone's sense of Jeffersonian possibility, was fully appreciated by Thomas Jefferson himself, who, so far as we know, never permitted his nephews' accomplishment to be mentioned in conversation. Yet the Lewis brothers are as much in the Southern tradition as their Uncle, rather more in the literary tradition which has developed, and so it is workaday that their furies should pursue them with homicidal chivalry, the pomp of Vestal Virgins—and the murk of Warren's four novels. Indeed these monstrous heroes are so extremely *literary* that their actual lives seem to have been imagined by anti-Romantic Southern moderns, and we are tempted to suppose that only gratuitous caprice caused Warren to blame their bestiality on the Deist idealism of their detached relative, Thomas, the first Democratic president. Portentous in their living characters, when Lilburn and Isham Lewis reach in 1953 their first artistic existence, they draw upon a long line of conventions established by their imaginary counterparts: it is as true inheritors that they speak a mixture of Faulkner's iron courtesies, country dialect, and Booth's *sic semper*. Like their ancestor Cain, these late-comers were prior to their poetic fulfillment. The disharmony between the brothers' high connections and their low conduct, however, is less astonishing than Warren's ability to make all his characters speak in unfaltering, unstilted blank verse. (I trust it is this Jeffersonian and noble technical feat, and not the lurid prose melodrama, which has three times caused me to read *Brother to Dragons* from cover to cover without stopping.)

The generals' war between the specialized arts and the specialized sciences is over. We have accepted our traumatically self-conscious and expert modern poetry, just as we have accepted our other perilous technological methods. Eternal providence has warned us that our world lies all before us and nowhere else. Only the fissured atoms which destroyed Hiroshima and Nagasaki can build our New Atlantis. This is what Paul Valéry meant when he wrote with cruel optimism that poetry before Mallarmé was as arithmetic to algebra. Valéry's education was more diversified than ours, and he wrote in a time when men still remembered the old Newtonian universe. We cannot be certain that we even understand the terms of his equation, but as poets and pragmatists we approve. Back in the palmy, imperialist days of Victoria, Napoleon's nephew, and Baudelaire, a kind of literary concordat was reached: the ephemeral was ceded to prose. Since then the new poetry has been so scrupulous and electrical, its authors seem seldom to have regretted this Mary and Martha division of labor. Poetry became all that was not prose. Under this dying-to-the-world discipline the stiffest and most matter of fact items were repoeticized—quotations from John of the Cross, usury, statistics, conversations and newspaper clippings. These amazing new poems could absorb everything—everything, that is, except plot and characters, just those things long poems have usually relied upon. When modern poets have tried to write dramatic and narrative works, neither genius, shrewdness, nor the most defiant good will have prevented most of the attempts from being puffy, paralysed, and pretentious. Outside of Browning, what 19th Century story poems do we still read? What poetical dramas since Dryden and Milton? Are Eliot's three plays, Auden's *Age of Anxiety*, Robinson's narratives, or Hardy's *Dynasts* much better? Yeats's later plays and Frost's monologues are short. Shorter still and more fragmentary are the moments of action and dialogue in *The Waste Land* and Pound's *Cantos*. Here stubborn parsimony is life-preserving tact. But *Brother to Dragons*, though tactless and voluminous, is also alive. That Warren, one of the bosses of the New Criticism, is the author is as though Professor Babbitt had begotten Rousseau or a black Minerva dancing in Congo masks. Warren has written his best book, a big book; he has crossed the Alps and, like Napoleon's shoeless army, entered the fat, populated riverbottom of the novel.

Brother to Dragons is the fourth remarkable long poem to have been published in the last ten or twelve years. *The Four Quartets, Paterson*, and *The Pisan Cantos* are originals and probably the masterpieces of their authors. Warren's poem is slighter, lighter and less in earnest. This judgment, however, is ungrateful and misleading. *Brother to Dragons* is a model and an opportunity. It can be imitated without plagiarism, and one hopes its matter and its method will become common property. In a sense they are already, and anyone who has read Elizabethan drama and Browning will quickly have opinions on what he likes and dislikes in this new work.

There *are* faults in this work. Warren writes in his preface, "I have tried to make my poem make, in a thematic way, historical sense along with whatever other kind of sense it may be happy enough to make." And more emphatically, ". . . a poem dealing with history is no more at liberty to violate what the writer takes to be the spirit of his history than it is at liberty to violate what the writer takes to be the nature of the human heart." Obviously the kind of historical sense claimed here is something more serious and subtle than the mere documentary accuracy required for a tableau of Waterloo or a romance set in 1812. The incidents in *Brother to Dragons* are so ferocious and subnormal they make *Macbeth* or Racine's *Britannicus* seem informal interludes in Castiglione's *Courtier*. Warren's tale is fact, but it is too good melodramatically to be true. To make sense out of such material he uses an arrangement of actors and commentators, a method he perhaps derived from Delmore Schwartz's *Coriolanus* in which Freud, Aristotle, and I believe Marx, sit and discuss a performance of Shakespeare's play. Warren's spirit of history has a rough time: occasionally it maunders in a void, sometimes it sounds like the spirit of Seneca's rhetoric, again it just enjoys the show. The difficulties are great, yet the commentary often increases one's feelings of pathetic sympathy.

As for the characters, nothing limits the length of their speeches except the not very importunate necessity of eventually completing the story. Warren improves immensely upon that grotesque inspiration which compels Browning to tell the plot of the *Ring* twelve times and each time in sections longer than *Macbeth*. Structurally, however, Browning's characters have the queer compositional advantage of *knowing* they are outrageously called to sustain set-pieces of a given length.

A few small points: Warren's bawdy lines—I sometimes think these are pious gestures, a sort of fraternity initiation, demanded, given, to establish the writer firmly outside the genteel tradition. Secondly, the word "definition" is used some fifty times. This appears to be a neo-Calvinist pun, meaning defined, finite and perhaps definitive and final, or "know thyself for thou are but dust." Warren used this word in his short poems and fiction and in an obsessive way I'm not quite able to follow. Time and History: the poet addresses these ogres with ritualistic regularity, reminding us a bit of a Roman proconsul imposing the Greek gods on the provinces, those gods which had already renounced the world in Eliot's *Four Quartets*.

Some stylistic matters: the hollow bell-sound repetition of

> I think of another bluff and another river.
> I think of another year and another winter.
> I think of snow on the brown leaves, and below
> That other bluff, how cold and far was light on that northern river.
> I think of how her mouth and mine together
> Were cold on the first kiss. Sparsely, snow
> Descended among the black trees. We kissed in the cold
> Logic of hope and need.

Passages of stage-direction blank verse, not bad in themselves (squeamishness in absorbing prose would have been crippling) but sometimes "sinking," like a suddenly audible command from the prompter's pit:

> From an undifferentiated impulse I leaned
> Above the ruin and in my hand picked up
> Some two or three pig-nuts, with the husk yet on.
> I put them in my pocket. I went down.

And these Thersites screams which modern writing channels on its readers like televised wrestlers:

> and in that simultaneous outrage
> the sunlight screamed, while urine splattered the parched soil.

Brother to Dragons triumphs through its characters, most of all through two women. Lucy and Laetitia Lewis, Lilburn's mother and wife, charm and overwhelm. They are as lovingly and subtly drawn as anything in Browning. Laetitia, the more baffled and pathetic, uses homely frontier expressions, and her speeches beautifully counterpoint those of the intelligent and merciful Lucy. Unlike the heroines in Warren's novels, those schizophrenic creatures more unflattering to womankind than anything in Pope, Lucy Lewis is both wise and good and proves Warren's point that neither quality can flourish without the other. Both women speak simple and straightforward blank verse, which is wonderfully emphasized by the messy rhetorical violence of the other speakers. As for Lilburn and Isham Lewis, Warren takes them as he finds them: ruins. Lilburn, the villain-protagonist, is a lobotomized Coriolanus, or, rather, that hollow, diabolic, Byron-Cain character who is so familiar to us from Warren's novels. He speaks few lines and is seen through the other speakers, because he is almost pure evil and therefore unreal. He sheds a sinister, absorbing glitter, which is probably all he was intended to do. Neither Ahab nor Satan, Lilburn is simply Lilburn—a histrionic void. Isham, Lilburn's younger brother and the subordinate villain, is a cowed imbecile. He is a sturdy, evil, stupified Laetitia. Unlike Lilburn, he is pure Kentucky and has no Virginian memories. (In *Brother to Dragons*, when the characters pass from Virginia to Kentucky they experience an immense social decline, as if this latter state were a "bad address." The Kentuckians are Elizabethan rustics, all a bit clownish and amazed to be speaking in meter.) Isham is drawn with amusement and horror, although as a key witness he needs a great deal of help from Warren's superior understanding of his own actions. The minor characters are quickly summarized: Dr. Lewis, the father, is shadowy; Aunt Cat is a mask; Laetitia's brother is a mildly amusing "humor," the sort of appendage who stands about, scratching his head, and saying, "I'm a simple country fellow." Meriwether Lewis seems altogether out of place in the work.

Jefferson! An original—mean, pale, sour, spoon-riverish! Hardy's Sinister Spirit. In the end, this Robespierre in a tub is converted by Lucy to a higher idealism, to "definition." (The Democrats are out of office and so perhaps Warren will not suffer public assault because of this black apotheosis.)

Finally there is R. P. W., the author, who speaks at greater length than any of the other characters and with greater imagination, power, and intelligence. He is Pilgrim, Everyman, Chorus, and Warren, the real person, who like everyone has his own birthplace, parents, personal memories, taste, etc. It is his problem to face, understand, and even to justify a world which includes moronic violence. As with Hugo at the beginning of *Le Fin de Satan*, the crucial catastrophic act is not the eating of the apple but the murder of Abel. Warren suggests that the pursuit of knowledge leads to a split in body and spirit, and consequently to "idealism," and consequently to an inability to face or control the whole of life, and consequently to murder. He is concerned with evil and with the finiteness of man. I'm not sure of Warren's position but it is often close to neo-Humanism and neo-Thomism, and so deliberately close that he frequently suffers from hardness. Yet sometimes you feel he is taking the opposite position and is merely a commonsense, secular observer. The character R. P. W., as we see him in the poem, is himself split between a love for abstractions and an insatiable appetite for sordid detail, as though Allen Tate were rewriting Stavrogin's "Confession." R. P. W. has his own troubles with "definition." The two halves embarrass each other: the character is at once unreal and again irresistibly energetic. I quote a passage—for its power rather than as an expression of character:

> Well, standing there, I'd felt, I guess, the first
> Faint tremor of that natural chill, but then
> In some black aperture among the stones
> I saw the eyes, their glitter in that dark,
> And suddenly the head thrust forth, and the fat, black
> Body molten flowed, as though those stones
> Bled forth earth's inner darkness to the day,
> As though the bung had broke on that intolerable inwardness,
> And now divulged, thus focused and compacted,
> What haunts beneath earth's primal, soldered sill,
> And in its slow and merciless ease, sleepless, lolls
> Below that threshold where the prime waters sleep.
> Thus it flowed forth, and the scaled belly of abomination
> Rustled on stone, rose, rose up
> And reared in regal indolence and swag.
> I saw it rise, saw the soiled white of the belly bulge,
> And in that muscular distention I saw the black side scales
> Show their faint flange and tracery of white.
> And so it rose and climbed the paralysed light.

On those heaped stones it was taller than I, taller
Than any man, and the swollen head hung
Haloed and high in light; when in that splendid
Nimb the hog-snout parted, and with girlish
Fastidiousness the faint tongue flicked to finick in the sun.

Of course Warren is a remarkable novelist, yet I cannot help feeling that this strange metrical novel is his true medium. It has kept the unique readability of fiction, a charm which is almost always absent from long poems. In this, at least, *Brother to Dragons* is superior to any of the larger works of Browning. And yet Warren almost *is* Browning. What this may mean is suggested by an observation by Gide. "Browning and Dostoevsky seem to me to bring the monologue straightway to perfection, in all the diversity and subtlety to which this literary form lends itself. Perhaps I shock the literary sense of some of my audience by coupling these two names, but I can do no other, nor help being struck by the profound resemblance, not merely in form, but in substance." After reading *Brother to Dragons*, I feel not only that Warren has written a successful poem but that in this work he most truly seems to approach the power of those writers one has always felt hovering about him, those poetic geniuses in prose, Melville and Faulkner. In Warren's case, it is the prose genius in verse which is so startling.

Poetry, LXXXIII (December, 1953), 167–71.

Parker Tyler

What foot to start out on? Mr. Warren has conceived another elaborate agon of the cultural conscience of the South, this time in a poem
of over two hundred pages, and not surprisingly its conceptual pivot,
the spring on which its phantasmagoria unwinds, is a man who stood
for a political ideal: Thomas Jefferson. Like literary critic or scientist,
who must become scholars in their subjects to be authoritative, Mr.
Warren the poet and liberal thinker fixes the American President with
the glare of a prosecutor and the charge—which Jefferson in this tale
"of voices" unhesitatingly admits—that his self-authored epitaph is
"a triple boast." The epitaph merely designates him as "Author / Of
the Declaration of / American Independence / Of / The Statute Of Virginia / For Religious Freedom, and / Father Of The University / Of Virginia." R. P. W. and Thomas Jefferson speak informally, as though not
for the undiscriminating public of newsprint, but for the special and
less naïve public of poetry; indeed, they speak in verse. It is there,
obviously, and only there—in the lucidity of poetry—that everyone
concerned will find *justice*.

This—regardless of the foot started out on or the metric itself—is
the thing. The feeling for poetry as a realm, almost a muse, of justice,
has been felt before. Robert Browning felt it in *The Ring and the Book*.
That was his inspiration: to reconstitute in living warmth and The
High Conclusive Words a human story that seems dishonored by the
form in which it appears to posterity. Mr. Warren found the crime of
Lilburn Lewis, Jefferson's nephew, in a few legal documents concerning his arrest and trial for the murder of a slave-boy, George. There
were curious factors—such as the escape of the convicted man from
hanging by a pact with his younger brother, his accomplice, to shoot

each other over their mother's grave—but the most curious factor was Lilburn Lewis' kinship with Jefferson and that behind the proud facade of the President's epitaph lies the tabooed subject of a family scandal. It seems that Jefferson totally ignored the event so far as leaving any trace of it in writing or known conversation goes. Mr. Warren saw his typical subject and took fire. The "brother" of his title is certainly the moral idealist no less than the vehicle of blood, his brother's and the Dragon's keeper, while the Dragon is the hybrid human, the Minotaur. As Jefferson is made to confess:

> . . . "Oh, this is Man!"
> And thus my minotaur.

What the Renaissance was able to derive from pagan culture in its conception of man was the Humanistic anatomy: a metaphor that corresponds directly to the man-beast, as in the Minotaur and other figures. Man owes his marvelousness, thought Pico della Mirandola, to the fact that to him alone, of all creatures, everything is possible. It is on this, the infinite metamorphose, rather than on a document such as Plato's *Republic*, that modern political idealism is actually based. "The seeds which each man cultivates," said Pico, "will grow and bear their fruit in him. If he cultivates vegetable seeds, he will become a plant. If the seeds of sensation, he will grow into a brute. If rational, he will come out a heavenly animal. If intellectual, he will be an angel and a son of God." Of course, the uses of the words "sensation," "rational," and "intellectual," have to be correlated with Pico's time. But there is no uncertainty about the heritage of the moral idea in its substance. *Brother to Dragons* is another reminder that the Classic idea was to exile the poet from the body politic, for it is in poetry that man may project his "intellect" and become—as Poe propagandized—an angel by virtue of literature. In any competent view, Mr. Warren seems to think, man's moral anatomy is violated by conceiving its heavenliness merely through poetry, through art. Verily, most of *Brother to Dragons* testifies that man's consciousness is on earth, not among the stars! The paradox is that it is in this poem that the members of Lilburn's family, who adore and defend him despite everything, are supposed to find the voice of a higher truth and to authorize his crime as substantially a ritual-sacrifice.

It is *here* that the axe wielded on George the slave really falls: on man the ethical complex. The poem emerges as an indictment of all political formalism which projects man as an image on such a public screen as the Declaration of American Independence. Therefore, says R. P. W., Jefferson's epitaph represents both moral and literary hypocrisy. Jefferson is forced here to adopt the mythic-metaphoric system and admit that common man, society, betrayed him through his own family and yet that he clung to the "heavenly" term of rational man in writing his epitaph. But as Mr. Warren finds this flaw in a personal political crystal through poetry, he has presumed to justify it, still through poetry, in a quite different perspective: that of the subject, Lilburn, who, having created a "Victor-victim" in George, alleged by R. P. W. in vivid lines to have *desired* his role in the ritual-sacrifice, is correspondingly a Victim-victor. As the physically powerful and magnetic hero, whose abnormal brutality in sex is vindicated by his wife's voice, Lilburn Lewis is the open metaphor of man; technically a "sensationalist" and, in modern psychological terms, a very frustrated and probably incestuous being, the poet weaves about him a considerable achievement in human portraiture. Various direct observations by R. P. W. on the elements of the narrative reveal his intention of transcending anything such as "folk simplicity" or specifically "the action"—of a ballad about the same subject begun but abandoned— "which is not explained by anything in the action." Courtroom records and traditional folk styles are equally inadequate. Nevertheless, poetry at large is the court to which Warren has appealed for justice to Lilburn's crime. The justification—in the eloquent, "interior" language of Laetitia, his wife, Lucy, his mother, Isham, his younger brother, and Aunt Cat, his old Negro nurse, all his "victims"—is to define Lilburn as Scapegoat.

The Scapegoat-image of man, in relation to Pico's Humanistic concept, would place the accent, assuredly, on the goat-foot, the club-foot, and the Devil's cloven hoof. The king is also the "slave" and the "animal." His queen is the "angel" as well as the "bitch": Pasiphaë in the cow's artifact. That this device, dominating the *poetic* calibre of the poem, is a wielding of the axe on the real social context of Lilburn's crime seems a point of which Mr. Warren is well aware but which actually he has overlaid in his poem. If, as his sister Lucy claims, Jefferson has wielded an axe on Lilburn as Lilburn wielded one on George, Warren has wielded an axe on the author of The Declaration of American Independence. It is the sharper through another relative, Jefferson's cousin. Meriwether Lewis, whose suicide in the wilderness the poem interprets as the product of his disillusionment with Jefferson's political gospel. The truth is that the air is full, in *Brother to Dragons*, of ideological axes (poetry is one, too), their edges more or less naked. Some grind, some fall. The only axe totally absent is that of the tragic fate.

The whole pathos of the tragic fate is that man knowingly falls short of ideal power over himself and his kind, that he can never be the happy and successful "son of God" indicated by Pico. Certainly not—or most probably not—if he is a ruler, a law-maker. But the creed is, superstitious or not, that he may succeed if he is a poet. *Brother to Dragons* contains a pure moment of the poet's ascendancy: R. P. W.'s encounter with the tremendous snake on his pilgrimage to the ruined home of the Lewises. He has mounted past natural barriers to achieve this hieratic instant; the most is made of it, and beautiful it is. But the symbolic snake, mythical emblem of evil who in this incarnation is "good," being a harmless species, is the dynamic opposite of the tragic fate. So we have, explained, the undramatic psychic metric of the "foot" Mr. Warren starts out on and keeps up till the end. There is no lucidity of the tragic fate reserved for Lilburn himself; he is never allowed to speak in his own behalf, not even once. Instead of having the maximum consciousness of the poem, he has—or seems to have—its minimum consciousness. He is a "natural," a man who moves in the simplicities of personal enigmas that are absolute. Mr. Warren has resurrected him as the protagonist of man in order to show him as the automaton, the passive victim of social, and implicitly political, action. It is a most reverberant note in Warren's works and in works of our time.

In its way, then, *Brother to Dragons* is a subjective fantasy. Warren wanted to pit the quick of his intuition of the meaning of Lilburn's crime against that ideological formalism, that political fraudulence, which made it severally the trite mark of Cain, a family scandal, and Jefferson's moral Achilles-heel. Mr. Warren is the poet as lawyer for the cause of "Lilburns" downtrodden by the mere judiciary conception of human experience. His dissent from the tragic fate signifies, I believe, some ineffable fondness for the humanly resonant figure of Lilburn, some desire to denounce and forgive and caress that is endemic to the words in the mouths of Lilburn's wife, his mother, and his old nurse. A search after truth, a recreation of fact, a justification and a thing of arguments, *Brother to Dragons* remains yoked to the Ineffable after all. One simply might have wished, in a poet, a more direct approach to poetry's inevitable triumph through virtue of the Ineffable. The approach here, apparently, is as it is because Mr. Warren found something intolerable, some tongue of venom, in the Ineffable's divine image. The poem is not a masterpiece, but it moves as a living thing, a scarred thing, something whose voices are all too universed in the supreme articulateness that Mr. Warren has sought to strike, out of the blue, from the red secrets of human life.

William Van O'Connor

Sewanee Review, LXII (Winter, 1954), 143–50.

Songs of innocence and songs of experience have not been peculiar to William Blake. A goodly portion of all literature, it would seem, is concerned with innocence vs. experience. Certainly it is a theme dear to American authors, as witness Henry James's *The American* and *Daisy Miller*, Edith Wharton's *The Age of Innocence*, Henry Adams's *Democracy*, Scott Fitzgerald's *The Great Gatsby*, and Robert Penn Warren's *All the King's Men*. And there is a literature of innocence vs. horror. Sometimes, as in Herman Melville's *Pierre* or Warren's *World Enough and Time*, a vision of the world as romantic innocence slowly darkens and in the ensuing half-light unsuspected horrors present themselves. *Brother to Dragons* has both themes, innocence vs. horror and innocence vs. experience, the former being the monstrous murder of a Negro boy and the latter being Meriwether Lewis's inability to suffer slander, dishonesty, and injustice. . . .

The whole conception of *Brother to Dragons* bespeaks the novelist-poet, and in this instance at least the genres merge beautifully. It is not, however, a novel in verse. Nor is it a play. Again, it is not a series of arguments held in focus by several historical documents. The poem says a good deal about history, but it is fiction, not history. A few of the characters, incidentally, were made up simply because they were dramatically useful. By and large the devices employed work quite well. The voices, "at an unspecified place and at an unspecified time," help give a sense of universality to the argument that is the theme. Only occasionally is one aware of a too sudden emerging, from out the dusk of eternity, of a character whose voice is needed at a particular moment. At first, the presence of "R. P. W." may seem a little disconcerting, especially in talking back to Mr. Jefferson or asking Isham to continue with the story, but soon we become accustomed to it and see certain advantages in having the poet in his poem. (Possibly we have been oversold, as E. M. Forster believes we have, on the need for an invisible author, sitting above the action paring his fingernails.) Through "R. P. W." Kentucky in mid-20th century lives more vividly than it might if presented by a fictional character. The poet in his own poem gives a sense of actuality, and helps relate the past to the present. For example,

> Just out of Smithland on the Louisville road
> You'll find the monument, a single shaft
> The local D. A. R.'s put up in '24
> Amid the ragweed and the cockleburr
> To honor Lucy Lewis for her good taste
> In dying in Kentucky. True, the stone
> Does name her as sister to the President,
> But quite neglects her chiefest fame, that she
> Gave suck to two black-hearted murderers.
> But let that pass, for the pious mind
> Our history's nothing if it's not refined.

Warren does not allow the Lewis story, however, to thin out in historical exposition. As the poet takes us up the mountain, owned now by Jack Boyle, fiction and poetry assimilate the history and turn it into a horrendous vision:

> And there it was: the huddled stones of ruin,
> Just the foundation and the tumbled chimneys,
> To say the human had been here and gone,
> And never would come back, though the bright stars
> Shall weary not in their appointed watch
> And the broad Ohio devotedly seek the sea.

One of the finest preliminary touches is the description, which continues for more than two pages, of the great black snake, Hog-snout or Chicken Snake, that rears in ugly indolence on the stones of the razed plantation house:

> I saw it rise, saw the soiled white of the belly bulge,
> And in that muscular distension I saw the black side scales
> Show their faint flange and tracery of white.
> And so it rose and climbed the paralyzed light.

> On those heaped stones it was taller than I, taller
> Than any man, and the swollen head hung
> Haloed and high in light; then in that splendid
> Nimb the hog-snout parted, and with girlish
> Fastidiousness the faint tongue flicked to finick in the sun.

Each character emerges clearly from the past, Dr. Lewis, his wife Lucy, Lilburn, Laetitia, and the rest. With rising tension the story of the murder is told: how, on that gloomy mountain in the days when Kentucky was frontier, mad Lilburn Lewis nursed a sentimental regard for his dead mother's silver and chinaware, how he invited young George to break one of her best-liked pitchers. . . . None of the horrors of that night are omitted:

> ISHAM: Yeah, that fool nigger spread his mouth to yell.
> You got to yell when they start chopping you.
> He must of yelled, but I ne'er heard a sound,
> Like all that nigger yelled was just a hunk
> Of silence—you don't even hear it when the meat-axe
> Gets in, gets through, goes *chunk*, and chunks on wood.
> It's funny how that *chunk* just won't come clear.

We watch the household waiting for the murder to out: guileful old Aunt Cat who bides her time, Laetitia running away, Lilburn and Isham drinking, the arrival of the sheriff, the indictment. . . . When this sequence has pretty much run its course, Meriwether Lewis appears, and we learn, in a more foreshortened manner, of the painful experiences that lead him to his melancholy end at the age of thirty-five.

Toward the closing pages of the book, and in recording a second visit, the poet recognizes that his vision has made the mountain growth thicker and more madly tangled, has made the snake, old *obsoleta*, loom as she once did in ancient Egyptian myths, and made the ghosts of the Lewises and Jefferson rise in Gothic horror. The catharsis achieved, the poem nearing its end, the poet comes down, past Jack Boyle's house, and rejoins his father, waiting for him in a car:

> But now I passed the gate and entered a world
> Sweeter than hope in that confirmation of late light.
> I walked down to the car where my father had been waiting.
> He woke from his cold drowse, and yawned, and said,
> "You finished what you climbed up there for, Son?"
> And I said: "Yes, I've finished. Let's go home."

It is unfortunate that Warren's verse play, *Proud Flesh*, has never been published, because it makes clear, more so than "The Ballad of Billie Potts," one of his contributions to the modern poetic idiom: a folk language, genuine folk, rising upon itself like ocean water in a rock pool. In *Brother to Dragons* there is passage after passage in which slang, cussing, and worn phrases become poetry. This particular passage is about the town of Smithland on the Cumberland River, a town that never came to much:

> Above Paducah, east some fifteen miles,
> Upriver, there it is, they call it Smithland.
> The town, I mean. It never came to much. . . .
>
> Smith had a right, all right; for the town-site
> Was noble where the Cumberland discovers
> The sober magnificence of the Ohio, and into that sweep pours
> All its own wash and wastage up from Tennessee,
> And the bluff was noble, and the beech it bore
> To guard that stately confluence and observe
> The traffic yawning westward, like a tide. . . .
>
> Haired hand on the sweep, and the haired lip lifts for song,
> And the leathery heart foreknows the end and knows it will not be
>   long,
> For a journey is only a journey and only Time is long,
> And a river is only water, Time only will always flow
>   *All the way from Shawneetown,*
>   *Long time ago.*
> That was the song the sweating boatman sang
> While sunlight shivered and the green bluffs rang
> All the way from Shawneetown, long time ago.

Because so much of *Brother to Dragons* is conversation, Warren's rhetoric in this poem is sometimes less dazzling than that in *Eleven Poems on the Same Theme* and other volumes, but it is an appropriate idiom, sustained, shifting from character to character, rising and falling with the intensity of the action or the scene being described. It may not be extravagant to say that of all English and American poets now writing, Warren has the greatest gift for the long poem. If anything, Warren's poetry spills over, in an excessive profusion. No other poet has his sustained emotional drive. And in an age of the eked-out line and the tortured lyric, we should not berate the prodigal Muse.

Certain readers may feel that Warren's dialectic would have more relevance to the norm of things if Meriwether's story were central and the murder peripheral. On the other hand, one might say in disagreement with this point: Of course it is right to set up Monstrous Man and Madness as the opposite pole from Jefferson's Noble Man and Justice, as Warren has it, because one has to know the worst before one can understand or begin to understand virtue. (Again, but this would be a different theme from the sort that engages Warren's imagination, there might even be a poem about the ways in which Jefferson's "lie" or partial lie has served good ends: the belief, however unfounded biologically, that men are born equal demands self-restraint and generosity, and it has given generation after generation a chance for kinds of happiness that a truer doctrine, or "truer" in certain contexts, would deny them. Every poet or novelist has a right to his theme—criticism should begin only after he has given it flesh and blood in his fiction.) Warren believes or knows that the ego is Mr. Number One, and try though we may our actions are never purely selfless or disinterested. And ironically the more impure the motive the harder we work to justify ourselves:

> No, Lilburn had no truck with the Evil One,
> But knew that all he did was done for good,
> For his mother and the sweetness of the heart,
> And that's the instructive fact of history,
> That evil's done for good, and in good's name.

Man does evil in the name of virtue, and his virtuous acts are rarely pure. The view of man as innately good, inherently noble, and natively innocent hardly accords with the evidence. The danger in the myth of natural goodness is that it invites sentimentality, self-righteousness, or even a monstrous egotism. It is far from Warren's intention to present Lilburn Lewis as a Jeffersonian idealist, but one implication of the poem would seem to be that cherishing the doctrine of innocence can lead to the creation of sentimental monsters. No group persecutes so intently as the one hundred percenters, whatever their doctrine, and Jefferson's idealism has begotten, or helped beget, a group of them.

Facing the fact of monstrousness in his own family's blood, as well as the violent end of Meriwether's life, Jefferson is forced to re-examine his idealism. He is also asked to contemplate some of the more ignoble items of our history:

And Pittsburg and Pinkerton and the Polak bleeding
In some blind angle while the snow falls slow,
And Haymarket, and Detroit, and Henry's goons,
And high engirt in whiskered smuggery
I recall a certain broad-browed scholar, the pride of Harvard, who
    made
Good learning pimp for brokers, and he became
The common hangman, and the Dagoes died,
And Boston slept, and Philadelphia, too,
And sleep was easy over the great continent. . . .

As the jacket of the book has it, Jefferson is forced to "re-examine his belief in the innate goodness and perfectibility of man and to fashion, on a broader and more realistic base, a new definition of hope."

So far as historians know Jefferson never referred to Lilburn's murder of the Negro boy, despite its being sensationally reported in the press, but Warren does not depend on such a fact as this. He is dealing with the spiritual consequences of Jefferson's idealism, not with the man Jefferson. Nor is he dealing with the man Meriwether. The skeptical reader might say something like this of Meriwether: He had suffered the hardships of crossing the plains and the mountains and had seen not merely the savages but his own men indulge in bestial and ignoble actions, all of which presumably would prepare him for putting up with the slanders and the conniving he was subjected to as Governor of the Louisiana Territory. But Warren prefers to think of those earlier experiences as weakening him, and of his experiences as an administrator being the final straw. No one knows why the historical Meriwether killed himself, or for certain whether he actually took his own life. But a poem, or a novel, is not history, and the action therein may or may not be an index to the norms of psychological and historical action. To heighten the point he is dramatizing, namely that a too innocent view of the world incapacitates one for action, Warren has Meriwether take his life and blame Jefferson for not having instructed him better about the nature of human conduct.

In a recent issue of *Sewanee Review* Warren protested the all too common inability of the literal-minded to distinguish between Willie Stark and Huey Long. That misunderstanding will be as nothing in comparison with what he will meet from those who will ask, Well, who is "Jefferson" if he is not Jefferson? The answer, of course, is that he is Jefferson's shade, a fictional character, a projection of a view of human conduct. It may be closest to the truth to say that Jefferson is the sort of idealist-gone-sour that one finds in Conrad or in Warren's own novels. He is hardly the sage of Monticello.

Warren, like Conrad, has created the fictional character who has what may be called an "angel complex" and the character who is blind to the complexities and intensities of the moral life. Like Conrad's Jim, the former is unable to contemplate his own weaknesses when these are discovered to him, and the latter, like Captain Brierly, commits suicide after, for the first time in his life, he learns that he and other "noble" men have been walking at the edge of a sharp precipice. Stein, in the same novel, says we all swim in a distructive element, and trying to live out of it is trying to live in an element too pure for human breathing. Warren has created characters in *World Enough and Time* that are very close to Jim and to Brierly. In Meriwether and Jefferson he has created characters who belong to the Conrad-Warren milieu, and it is not whimsical to say that the voice of "R. P. W." is close to the voice of Stein. Jefferson, as the idealist-gone-sour, tells his sister Lucy that it would have been better if someone had swung the infant Lilburn by its ankles and popped its head like a pod on a stone wall. His cynicism, as he recognizes, is only a means to separate himself from "the common collusion." Neither Lucy nor "R. P. W." will allow him the bitter joy of his cynicism, and eventually his statements are close to the thematic center of the poem itself:

> I think I begin to see the forging of the future.
> It will be forged beneath the hammer of truth
> On the anvil of our anguish. We shall be forged
> Beneath the hammer of truth on the anvil of anguish.

The Jefferson of the poem, prior to this, is a fictional projection of the Jeffersonian ideal as it has become the dogma of the naïvely innocent. His acceptance of a more complicated view may be read as a wish for the future. The burden of innocence, as Lucy tells her brother, is heavier than the burden of guilt.

Harold Bloom

New Republic, September 1 & 8, 1979.

Warren's *Brother to Dragons: A Tale in Verse and Voices* was published in 1953. A quarter century later, he gives us a new version that is, as he says, "a new work." His poetic style changed radically with *Incarnations: Poems 1966–1968*, a change that continues in his increasingly distinguished canon of poems. He stands now, at almost 75, as our most impressive living poet because of his work since 1966. Reading *Brother to Dragons* in this new version, side by side with the 1953 text, is an instructive experience, particularly in regard to the vexed problem of poetic revisionism. The famous dictum of Valéry, that a poem is never finished but is abandoned, is severely tested by Warren's rigorous reworking of his longest poem.

I myself was one of the readers, previously cold to Warren's verse, who converted to him on the basis of *Incarnations* and the subsequent long poem *Audubon: A Vision*. Reading *Brother to Dragons* in 1953, I was made uneasy, acknowledged the poem's vigor, disliked its ideological tendentiousness, and gloomily admired the Jacobean intensity of its more violent passages. The poem seemed then a good enough extension of the tradition of T. S. Eliot, sounding at times the way Eliot sounded when he was deliberately closest to Webster and Tourneur. Warren's quite explicit argument seemed to be another churchwardenly admonition that original sin was indeed the proper mental burden for *our* poetry. Thus, poor Jefferson received a massive drubbing, for being an Enlightened rationalist, and the drubber, a tough interlocutor named R. P. W., prodded the author of the Declaration of Independence into saying: ". . . I once tried to contrive / a form I thought fit to hold the purity of man's hope. / But I did not understand the nature of things." The nature of things was that Jefferson's nephew, wielding a meat-axe, had butchered a 16-year-old black slave, in December 1811, for having broken a pitcher belonging to his deceased mother, Jefferson's sister. In his "Foreword" Warren dismissed with polemical gusto the evident fact that Jefferson never referred to this family debacle:

> If the moral shock to Jefferson caused by the discovery of what his own blood was capable of should turn out to be somewhat short of what is here represented, subsequent events in the history of America, of which Jefferson is the spiritual father, might still do the job.

A reader more Jeffersonian and Emersonian than Warren was could be forgiven for muttering, back in 1953, that if there was something nasty in the meat-house, there was something pretty nasty in the "Foreword" also. But I too am a quarter century older now, the age indeed that Warren was when he first published the poem. I am not any happier with the implicit theology and overt morality of *Brother to Dragons* than I was, but subsequent events have done the job all right, to the degree that I am not tempted to mutter my protest anymore. Warren does seem to me the best poet we have now, and the enormous improvement in the poem's rhetorical force is evident upon almost every page. I am never going to love this poem, but I certainly respect it now, and a poem that can overcome one's spiritual distaste probably has its particular value for other readers in my generation besides myself.

The difference in the tale comes in both verse and voices, especially in the voice of R. P. W., which has an authority and resonance that little in the 1953 text prophesied. I could argue back at what seemed only another Eliotician, but I just want to listen to this sublime sunset hawk of 1979:

> . . . and lift our eyes up
> To whatever liberating perspective,
> Icy and pure, the wild heart may command,
> And so the glimmering night scene under
> The incalculable starlight serves
> As an image of lethal purity—
> Infatuate glitter of a land of Platonic ice.

In the 1953 version those six and a half lines appeared as eight and a half and between the "lethal purity" and "Infatuate glitter" came, most tendentiously, "the incessant / And whirling dream of desperate innocence." Warren now trusts his reader to interpret the trope of the passage's final line on his own, and a poem of 216 pages has been reduced to 133. In the central poem of *Incarnations*, "The Leaf," Warren has celebrated being blessed by a new voice "for the only / Gift I have given: *teeth set on edge.*" This grim Biblical trope epitomizes the ethos and the style of Warren in his major phase, and is realized in the new *Brother to Dragons*. Our teeth are set on edge by the harsh power of this verse.

Warren, in his revised "Foreword," asserts that the dramatic effects of his poem have been sharpened, which is true, particularly in the exchanges between Jefferson and R. P. W., where the poet no longer maintains a rhetorical advantage over the president. That Warren is still dreadfully unjust to Jefferson could go unsaid, except that I fear no one else is going to say it. If presidents were morally responsible for their nephews, then our twice-born incumbent would have to confront a parody of Warren's dramatic situation, since I believe a son of one of President Carter's sisters is currently serving an extended term for armed robbery.

Warren might argue that his sense of Jefferson's greatness is dialectically demonstrated throughout the poem, in much the same way as there is a projection of Emerson's adversary power in the ironic sequence "Homage to Emerson, on Night Flight to New York," which preceded the *Incarnations* volume. Still uneasy with his ideological ferocity, I content myself here with expressing admiration for the revisionary skill and intellectual persistence he has shown in this new *Brother to Dragons*. There is a greater Warren, the poet of "Evening Hawk," "Sunset Walk in Thaw-Time in Vermont," "Red-Tail Hawk and Pyre of Youth," and scores of other visions of an authentic American sublime, including *Audubon* and the work in progress, a volume intended for his 75th birthday. That greater Warren compels homage, and has transcended his polemics against Jefferson and Emerson.

Irvin Ehrenpreis

New York Review of Books, February 21, 1980.

In 1811 a nephew of Thomas Jefferson nearly chopped off the head of a young slave named George. The seventeen-year-old boy had broken a pitcher belonging (we are told) to the deceased mother of his master, Lilburne Lewis. The drunken master, with the help of his own brother Isham, dragged George into the kitchen cabin, tied him down, and assembled the other slaves to witness the punishment that followed. Then Lilburne sank an axe into George's neck, killing and almost decapitating him.

He forced one of the black men to dismember the body with the same axe. The pieces were thrown into the fireplace, where roaring flames had been built up. Lilburne Lewis warned the slaves to tell nobody what had happened.

At two o'clock the next morning a violent earthquake struck the region of western Kentucky where the Lewises lived. The chimney of the kitchen cabin fell down, smothering the fire and halting the process of cremation. Lilburne had the slaves rebuild the chimney and fireplace, hiding the fragments of George's body in the masonry. But the quakes continued, exposing the remains; and a dog carried off the head, to gnaw on it until a neighbor noticed and turned the skull over to officers of the law.

Three months after the crime, a grand jury indicted Lilburne and Isham Lewis for murder; but both men were admitted to bail while awaiting trial. Three weeks later, in keeping with a pact they had made, the two brothers went to a graveyard intending to shoot one another. Lilburne showed Isham how to commit suicide if the flintlock misfired, but he accidentally shot and killed himself during the lesson. Isham left the graveyard and was jailed two days later as accessory to his brother's self-murder. But he escaped, and we do not know what became of him.

My story of these events is taken from the handsomely documented and well-told account by Boynton Merrill, Jr., in his book *Jefferson's Nephews*. Mr. Merrill asks what Jefferson knew or said about the monstrosities of his sister's children, and he tells us, "No evidence has been discovered . . . that Jefferson ever wrote or spoke a word directly concerning this crime, or that it changed his life or attitudes."

In 1953 Robert Penn Warren published *Brother to Dragons*, a narrative poem based on the crimes I have reviewed. He organized it as a dialogue of disembodied voices conversing long after the event, in an unspecified place. Instead of making the incidents themselves the substance of his poem, Warren treated those as starting a debate on "the human condition," particularly the extent of man's innate virtue or depravity. To suit his plan, he not only altered some of the facts; he not only added some fictitious characters; but he also planted himself and Thomas Jefferson in the poem, giving these outsiders many long speeches. Warren has now carefully revised and shortened *Brother to Dragons* for a new publication, altering many details, reassigning speeches, breaking up long lines, and giving the verse a dryer texture.

In Warren's telling, although the sickening episodes emerge gradually from the give and take of the speakers, the element of suspense seems weak; and a reader unfamiliar with the story would not gather it easily from the poet's presentation. Warren diversifies the main line of his narrative with other ingredients: memories of his own research into the historical evidence, fictitious incidents of sexual passion and family tension, monologues in which real and imaginary persons tell us about their feelings of love and guilt. We hear Lilburne's wife recall the stages of her courtship and marriage, and the sexual abuse practiced on her by Lilburne. We hear Meriwether Lewis review his exploration of the northwest territories and supply graphic details of his suicide.

Such secondary narratives, mainly fictitious, illustrate the depravity of human nature. Warren attributes the death wish of Meriwether Lewis, for example, to the failure of the optimistic philosophy which Jefferson supposedly taught him. The other autobiographical speeches lead us in the same direction.

In the choral commentary of the poet's dialogues with Jefferson, Warren suggests that we are all responsible for the mischief done by any one of us; the victim of evil, however weak and vulnerable he may be, participates in the beastly motivations which lead to his destruction and so does the righteous denouncer of the crime. Jefferson himself, we are told, shared the potentiality for evil which his nephew realized in action. Unfortunately, this doctrine transpires in such a way as to darken Jefferson's character and to brighten Warren's. It is hard for one not to feel that the author takes advantage of his place as inventor of the fiction when he assigns to Jefferson a less perceptive morality than that of the poet who confronts him.

One may ask as well whether a plain historical account, even in my few words, is not more absorbing than Warren's self-indulgent, highly reflexive work. It would take a most dramatic discussion of the problem of original sin to hold us better than a bare chain of startling but true events. Warren composed the poem in flexible, varied free verse, often approximating blank verse. Is the poetic element attractive enough to carry us over the difficulties of Warren's theme?

If we do listen to the verse, we find that the poet's style is more lyrical, descriptive, or reflective than narrative, dramatic, or discursive. When he remembers a landscape or evokes passionate love, Warren's poetic energies seem more deeply engaged than when he rehearses a story or produces moral arguments. His speakers often sound alike, or they talk out of character. They are given to clichés of language or sentiment. Consequently, the ingredients which ought most to please us receive inadequate support from Warren's style. As for the lyrical and descriptive passages themselves, one may judge their freshness and power from a specimen on the coming of spring:

> The red-bud shall order forth its flame at the incitement of sun.
> The maple shall offer its golden wings for the incitement of air,
> Powder of oak-bloom shall prank golden the deerskin shirt
> Of the woodsman, like fable.
> Gleaming and wind-tossed, the raw
> Conclamation of crows shall exult from the swale-edge.
> The redbird whistles, the flame wing weaves,
> And the fox barks in the thicket with its sneezing excitement.
> The ceremony of joy is validated in the night cry,
> And all earth breathes its idiot and promiscuous promise:
> Joy.

If the narrative and the verse are open to censure, the scheme of debate becomes peculiarly important; for it could supply the challenge which an audience seeks from a poem of this length. If the disagreement set forth between the poet and Jefferson—the quarrel over the meaning of the Lewis brothers' crime—were handled forcefully, if the reader found himself drawn into the substance of the controversy (regardless of the data which provoked it and regardless of the poet's limitations of style), *Brother to Dragons* might deserve the attention it invites.

But when an author supports his moral doctrine by a mixture of fact, speculation, and invention, it cannot seem sturdy. The last fifty years of human events have provided abundant evidence of the ugliness of man's inborn character. I suspect that the power of Warren's poem when it first appeared sprang from the precipitate decline of American moral optimism, a decline which followed the full disclosure of the German nation's bestiality, made known in the years after 1945. Since that period, the conduct of other nations, including our own, has not reversed the decline. On this issue, history has overtaken poetry.

Warren dwells on the betrayal of the vision of men like Jefferson by the sins of the republic they conceived. In America—many used to think—history had been granted a fresh opening. Jefferson himself sometimes claimed that for the United States the present was independent of the past. For this people to practice abominations was the last offense to minds that thought of it as a proving ground of human potentiality. Warren lists the disgraces: the destruction of the Indians, the institution of slavery, and so forth; and he declares that all of us— high and low, Southern aristocrat and humble slave—are, like the rest of the world, caught in history. The peculiar loathsomeness of Lilburne Lewis was his kinship with the most splendid type of American manhood, Jefferson.

Unfortunately, every aspect of Warren's analysis is not overfamiliar. The failure of our national character is a favorite theme of the American literary imagination. The myth of Southern aristocracy has been stripped bare too often for another exposure to move us. Moreover, the appeal to fact, which the poem urges upon us, works against the drift of Warren's argument. Whoever examines the scholarly accounts of Jefferson, the Lewis brothers, or Meriwether Lewis will undermine Warren's case.

So far from being taken in by any optimistic misrepresentation of Jefferson's, Meriwether Lewis himself said, "I hold it an axiom incontrovertible that it is more easy to introduce vice in all states of society than it is to eradicate it, and this is more strictly true when ap-

plied to man in his savage than in his civilized state." When Warren
says, "We must believe in the notion of virtue," he hardly disagrees
with Jefferson, who thought a moral conscience was an integral part
of human nature.

Returning from the meaning to the form, I have to wonder
whether the enterprise of such a poem as *Brother to Dragons* does not
represent one more desire to equip the United States with a verse
epic. The ambition to do so goes back to the early years of the republic. But by that date, large-scale narrative had already become the
responsibility of the novel. When poets finally accepted this truth,
they altered their definition, and spoke of writing a "long poem,"
which should be neither narrative in the manner of Virgil nor exposition in the manner of Lucretius. One of the monuments of the revised
hope is W. C. Williams's *Paterson*. But for all the praise that *Paterson*
and efforts like Charles Olson's *Maximus Poems* have received, no one
ever wished them longer; and in search of honest pleasure, readers
without a vested interest in duration are likely to turn to the shorter
pieces in Williams's *Selected Poems*.

American poetry became mature when the novel, the film, and
the theater supplied dramatic and narrative works that required hours
for their consumption. The genius of our poetry is indeed lyric and
reflexive. If we need a verse epic, the want is satisfied by Whitman's
Song of Myself, which is a cluster of poems kept together by the
spirit and theme of the author. The transformations of the self give
our poets their best starting point, as they gave Whitman his. Self-
conscious, self-dramatizing, self-mocking, self-awed, the poet looks
out on a world whose contents are sanctified by his inspection; and it
is by identifying himself momentarily with the figures and scenes of
that world that he nourishes his identity.

For Whitman, as Richard Chase said, the drama of the self was
essentially comic. For poets today, that drama must modulate unfore-
seeably from pathos to humor, from despair to irony. Poems like Elizabeth Bishop's "Poem" ("About the size of an old-style dollar bill"),
Robert Lowell's "Skunk Hour," Richard Wilbur's "Walking to Sleep,"
and James Merrill's "The Thousand and Second Night" are suitable
models, not because they reveal any scandal about the poet but because they involve world and self in the fascinating, funny, terrible
work of connecting and disconnecting the immediate sensibility and
the experiences that produced it. A group of such poems is the grandest epic we can use.

Warren himself, in his recent and best poems, shows an affinity with this tradition rather than with the evasions of Ashbery, the surfaces of Strand, or the monotones of James Wright. His last collection, *Now and Then*, has at least half a dozen good poems. In them the poet looks at himself from the remoteness of old age eyeing death; and he searches for the meaning of experiences embodied in his identity. The strength of remembered emotions, the montage of past and present, the crescendos and diminuendos of sensation provide satisfactions that almost make up for the carelessness of the language. One wishes that Warren's flights were less effortful and that his earthiness were less commonplace, just as one wishes that his metrics were more purposeful. There is also the lushness which troubles one in *Brother to Dragons*; but it is undercut here by the critical perspective of memory.

Although the attitude, in these poems, is highly serious, the intensity of the poet's self-consciousness and the sense one has of extremes in time being pressed quickly together infuse irony into the tone. The themes include earthly and spiritual aspiration, the desire for glory; they include the transformation of the self through faith, the need to make a self that will not merely vanish—the possibility of resurrection. As with Whitman, the egoism (for Warren rarely delights in self-effacement) is redeemed by typology, and the poet becomes Everyman.

In this autobiographical verse, the narrative part is easy to manage, because it springs from personal anecdote. Actor and setting partake of each other:

> In the dark kitchen the electric icebox rattles.
> It whispers like the interior monologue of guilt and extenuation. . . .
> ("The Mission")

Dramatization is no problem, since the poet speaks of and for himself. Instead of argument and morality, he strives to convey insights and feelings; and we are not troubled with self-conferred rectitude.

Death closes the process of metamorphosis. In "Departure," Warren makes the end of summer into a hint of the end of life. In "Heat Wave Breaks," he turns a summer storm into a foreshadowing of Judgment. In "Heart of Autumn" the passage of Canada geese overhead becomes a premonition of the poet's own passage—

> And my heart is impacted with a fierce impulse
> To unwordable utterance—
> Toward sunset, at a great height.

The poems comment on and reply to one another. They cohere naturally and give the reader a beautiful impression of a brave ancient gathering the resources of intellect and spirit against the challenge of finality. For ambitious young poets a sequence of such lyrics could, I think, be more powerfully suggestive than Crane's *The Bridge* or Pound's *Cantos*.

Interpretations: 1979 Edition

Original Sin on the Dark and Bloody Ground

C. Hugh Holman

Few novelists and poets have made more explicit comments about history than Robert Penn Warren. At the Fugitive's reunion in 1956, he said: "your simpler world is . . . always necessary—not a golden age, but the past imaginatively conceived and historically conceived in the strictest readings of the researchers."[1] In *All the King's Men*, Jack Burden tells Anne Stanton, ". . . if you could not accept the past and its burden there was no future," and then they are ready to go "out of history into history and the awful responsibility of Time."[2] In both the published versions of *Brother to Dragons: A Tale in Verse and Voices*, Warren says in the foreword: "I have tried to make my poem make, in a thematic way, historical sense. . . . Historical sense and poetic sense should not, in the end, be contradictory."[3] Such remarks, and there are many of them in Warren's work, would lead us to see him as a practitioner of historical fiction, as one subscribing fully to the author's comment in *World Enough and Time* that "we are like the scientist fumbling with a tooth and a thigh bone to reconstruct for a museum some great, stupid beast extinct from the ice age. Or we are like the louse-bit nomad who finds, in a fold of land between his desert and the mountains, the ruin of parapets and courts, and marvels what kind of men had held the world before him. But at least we have the record: the tooth and thigh bone, or the kingly ruins."[4]

A modified version of this paper was presented at the MLA convention's special session, "Robert Penn Warren's *Brother to Dragons* (New Version): A Discussion and a Tribute on the Occasion of His 75th Birthday," December 29, 1979, San Francisco, Calif.

1. Rob Roy Purdy (ed.), *Fugitive's Reunion* (Nashville, Tenn.: Vanderbilt University Press, 1959), 210.

2. Robert Penn Warren, *All the King's Men* (New York: Harcourt, Brace, 1946), 461 and 464.

3. Robert Penn Warren, *Brother to Dragons: A Tale in Verse and Voices* (New York: Random House, 1953), xii; *Brother to Dragons, A New Version* (New York: Random House, 1979), xiii. All quotations from and citations to the text will be to the 1979 New Version, unless otherwise noted, and will be given parenthetically in the text.

4. Robert Penn Warren, *World Enough and Time* (New York: Random House, 1950), 4.

When we examine Warren's use of history in *Brother to Dragons*, however, a substantial doubt about how he is using it arises. In the foreword to both versions, he recounts briefly the events of the slaughter of the slave George by his master Lilburne Lewis in Kentucky in 1811. This account, although brief in each case, is persuasively circumstantial. Then Warren adds to the disingenuous statement, "I have stayed within the general outline of the available record, but have altered certain details" (p. xi),[5] a seemingly frank acknowledgment of some of the changes he has made. In the notes at the end of each published version, he quotes from documentary sources to explain, or substantiate, material in the text. The unwary reader, looking at these Scott-like acknowledgments of conscious historical inaccuracy and at this parade of documents, in the absence of historical accounts of the actual occurrences, may be led to declare, as I did in 1976, that "this long poem . . . deals with the past with great accuracy."[6]

There is no longer any excuse for such a judgment, for late in 1976 Boynton Merrill, Jr., published his detailed, thoroughly documented account of Lilburne Lewis's crime, *Jefferson's Nephews: A Frontier Tragedy*,[7] and the historical data is now clearly before us. Those who wish to examine the historicity of the poem may do so. Merrill, with a recognizable and understandable touch of asperity, says, in his "Discussion of Sources," "In regard to the historicity of *Brother to Dragons*, Warren states in the preface: 'I am trying to write a poem and not a history, and therefore have no compunction about tampering with facts.' Warren succeeded admirably, both in his poem and in tampering with the facts. However, it might be ventured that facts usually do stand in the way of poetic expression and artistic triumph, such as Warren has achieved."[8] Warren has twice responded to Merrill's account, which differs from his in the poem in many respects, even indeed in its "outline of historical fact." In a footnote to the dramatization, *Brother to Dragons, A Play in Two Acts*, he acknowledges several of the discrepancies, but asserts, about his mislocation of Lucy's burial place, "This discrepancy no more than the others affects the mean-

5. In the 1953 version he writes, "have modified details in two respects" (p. x).
6. C. Hugh Holman, *The Immoderate Past* (Athens, Ga.: University of Georgia Press, 1977), 83.
7. Boynton Merrill, Jr., *Jefferson's Nephews: A Frontier Tragedy* (Princeton, N.J.: Princeton University Press, 1976).
8. *Ibid.*, 426–27.

ing of the play."[9] In the foreword in the 1979 version, he declares the
Merrill book to be "a conscientious and scholarly account" (p. xi) but
denies its relevance to the poem, repeating a statement made in the
1953 foreword: "Any discussion of the relation of this poem to its historical materials is, in one perspective, irrelevant to its values" (p. xiii).

I shall not attempt the task of demonstrating that *Brother to Dragons* is not historically accurate in detail or even in broad outline. I shall
simply mention a few basic situations in the poem that are false to the
facts. Letitia was Lilburne's second wife; his first, whom he dearly
loved and over whose grave the suicide pact was to have been carried
out, had borne him five children. Letitia did not leave on the night of
the murder; she stayed on at Rocky Hill and in January bore him a
son. She was taken away by her father and brothers after Isham's indictment as an accessory. The murdered slave was not dismembered
in the meat-house on a butcher's block, but in the kitchen-cabin on
the floor. Warren seems to follow the account of the abolitionist the
Reverend William Dickey, but not very accurately. Lilburne did not
trick Isham into killing him, but rather killed himself, probably accidentally, before the double suicide pact could be put in motion. There
are many other discrepancies than these. Indeed, one is forced to the
conclusion that the suggestions of deranged motives for Lilburne—
the Oedipal struggle, Letitia's sexual frigidity, the suggestions of class
hatred between her family and the Lewises, and Lilburne's domi-
nance of Isham—all have little or no support in historical fact.

One interpretation of the great discrepancy of *Brother to Dragons*
with history might rest on the Warren poem which most clearly ad-
umbrates the verse play, *The Ballad of Billie Potts* (1935), which is laid in
Kentucky about the same time and rests on oral legend heard from a
kinswoman when Warren was a child, and which tried—most successfully it seems to me—to combine that traditional ballad quality:
"Big Billie Potts was big and stout / In the land between the rivers /
His shoulders were wide and his gut stuck out"—with rhetorical,
philosophical discourse—"Weary of innocence and the husks of
Time, / You come, back to the homeland of no-Time, / To ask forgiveness and the patrimony of your crime."[10] In 1950 he had turned to

9. Robert Penn Warren, *Brother to Dragons, A Play in Two Acts, Georgia Review,* XXX
(Spring, 1976), 67 [q.v., p.297]. The play is on pp. 65–138.
10. Robert Penn Warren, *Selected Poems, 1923–1975* (New York: Random House, 1976),
271 and 281.

documents as the source for an historical romance, *World Enough and Time*, using the documents of the Beauchamp-Sharp murder case, as he would use the Lewis court records, but also relying heavily on tradition yet changing names, inventing characters, and giving a new and highly melodramatic ending.

Brother to Dragons had a similar origin. Warren says in the foreword to the New Version: "My poem, in fact, had its earliest suggestion in bits of folk tale, garbled accounts heard in my boyhood. Then came a reference or two, years later, in print. Then . . . I . . . sought out . . . the little bundles of court records . . ." (p. xii). Thus, in the beginning it was not formal history but legend with which he was dealing, and not with fact—aside from the few court records—but the meaning those data could embody or express. So, "when Truth broke in / With all her matter-of-fact,"[11] Warren could hardly be expected to greet her with open arms. Indeed, the change of the victim's name from the historical George to John is a quiet but emphatic declaration to Clio, in the guise of Boynton Merrill, of "non serviam."

But the true and basic issue is really the purpose to which material—whether from folk tradition or from the unquestioned annals of history—is put. On this issue Warren embraces a purpose and a method older by far than that of historical fiction as it was practiced by Sir Walter Scott. Historical fiction, in what Georg Lukacs, its most important critic, calls "the classical form" is a social and essentially—despite the frequent extravagance of its plots—realistic form.[12] It explores man in society, the individual caught in the inexorable trap of social and economic forces. Its protagonists are average citizens, helplessly in the middle, caught, in Hegelian terms, in the struggle of antithesis against thesis. It reconstructs the social texture of an age and dramatizes the tensions that tore average citizens in that time. It speaks with the authority of demonstrable fact of the pressures unique to one age upon a person whose essential nature is common to all ages. It is to these aspects of the tragedy of Lilburne Lewis that Boynton Merrill quite properly addresses himself. He explains and defines the issues, as an historian should, in such terms as the nature of the frontier, the inherent violence of Kentucky, the financial de-

---

11. Robert Frost, "Birches," *The Poetry of Robert Frost* (New York: Holt, Rinehart and Winston, 1967), 152.
12. Georg Lukacs, *The Historical Novel*, trans. Hannah and Stanley Mitchell (Boston: Houghton Mifflin Company, 1963).

pression of the early 1800's, the sense of class and caste, the practice of slavery. The historical novel, like the scientific history whose development made it possible, whether Hegelian in doctrine or not, sees history as process, and it seeks to displace myth with fact.

On the other hand, myth exists when what is unique about periods is dissolved away, when time becomes meaningless and space replaces time as the dominant ingredient in fiction. Myth tries to tell us what is eternal not temporal. The order of its meaning is ultimately cosmic not terrestial, and what it means it means independent of time and place. It speaks not of social forces but of philosophical propositions.

It is no accident and in no sense whimsical that Warren locates *Brother to Dragons* in "no place" and at "no time," and then adds, "This is but a way of saying that the issues that the characters here discuss are, in my view at least a human constant" (p. [xv]). It may be argued that he is really talking about the scene wherein Jefferson and R. P. W. reconstruct and interpret events and not about the actions or the motives of Lilburne, Isham, Letitia, or Lucy. But such an objection is not valid, for these characters, like Jefferson and Meriwether Lewis, who had, in fact, been dead two years when the murder occurred, exist not in time or space but in memory. They all function as counters in a structure of meaning rather than as persons in time and space.

In all of Warren's fictions, he seems to feel the need to express the meaning that is, he feels, inherent in his materials. In *All the King's Men* not only does the witness—narrator Jack Burden—have the ability to explain and discuss meaning with dramatic propriety, but the interpolated story of Cass Mastern constitutes a commentary on the main action. In "The Ballad of Billie Potts," the mediating voice of the poet, as opposed to the balladeer, explores meaning intensely, as in:

> The answer is in the back of the book but the page is gone.
> And Grandma told you to tell the truth but she is dead.
> And heedless, their hairy faces fixed
> Beyond your call or question now, . . .
> Sainted and sad and sage as the hairy ass, these who bear
> History like bound faggots. . . .[13]

In *World Enough and Time* Warren as discursive author can and does discuss the significance of the actions. In *Band of Angels* a first person narrator can and does express the meaning.

13. Warren, *Selected Poems*, 273.

In *Brother to Dragons* he makes his strongest and most concerted effort to force the reader to see the fiction in terms of meanings and values by making the entire work an inquiring meditation not on history but on the permanent meaning of history. In order to do this, he frames the action with Thomas Jefferson, in a role not unlike that of Hawthorne's Young Goodman Brown, this time contemplating his Faith put to the crucial test in Kentucky. Like Hawthorne's Brown, who after seeing Faith in Satan's embrace in the wilderness, became "a stern, a sad, a darkly-meditative, a distrustful, if not a desperate man,"[14] Jefferson, after the Lewis atrocity, says:

> But I could not accept it. I tried
> To buckle the heart past fondness or failure.
> But the pain persisted, and the encroachment of horror.
> I saw the smile of friendship as a grimace of calculation. (85)

This Jefferson, his faith in man's essential goodness and perfectibility shattered by the depravity of his nephews, is totally unhistorical. As Merrill says, "No evidence has been discovered to date indicating that Jefferson ever wrote or spoke a word directly concerning this crime, or that it changed his life or attitudes."[15] Warren's intention is clearly not to describe an historical Jefferson but to criticize the view of man and human possibility which Jefferson is generally considered to embody, and which the Lewis atrocity teaches him in the dialogue with R. P. W. to call "a lie." To the ghost of Meriwether Lewis, who followed this optimistic dream of the West to his suicidal fate, Jefferson says:

> If what you call my lie undid you,
> It has undone me too. For I, too,
> Was unprepared for the nature of the world,
> And I confess, for my own nature. (117)

For ultimately *Brother to Dragons* is an extended and dramatized gloss on Warren's poem, "Original Sin: A Short Story," in which he says:

> Not there when you exclaimed: "Hope is betrayed by
> Disastrous glory of sea-capes, sun-torment of whitecaps

14. Nathaniel Hawthorne, "Young Goodman Brown," *Mosses from an Old Manse* (New York: American Publishers Corporation, n.d.), 86.
15. Merrill, *Jefferson's Nephews*, 327.

—There must be a new innocence for us to be stayed by."
But there it stood, after all the timetables, all the maps,
In the crepuscular clutter of *always, always*, or *perhaps*.[16]

In fact, *Brother to Dragons* might be aptly subtitled *Original Sin on the Dark and Bloody Ground*.

Jefferson is another of Warren's absolutist protagonists who pursues an impossible ideal until he is destroyed by the reality of evil, darkness, sin, depravity, and suffering—from which, at the last, his ideal cannot shield him. And the poem in which his disillusionment is recorded takes people and events from history and uses them to a most unhistorical, very mythic purpose, to state a universal truth about the nature of man and his world and not a local or temporal truth about a crime in Kentucky in 1811. Such a use of history is very old. Shakespeare uses it in *Hamlet* and *Lear*, in *Julius Caesar* and *Richard the Second*. Homer has used it in the *Iliad*. And, dear probably to the hearts of Warren's feminine ancestors, Jane Porter has used it in her very unhistorical celebration of Scotch virtue in *Scottish Chiefs*. Questions of accuracy pale to nothingness before such a purpose, for the author intends his readers to grieve on universal bones.

16. Warren, *Selected Poems*, 289.

Brother to Dragons and the Craft of Revision

Victor Strandberg

Among the vast assortment of manuscripts that Mr. Warren has put on deposit in the Beinecke Manuscript and Rare Book Library at Yale, those relating to *Brother to Dragons* have acquired a renewed topicality with the appearance of his "rewritten" *Brother to Dragons* in the fall of 1979. In this discussion I shall make some comparisons between the published and unpublished versions of the poem in order to look more closely at this remarkably prolific artist's creative process.[1]

The manuscripts at Yale show that prior to the three versions of the poem which have entered the public domain,[2] the work underwent a number of substantial revisions. Presumably the earliest version was that which Warren refers to in the 1953 edition and which he repeats almost verbatim in the rewritten 1979 publication (cf. 31):

> R. P. W.: Yes, I have read the records. I once intended
> To make a ballad of them, long ago.
> And I remember how the thing began:
> *The two brothers sat by the sagging fire.*
> *Lilburn and Isham sat by the fire,*
> *For it was lonesome weather.*
> *"Isham," said Lilburn, "shove the jug nigher,*
> *For it is lonesome weather.*

A modified version of this paper was presented at the MLA convention's special session, "Robert Penn Warren's *Brother to Dragons* (New Version): A Discussion and a Tribute on the Occasion of His 75th Birthday," December 29, 1979, San Francisco, Calif.

1. In citing excerpts from the unpublished manuscripts, I risk offending the author's good will—for they are restricted sources—but this material should be of interest to Warren scholars and quite harmless, I think, from the author's point of view.

2. Robert Penn Warren, *Brother to Dragons* (New York: Random House, 1953), published August 21, 1953; excerpts in *Kenyon Review*, XV (Winter, 1953), 1–103, *Poetry*, LXXXII (June, 1953), 125–33, and *Partisan Review*, XX (July–August, 1953), 393–96; and *Brother to Dragons, A New Version* (New York: Random House, 1979), published September, 1979.

> *It is lonesome weather in Kentucky,*
> *For Mammy's dead and the log burns low*
> *And the wind is raw and it's coming snow*
> *And the woods lean close and Virginia's far*
> *And the night is dark and never a star. . . ."* (42–44)

Disappointingly, no such ballad exists among the Beinecke manuscripts, evidently because the poet found the ballad form unworkable
almost from the outset. According to the final two versions (1953 and
1979) of the poem, the ballad form failed to serve either the poet's
philosophical or psychological purposes. Possibly one might also infer an interesting retrospect on "The Ballad of Billie Potts" in these
lines:

> Yes, it began about like that, but the form
> Was not adequate: the facile imitation
> Of a folk simplicity would never serve,
> For the beauty of such simplicity is only
> That the action is always and perfectly self-contained,
> And is an image that comes as its own perfect explanation
> In shock or sweetness to the innocent heart.
>
> But first, our hearts are scarcely innocent,
> And any pleasure we take in the folk simplicity
> Is a pleasure of snobbish superiority or neurotic yearning.
> And second, the action here is not explained.
> But anything in the action. It is explained,
> If explainable at all, by our most murderous
> Complicities, and our sad virtue, too.
>
> No, the action is not self-contained, but contains
> Us too, and is contained by us, and is
> Only an image of the issue of our most distressful self-definition.
> And so to put the story in a ballad
> Would be like shoveling a peck of red-hot coals
> In a croker sack to tote them down the road
> To start the fire in a neighbor's fireplace.
> You won't get far with them, even if you run—
> No, the form was not adequate to the material. (43–44)

But although Warren renounced the ballad form, his earliest manuscripts of *Brother to Dragons* show that, up through the *Kenyon Review* typescript, he retained the notion of a ballad in their title: *Ballad*

of the Brothers: A Murder Mystery. The first draft of the poem we now recognize as *Brother to Dragons,* written in the poet's almost illegible longhand, begins with notes scribbled on stationery of the Dinkler-Tutwiler Hotel in Birmingham, Alabama (no date). After marking an *N.B.* by his sources, Claiborne's History of *Mississippi* and C. J. Latrobe's *Rambler in North America,* Warren lists three notes under the heading "Material" ("1. Use in past 2. My acquaintance 3. Narrative") and then arranges the substance of the work under the heading "problems—":

1. Novel?—play—poem
2. Theme—light carrier etc.
3. Jefferson as key
4. Jefferson as narrator
5. Jefferson as a "role"
6. How convert Jefferson
7. Meriwether Lewis
    light carrier
    related to Jefferson
8. Jefferson's "Crime"
    parallel to Lilburn's crime
9. Negro as "dark parody" of self
10. Laetitia as "parallel"
11. Mother as "resolution"
Need for Perspective
  My visit—Smithland now
Need for "feel" of land
  December visit
  "common world."

That the question of genre heads the list—"Novel?—play—poem"—should not surprise us in a writer who began his career as a poet and whose most celebrated novel originally took shape as a play. The curious thing is how Warren conjoined the "play-poem" genres together to solve his problem in this instance. The other items in the list of "Problems" are interesting mainly for their early sense of design, centering on Jefferson's "conversion," and for their debt to Joseph Conrad implicit in the "light carrier" motif.[3]

If Conrad implicitly contributed to the genesis of the poem, War-

---

3. The fact that Warren was composing his masterly essay on Conrad at the same time he was working on *Brother to Dragons* helps explain the poem's general effect of an American *Heart of Darkness,* with Marlow's role as meditative witness emerging in

ren's more explicit thoughts at the start were fixed upon the literature of antiquity. Perhaps indicative of an "American epic" intention, the poem's first draft cites, with a sprinkling of N.B.'s, excerpts from the *Aeneid* and the Bible. Originally the epigraph to the poem was to be a Biblical analogy to the December, 1811, earthquake taken from the prophet Amos, VIII:9: "And it shall come to pass in that day, saith the Lord God, that I will cause the sun to go down at noon, and I will darken the earth in a clear day." I suspect that the poet's eventual choice of *Brother to Dragons* as the title (from the book of Job) led him to shed this epigraph in favor of the one from Lucretius, so as to avoid too heavy a Biblical emphasis.

Warren's classical affinities—which gave the poem the Pasiphaë-minotaur episode, Jefferson's visit to Nîmes, and a reference to Homer as "that vagrant liar from Ithaca"—appeared even stronger in the beginning than the Biblical flavor. In a passage marked *N.B.* and circled for extra emphasis, Warren's Prefatory Notes insist upon the theistic significance of the *Aeneid* (pointed brackets indicate illegible longhand).

> *N.B.*   As the Gods strove above the battlements of
> gods strive in ⟨per viscera?⟩
> At end—realization of Aeneas in Virgil at fall of Troy that it was not a matter of the struggle of men—that Gods strive above the battlements.

Here, too, Aeneas appears as a "light carrier" of antiquity—"Aeneas then flees, but flees into 'action' . . . all men must 'found Rome'—etc."—and Warren relates the Anchises image, in particular, to his own work both past and to come:

> Always we must carry Anchises (the "father") from the ruin of the human establishment—he is . . . the necessary burden of "piety"—one cannot flee to the "new land" without him . . . Cf. Billie Potts . . . N. B. Jefferson—the "Founding Fathers" in the strip of wilderness . . . .

Two final points of interest in the Prefatory Notes are (first) the "sinking into common day" that Warren hoped to achieve by returning to the Lewis and Clark expedition to discuss "the ordinary sol-

---

R. P. W. and Kurtz's schizoid character being apportioned between Jefferson and Lilburn. And, of course, the Secret Sharer motif is strong in the poem, too, as the theme Jefferson must come to terms with.

diers who went on out," and (second) the empathy with Lilburne, which is built into the narrative design:

> *N.B.* Everybody "betrays" Lilburne—his dog with the bone, his wife after she leaves the house, his mother in dying, his father in going back to Virginia, his brother in shooting before the count, etc.
>
> Lilburn is a "victim"—

In the text proper, many of the finest poetic passages—the rape of Pasiphaë, the two visits to the Lewis homesite, the coming of the *annus mirabilis*—are carried over largely intact from the first draft ("Finished in New York City, October 5, 1952") through the 1979 version. Nonetheless, the changes rendered over a quarter century result in so substantial an effect as to motivate the poet's insistence that the recent version is a rewriting, not merely a revision, of its predecessor. Some of the changes in the published versions are obvious, like the division of the text into numbered sections; some are curious, like the disappearance of R. P. W.'s father from the poem's coda (an ellipsis that occurred only after Mr. Warren himself became the father of two children); some involve subtle reworkings of meter and rhythm; and some changes represent a new departure in theme.

One approach, perhaps the most efficient approach, may be to classify a number of revisions in terms of diction, tone (two somewhat interchangeable elements), meter and rhythm, imagery, and philosophic attitude. Of special interest to Warren scholars are such revisions in response to criticism bearing Allen Tate's initials in the margins of the *Kenyon Review* typescript; I shall indicate this influence when relevant.[4]

Of the many revisions in diction, by far the greater number had the effect of elevating the tone of the poem. The opening lines include a most engaging example of this principle. Originally the *Kenyon Review* typescript has Jefferson introducing himself as "he / Whose body yet, beneath the triple boast / On my green mountain, rots." But by publication day, that final verb had vanished, to be replaced by R. P. W.'s discreet interruption: "your body still waits / On your green mountain."[5] A similar thoughtfulness toward diction produced a soft-

---

4. Allen Tate was one of four readers in this enterprise, and the only one whose suggestions were manifestly efficacious.
5. In the 1979 version, Jefferson's body neither rots nor waits; it no longer rates a mention.

ening of expletives throughout the poem—e.g., "I scarcely held that meditation on the nurture of roses / Is much comfort to a man who had just stepped in dung" [1953, p. 37, 1979, p. 26]—and in one instance an excretory expletive was reduced to "Oh, fudge" before being deleted entirely.

Occasionally, a reader may regret this dignifying of tone. The manuscript line, "But hit the gas and pretty quick you're gone" ("omit?" Tate marked in the margin) seems more forceful and metrically appropriate than, "But touch the accelerator and quick you're gone" in the 1953 and 1979 volumes (p. 15 and p. 12 respectively). Elsewhere a sardonic little couplet (like T. S. Eliot, Warren sometimes rhymes to point up sarcasm) survived Allen Tate's doubts ("You want this rhyme?—A. T.") in the 1953 book, only to vanish from the 1979 rewriting (the occasion here was a D. A. R. marker that purified the Lewis family history): "But let that pass, for to the pious mind / Our history's nothing if it's not refined" (1953, p. 21; cf. 1979, p. 17).

The manuscript passage most happily deleted, I should say, is a digression I must refrain from reproducing here. Extending its ridicule of "a certain breed among professors of American literature" (the "hurrah America!" breed) to a dozen lines, it would certainly have diminished the main text of the poem, as Tate's reaction indicated ("drop?—A. T."). Another problem passage has been Jefferson's greeting to Meriwether (who had shot himself in the head) as "Crack-head." The 1953 volume, which added two more Crack-heads to the dialogue ("Yes I am Crack-head, but if I'm Crack-head now / You ought to recognize your handiwork"—p. 175), prompted J. L. Stewart's protest that one is tempted to lay aside the book in disgust, to see Jefferson so crudely travestied. In the 1979 version, the poet reduced his Crack-heads to two, and in the *Kenyon Review* typescript there was just one; in all three versions, however, the identical phrase is assigned to Jefferson: "Well, Crack-head, who are you?"

So far as meter and rhythm are concerned, one senses that—especially in a long poem—the urge to revise is an itch that is never satisfied. Warren himself stated, concerning his new *Brother to Dragons*, that to change a single syllable may sometimes alter the rhythmic effect of a line dramatically—a point he illustrated back in the *Kenyon Reivew* typescript by rearranging a line (at Tate's suggestion) from "[I] Sought the new world, tension and test, terror perhaps," to "[I] sought the new world, tension and test, perhaps terror" (1953, p. 13, 1979, p. 11). The major difference between the recent version and the metrics of the early 1950's, however, stems from the onset during the intervening period of the "new American Poetry." "I was caught in a blank verse trap," Warren recently remarked concerning those earlier versions.[6] The Beinecke manuscripts reveal a very strong allegiance to the blank verse tradition, but this form was already yielding to the loosening effects of the new style in the 1953 book version, as a comparison between it and the *Kenyon Review* typescript indicates:

> The West, my West, the West I bought and gave and never
> Saw, or but like the Israelite,
> From some high pass or crazy crag of mind, saw,
> Saw all, swale and savannah and the tulip tree
> Immortally blossoming to May, Hawthorn and haw,
> Valley's vast and prairies idle and the land's
> Long westward languor lifting to the scarped day.
>
> (*KR*)

> But it was my West, the West I bought and gave and never
> Saw, or but like the Israelite,
> From some high pass or crazy crag of mind, saw—
> I saw all,
> Swale and savannah and the tulip-tree
> Immortally blossoming to May,
> Hawthorn and haw,
> Valleys extending and prairies idle and the land's
> Long westward languor lifting toward the flaming escarpment at the
>   end of the day.
>
> (1953, p. 11; 1979, p. 10)

Like the tone, diction, and metrics, the poem's imagery sometimes yielded to the influence of Allen Tate's criticism. "Not clear," Tate objected when Warren described the town-site "where the Cumberland uncoils / To kiss the broad Ohio's flank and pour / All that sweet poison up from Tennessee." Thereafter, Warren erased his images in favor of a clearer though more prosaic and Latinate etching: "where the Cumberland discovers / The sober magnificence of the Ohio, and into that sweep pours / All its own wash and wastage up from Tennessee" (1953, p. 16; 1979, p. 13). In another instance the *Kenyon Review* typescript develops an elaborate metaphor—

> ISHAM: But he leaned closer then,
> And leans at me—

6. Robert Penn Warren to Victor Strandberg, summer 1979.

R. P. W.: And leans, and from his heart
That dark plant stands, and the buds now swell and pulse.
Yearn to divulge. They glisten in the light.
In that light of the late fire the plant's leaves
Glisten—bedewed by what?—by a dark ichor,
By blood, by tears? Or simply a splash of that stuff
From Lilburn's jug, no doubt just sprinkled there
Like water to refresh some widow-woman's pet hyacinth in a pot.
Well, anyway, it glistens there and grows.
And the night grows big with possibility. . . .

—to which Mr. Tate objected, "This bothers me a little. It's a symbol before it's a specific plant." Subsequently, Mr. Warren uprooted the plant completely out of the poem:

ISHAM: And he leans at me—
R. P. W.: And leans, and his heart knows
That the night grows big with possibility. . . .

(1953, p. 124; 1979, p. 78)

So as not to overstate Tate's influence on his fellow poet, it were best to include a few examples of Warren ignoring his old friend's counsel. "This strikes me as bad," Tate scribbled beside the following lines—

Broadhorn and keelboat and the boatman's hail
That shook the shallows while the fiddle skirled—
Half-horse, half-alligator, prodigal
Of blood, sweat, semen, and the God-damn world.

—but this rhyming quatrain survived unchanged from the typescript through the 1953 (p. 16) and 1979 (p. 13) publications. Tate also spotted an anachronism, and queried whether R. P. W. shouldn't be speaking these lines, but Warren continued assigning them to Jefferson:

Oh, it's always the same.
Always the same, and the dust always drinks blood,
And Bloody Angle, and the Bloody Pond—
Listen, flames crackle through the Wilderness. . . .

(1953, p, 136; cf. 1979, p. 86)

A final instance of resistance to change—a little favorite of mine—describes Jefferson's infanticidal rage toward his nephew: ". . . that parcel of unformed flesh. They should have thrown it / Out where the hogs come to the holler, out with the swill." One reviewer (not Tate) took these lines as confirming evidence of Warren's hatchet work on our most intellectually accomplished President: would Jefferson have really said "holler" instead of "hollow"? But the reviewer misunderstood the word: Warren was not referring to a forest dell but to a voice hollering "hoo, pig!" and so the offending word carried over from the 1953 book (p. 61) to the 1979 rewriting (p. 42).

I have reserved for last what I consider a greatly important revision that distinguishes the 1979 rewriting from its 1953 predecessor. I quote the original passage at some length in this case, both to clarify the ensuing revision and at the same time to savor the splendid imagery in the last half of this:

> . . . and I,
> In that cold light, was impelled to apostrophize:
> "O you [Ohio River] who have on your broad bosom borne
> Man and man's movement, and endured the oar
>
> . . . .
> You who have suffered filth and the waste of the human establish-
>   ment,
>
> . . . .
> I take you now as image and confirmation
> Of that deep flood that is our history,
> Of that deep flood that makes each new day possible
> And bears us westward to the new land.
> I take you as the image and confirmation
> Of some faith past our consistent failure, and the filth we strew."
>
> But even as I experienced this mood,
> I knew that though the great river might be
> Image, it could not be confirmation,
> For even the grandeur of Nature may not be
> Our confirmation. It is image only.
> There is, indeed, the bickering glitter of waters sun-bit to glory.
> There is the taciturnity of stone black at the massif's jut of noblest
>   exposure,
> Beyond the bloom-gaud of cirque, and the balsam's silence.
> There is the wing-whistle of bomb-plunge of gannet, and the moon-
>   lit unwhisper of owl-swoop.
> And there is, always, the philosophic peace of a certain pasture at
>   evening, not seen since boyhood.
> But whatever the gleam of massive magnificence or glimmer of shy
>   joy

> May be, it can only resemble the moon
> And is but mirror to the human heart's steadfast and central
>   illumination.
> If there is glory, the burden, then, is ours.
> If there is virtue, the burden, then, is ours.
>
> And so I thought of the dead beneath my feet. . . .
>
> (1953, pp. 210–11)

Deleted from the 1979 volume are the lines from the middle to the end; thus the new version reads:

> . . . and I,
> In that cold light, was impelled to apostrophize:
> River, who have on your broad bosom borne
> Man and man's movement, and endured the oar,
> . . . .
> You who have suffered filth and the waste
> Of the human establishment,
> . . . .
> I take you as an image
> Of that deep flood that is our history,
> And the flood that makes each new day possible
> And bears us westward to the new land.
> I take you as image and confirmation
> Of some faith past our consistent failure,
> And the filth we strew.
>
> And so I thought of the dead beneath my feet. . . .
>
> (1979, pp. 129–30)

In this revision, we find Warren risking a very unusual transaction, one that is almost invariably a losing proposition in poetry: the richness of sensuous detail in the earlier version was sacrificed so as to permit a new philosophic mood in the sequel. What intervened between the deleted lines, which sustain the idea that "even the grandeur of Nature may not be / Our confirmation. It is image only," and the stripped-down sequel was the poet's growing conviction that Nature is not merely a reservoir of stimuli for "image only." From *Promises* (1957) on, Warren has repeatedly portrayed Nature as radiant with "vital meanings," a motif that has deepened towards a quasi-Romantic pantheism in more recent poems like *Audubon: A Vision* (1969), "Trying to Tell You Something" (1975), and "Code Book Lost"

(1978). In Warren's total canon of poetry, now over sixty years in the making, this turning toward Nature for ultimate meanings has emerged as perhaps his most significant thematic development.

Eventually, when the definitive study of the Beinecke manuscripts is made—and a greatly ambitious project it will be—we are certain to have a much clearer picture of this artist's craft of revision. For now, to conclude this fragmentary study, two overall impressions may be rendered. First, the lapse of time now permits us to see the earlier *Brother to Dragons* as a watershed in Warren's poetic career. His lengthiest, most ambitious, and most experimental poem, it was the first major work in which he risked openly using himself—R. P. W.—as a voice in the poem. In so doing, he fashioned the persona that has unified the widely admired volumes of his later career—volumes such as *Promises*, "Tale of Time," *Or Else*, and *Now and Then*. Now the rewritten version of the poem tells us something new about the person behind that persona. When *Brother to Dragons* was first published as a book in 1953, it received lavish praise from many reviewers, including such fellow poets as Robert Lowell, Randall Jarrell, and Delmore Schwartz; and some fifteen years later, speaking from the cooler distance of Academe, Hyatt Waggoner pronounced a judgment that many of us share, that the book is "certainly a major *document* in American poetry." It is a measure of Mr. Warren's dedication to his art that neither this reception of his work nor his prolific yearly output since that time has prevented him from reshaping that work of a quarter-century ago toward an even higher standard of excellence. In the end, the path from the Dinkler-Tutwiler stationery to the recent volume reveals something beyond the craft of revision: it bespeaks a remarkable career, a Jamesian will to pursue the prize.

Brother to Dragons or *Brother to Dragons, A New Version?* A Case for the 1953 Edition

Richard N. Chrisman

Two texts of Robert Penn Warren's *Brother to Dragons* are now available. The original appeared in 1953 and a "new version" in September, 1979.[1] With the publication of a second, revised edition of his most famous poem, Warren has set before his readers a conception of *Brother to Dragons* which he apparently prefers but which may not ultimately replace the first version. We will have to wait, of course, for posterity to make its judgment; but at present, of the two editions, that of 1953 has far greater interest. Historical reasons alone would make it necessary for the first edition to be the object of any comprehensive study of Warren, since it has a fixed place in the sequence of long poems he wrote and has stood until just now—a period of twenty-five years—as the only text. But on other, aesthetic grounds, as I hope to demonstrate, the first version remains the preferable text.

The new version of *Brother to Dragons* differs enough from the original to raise the same questions provoked by the nine editions of *Leaves of Grass* that Walt Whitman published over a forty-year period: Which shall be regarded as the "authoritative" text? The most faithful to what we think of as the poet's true vision? The most original? The best poetry? When it comes to literary matters, we seem unable to accept the stereoptical perspective which in physiology produced the satisfying impression of depth. Where two texts vie for legitimacy under the same title, only one, it seems, may prevail while the other has to be an imposter.

On the other hand, while Warren regarded his revision as a "new work" (p. xiii), there is cause to ask to what extent it actually amounts to a substantially different poem. The changes, which by any reckon-

---

This article appears in print for the first time in this collection.
1.   Robert Penn Warren, *Brother to Dragons* (New York: Random House, 1953); *Brother to Dragons, A New Version* (New York: Random House, 1979). Hereinafter, references to these editions are cited parenthetically within my text.

ing are extensive, nevertheless prove in large part to be superficial. So it becomes a question, in the last analysis, whether for all his trouble Warren succeeded in improving his poem.

Warren's reworking of *Brother to Dragons* results in a reduction of the great bulk of the original book, an alteration unprecedented in Warren's career. The new poem, however, is not shorter by quite as much as Harold Bloom approvingly suggests.[2] Bloom compares page-counts, where the difference between 214 pages in the old version and 132 pages in the new comes to nearly half. But type-setting economies in the later edition increased the number of lines printed on a page. So the actual reduction amounts only to about one fifth, from 5,100 lines to 4,100 lines. Still, this reduction represents no small alteration. It is greater than any of the others to which Warren, an inveterate "tinkerer," subjected his poems. Warren frequently pared away ob-scurities from his lyrics as they went through successive editions and, except in the case of "The Ballad of Billie Potts," he emended only a phrase or two at a time and almost never entire lines. When he pre-pared "Billie Potts" for inclusion in a new edition of his poetry in 1966,[3] Warren trimmed about two dozen lines from the poem, among them four of the seventeen repetitions of the refrain, "In the land be-tween the rivers." This small change purged the bumping jauntiness from the ballad-like effect Warren was trying to create and vastly im-proved the poem, but no one would say that the 1966 version was a different poem from that published in 1944. In the case of *Brother to Dragons*, however, the new version's length and content present us with the appearance, at least, of a very different poem. Warren's changes are of three kinds: first, deletions; second, expansions and rewriting of some passages; and, third, reshaping of the lines and of the poem as a whole. I want to structure my analysis according to these three categories. At the same time I will, as appropriate, show how they affect characterization, rhythm, theme, and structure of the poem.

Even though it comes to a fifth of the poem, the thousand lines worth of deletions Warren has made does not manage to obscure its main features because there appears to be no systematic method of excision, no particular object—no theme, or set of images—that is

---

2. Harold Bloom, review of Robert Penn Warren's *Brother to Dragons: A Tale in Verse and Voices, A New Version,* in *New Republic,* September 1 and 8, 1979, p. 31 [q.v., p. 183].
3. Robert Penn Warren, *Selected Poems: New and Old, 1923–1966* (New York: Random House, 1966), 223–39.

singled out. Rather, the work of editing addresses what must have appeared to the author as repetitions or redundancies, since his cuts in any one area are never consistently or thoroughly executed. Although he removes much of the philosophical reflection in the mode of T. S. Eliot from the part of "R. P. W.," for instance, he does not remove it all. There are at least four places where Warren edits "R. P. W.'s" speeches this way, cutting 23, 19, 47, and 54 lines respectively. In each case, however, the economies are incomplete. The effect of the remaining speculations, now abbreviated and more terse, is to exacerbate the impression of lofty, sonorous abstraction rather than to eliminate it. Harold Bloom finds, to the contrary, that such emendations remove offensively "tendentious" verse, showing that Warren "now trusts his reader to interpret the trope of the passage's final line on his own."[4] Because Bloom objects, as he says later, to Warren's "ideological ferocity," he welcomes any and all excisions of what he sees as presumably ideological language. But with Warren the task of purifying his poetry along these lines would require far more surgery than he in fact performed. The result has been not so much to call forth our abilities to interpret the remaining lines as to throw us back into more inconclusive, and more frustrating guesswork. That Bloom could find in the revised poetry "an authority and resonance that little in the 1953 text prophesied" can only mean that Bloom prefers the elliptical rather than the discursive in poetry, perhaps at all costs.

The example Bloom uses demonstrates my point. Due to Warren's revision, the following passage wins Bloom's approval:

> . . . and lift our eyes up
> To whatever liberating perspective,
> Icy and pure, the wild heart may horizonward command,
> And so the glimmering night scene under
> The incalculable starlight serves
> As an image of lethal purity—
> Infatuate glitter of a land of Platonic ice.
>
> (1979, p. 62)

Between the last two lines, Warren has lifted "the incessant / And whirling dream of desperate innocence," thereby removing the objectionable similarity to Eliot that makes Bloom want to argue with Warren. Without that reference to natural beauty particularly as a "dream," as an illusion of goodness, *is* the reader likely to conclude on his own

4. Bloom, review of new version, 31.

that Warren means that nature traduces people who look upward, toward "whatever liberating perspective"? Bloom does not mention the other lines in this passage, now emended, which originally made clear that the upward gaze succeeded only in averting our eyes from the ineluctable "tightening coil" and "mathematical constriction" of earth-bound existence (1953, p. 95). Also, Bloom erroneously quotes Warren, omitting the poet's addition of the word "horizonward," itself a very awkward insertion that belies Warren's mastery of long lines. Warren's apparent attempt at clarification—in compensation for the lost lines—only calls attention to itself.

Bloom's example from Warren's revision happens to be the best he could have chosen. Others fail much more flagrantly. To take just one more of "R. P. W.'s" speeches, consider the diminution of the tragic consciousness evoked by the narrator's recollection of his father's limitations between original and revision:

> And thus I saw his life a story told,
> Its glory and reproach domesticated,
> And for one moment felt that I had come
> To that most happy and difficult conclusion:
> To be reconciled to the father's own reconciliation.
>
> It is most difficult because that reconciliation
> Costs the acceptance of failure. And can we,
> Sunk in our saeculum of desire,
> Pay that cost?
> Most difficult because that reconciliation
> Signifies the purification of vanity.
> And can we lift the hand,
> Even to the most secret and worthy work,
> If that hand be not sustained, and stained, in vanity?
> Therefore, most difficult because we know
> The failures of our fathers are the failures we shall make,
> Their triumphs the triumphs we shall never have.
>
> (1953, p. 28)

He then cuts thirteen of these lines for the new edition, which reads:

> And thus I saw his life a story told,
> Its glory and reproach domesticated.
>
> The failures of our fathers are failures we shall make,
> Their triumphs the triumphs we shall never have.
>
> (1979, p. 21)

The abbreviation admittedly eliminates a certain sententiousness in the commentary, but it costs Warren the development of his thought and something of the original pathos in the observation. His emendations do spare us triple repetitions of the words "reconciliation," "difficult," and "failure." And his pruning also spares us moral abstractions like the word "vanity" and the melodramatic expression "Sunk in our saeculum of desire," with its sound of drawing-room superiority. But we also lose his central idea, namely, the futility of our pretenses to goodness which are, paradoxically, essential to our attempts at doing the good. This is an argument worth preserving, if only because without the preceding argument the retained punch line makes little sense and has less emotional impact. The final couplet strikes an unprepared ear as unnecessarily aphoristic or, at worst, as mystification.

Occasionally Warren's lifting of the philosophical lines leaves a less jagged edge. Perhaps the most quoted lines of the poem, and those most reminiscent of Eliot, disappear quite inconspicuously:

> The recognition of complicity is the beginning of innocence.
> The recognition of necessity is the beginning of freedom.
> The recognition of the direction of fulfillment is the death of the self,
> And the death of the self is the beginning of selfhood.
> All else is surrogate of hope and destitution of spirit.
>
> (1953, pp. 214–15)

And other equally abstract lines also disappear:

> Thus though the act is life and without action
> There is no life, yet action is a constant withering
> Of possibility, and hence of life.
> So by the act we live, and in action die.
>
> (1953, p. 55)

and

> If there is glory, the burden, then, is ours.
> If there is virtue, the burden, then, is ours.
>
> (1953, p. 211)

Yet, others just like them have been saved:

> . . . every act to become an act must resolve
> The essential polarity of possibility . . .
>
> . . . .

> Yet all we yearn for is the dear redemption of
> Simplicity.
>
> (1979, p. 39)

and

> We have yearned in the heart for some identification
> With the glory of the human effort. We have devised
> Evil in the heart, and pondered the nature of virtue,
> We have stumbled into the act of justice. . . .
>
> (1979, p. 131)

Warren has by no means consistently eliminated the kind of diction Bloom faults in "R. P. W.'s" speeches. But, having stricken so many, much of the poem's reflective quality—so typical of all Warren's poetry—is lost. The authorial presence and its primarily philosophical concerns, though still in considerable evidence, are now muted by contrast with the original version. It is as if he were trying at this point to efface his own authorship—what he is and has been—his own past poetic identity.

After "R. P. W.," the character most abbreviated is that of Laetitia.[5] The reduction of her part has two discernible effects. First, as the wife of Lilburn, Laetitia provides the reader with the most direct perspective on his character that we have, since he himself only has two or three lines of his own. Shortening her part with its lengthy descriptions of her relation to him truncates his characterization. Since Lilburn is the agent of the primary action and the chief evidence in the debate about human nature in the poem, the loss of insight into his motivation really cannot be afforded. Second, through Laetitia's fragile personality Warren projects the horror that the events and the environment inspire in all the characters. Laetitia's hysteria is an index of the magnitude of evil in Warren's universe. With her excised lines, some of the terror of the poem goes out. Warren reduced the following nineteen lines to thirteen in the revision.

> LAETITIA: Yes, yes, that's right, it just filled up the room,
> And the dark outside the room, and the whole world,
> Or seemed to. Yet it wasn't loud, far off,
> Being so far off, down there in the meat-house.
> But soon as I heard it, it was like the world
> Just started screaming by itself, and like I
> Had just been waiting years for it to start,

5. Even her name is shortened in spelling from "Laetitia" to "Letitia."

And all my life had been waiting for it, and every
Dead leaf in the woods just screamed just like a tongue,
A little tongue, not loud, and maybe you couldn't
Hear one alone, it was so weak, but together
All screaming they made a big scream filling
Up all the world, and filled my head, and my poor head
Was one big hollow echo full of dark,
Big as the world, and the whole world, all the mountains,
The rivers, creeks, and fields and hills and woods and every
Leaf screaming in the dark, and all the stars,
Was in my head and lost, and my poor head
Kept whirling bigger. And I tried to scream.

> (1953, pp. 50–51)

LETITIA: And the whole world so dark!
Yet wasn't loud, being
Far off—down in the meat-house, they say—
But I heard it, and then the world
Started screaming too, by itself, like I
Had been waiting for years for it to start, and every
Dead leaf in the woods just screamed like a tongue,
Each little leaf weak, but all together
One big scream filling
My head,
Like one big hollow echo, my poor head big enough
To hold the world, and all the stars,
The stars all screaming.

R. P. W.: And you tried to scream?

> (1979, p. 36)

The revision seems to have all the essentials of the original—the death-scream of the slave in the night, the sympathetic response of nature, and Laetitia's horror. But the magnitude of the experience diminishes: What is left of the terror seems unconvincing. Laetitia's articulation of the invasion of evil by repeated images—screams filling the world, filling her whirling head—gives what psychological credibility a poem as "undramatic" as this one can have. A positive breathlessness emerges from the unrolling of fifteen long lines without full stop. The few and much shorter lines of the revision reduce the tone almost to that of casual reportage. Thus, the remaining lines, as in the case of Warren's treatment of "R. P. W.," have sufficient substance to arouse certain expectations but not enough to satisfy them.

Overall, the alterations in the speeches of "R. P. W." and Laetitia
do not eradicate their original content but trim from them their former extremes. Both the slightly overwrought thoughtfulness of the
narrator and the slightly overwrought hysteria of Laetitia shift to
moderate levels of intensity. With this decision Warren has retreated
from the poetic gamble he had originally set out to take and had, in
large measure, won. In the original, these extremes were held together, albeit with considerable tension, by the whole.

Emendations like those made in the parts of "R. P. W." and Laetitia also occur randomly throughout the poem with similar, if somewhat less concentrated, effects. A description of the Kentucky springtime in the revision reads thus:

> The month is March—and for a background the arabesques
> Of leafage dappled with gold, to fret
> And freak with joy the dark margin
> Of forest.
>
> (1979, p. 32)

the original presents this picture:

> The month is March—and for a background the incredible
> Complication and arabesque of tender tendril,
> Leafage, and bud, dappled in gold, and that heartbreaking
> New delicacy of green—oh, sweet as hope—
> That frets and freaks with joy this dark margin
> And massive dark of forest.
>
> (1953, p. 45)

The vivid accuracy of detail in the depiction of nature, a hallmark of
Warren's poetry during his entire career, apparently offends the author here. These cuts destroy the sense of luxuriant pleasure he was
taking in the poignant scene. And in the revision a syntactical anom-
aly obscures an important contrast between young growth and ominous maturity. Warren changes a dependent clause clearly modifying
"delicacy" to an infinitive of purpose describing either "background"
or "arabesques," we cannot be certain which. But it is certain that neither "background" nor "arabesques" constitutes the quality Warren
originally juxtaposed with the "massive dark" of the forest. The quality exactly opposed to the forest is the "New delicacy of green" in the
original text. With this change we have lost a contrast between innocence and experience expressed here with natural images in a vein
reminiscent of Hawthorne.

A simpler example of the loss caused by Warren's emendations appears in the tiny clippings from this line in the original: "It spoke / Of a fair time yet to come . . ." (1953, p. 41). In the revision, Warren drops only two words but undercuts rhythm and image and meaning: "It spoke / Of a time to come (1979, p. 29). The new version is less wordy as a result, but almost to a fault: Warren's expression strikes our ear too sharply. The words are Jefferson's, and he is describing an eighteenth-century government building in southern France that epitomizes, for him, the great prospects of human civilization. The revision cramps the elevated spirit that had just praised the building's "proportion" as "a shape that shines." This economy, so typical of Warren's whole revision, renders up extremely minimal benefit.

The second kind of editing to be examined in Warren's revision will be the rewriting of passages and the additions to the text. While far less numerous than the cuts enumerated above, these alterations have just as deleterious an effect upon the poem. Here, Warren's rationale appears to be one of clearing up obscurities or possible misunderstandings, but the passages he augments or restates in fact hardly asked for clarification. "I'll tell you quietly, in order, what I saw" (1953, p. 6) becomes "I'll tell you quietly, in system, what I saw" (1979, p. 5). He changes "So you'd make the pain the final obscenity" (1953, p. 139) to "So you'd make what you call masochism the final obscenity" (1979, p. 87). A "curtain rent" becomes a "curtain split." Warren revises "the immitigable ferocity of self" (1953, p. 47) to read "the unuprootable ferocity of self" (1979, p. 33), a change for which no metrical, aesthetic, or semantic justification is apparent. And surely it was not necessary for him to alter "your name means light" (1953, p. 23) to read "Your name means, etymologically, light" (1979, p. 18). "Human alienation" (1953, p. 47) becomes the less forceful "human lot" (1979, p. 33); "mystery" (1953, p. 52) gets demoted to "puzzle" (1979, p. 36). The murdered slave, George, is unaccountably renamed "John" and referred to not as "the colored boy" (1953, p. 63), in keeping with the period, but as "the black boy" (1979, p. 43), our contemporary idiom. For "the inexpugnable error," (1953, p. 24) Warren substitutes "the inexpungable error" (1979, p. 19) which, as spelled, is not a word. If, in fact, "inexpungible" or "inexpungeable" was meant, Warren has slightly changed "error" from being unvanquishable to unerasable, a probably insignificant difference in this context. Throughout these examples, and the many more like them, one can only sense an alien hand behind the revision, as if someone were doing Warren the du-

bious favor of advising him on acceptable language for a successful
poem in this age.

Such revisions occur, for the most part, randomly throughout the
book. The most conspicuous and objectionable example occurs, de-
cisively, in the first page and the first speech of the poem. In place of
his effective entrance into the original poem, Warren inserts twelve
new lines. Their tone and imagery momentarily confuse the reader
because the passage introduces prematurely and inadequately the
poem's major themes of knowledge and guilt. The new opening reads
thus:

> My name is Jefferson. Thomas. I
> Lived. Died. But
> Dead, cannot lie down in the
> Dark. Cannot, though dead, set
> My mouth to the dark stream that I may unknow
> All my knowing. Cannot, for if,
> Kneeling in that final thirst, I thrust
> Down my face, I see come glimmering upward,
> White, white out of the absolute dark of depth,
> My face. And it is only human.
>
> Have you ever tried to kiss that face in the mirror?
> Or—ha, ha—has it ever tried to kiss you? Well,
> You are only human. Is that a boast?
>
> (1979, p. 5)

Before his character is established, Jefferson in the revision is made to
assume an ironic posture, mocking our humanity, while the poem
and Jefferson himself eventually develop a different tone. Jefferson's
disappointment with human nature is generally expressed in both
poems with more pathos than irony. Warren's new introduction momentarily undercuts the precarious dignity that later accompanies
Jefferson through his fulminations against human depravity. With respect to imagery, Warren has replaced references to Jefferson's "green
mountain," both his burial place and an image that assimilates Jefferson's Enlightenment views to American pastoralism, with an overly
compressed statement of the poem's themes. The reader is unprepared for Warren's evocation of death as a false opportunity for the
forgetfulness (drinking at the River Lethe) Jefferson desires. It seems
melodramatic at first and then verges on the inappropriately comic.

Besides the random additions of lines to the original text, a concentration of them in the speeches of a particular character occurs only in the case of Meriwether Lewis. He appears late in the original book and with no prior reference whatever, extending the story somewhat anti-climactically. For the apparent reason of correcting this fault, Warren introduces Meriwether into the dialogue on page nine of the revision and regularly thereafter. The contribution of these additions to the theme or action is, however, negligible. In fact, the device only compounds the seeming arbitrariness of Meriwether's role. In the revision Meriwether, from out of nowhere, interjects questions or brief challenges to what is being said; but all of his statements go unacknowledged by the other speakers. Furthermore, Warren expands Meriwether's role often by assigning him parts of other characters' speeches. This expedient might not be noticeable to the reader acquainted only with the revision. But because the parts are interchangeable, even in this poem where the voices of all the characters seem subsumed in the author's voice, as Leslie Fiedler has pointed out,[6] an occasional reassignment of lines rings falsely. A glaring example occurs in the conclusion when we encounter a paean to "the shining land" in the mode of Hart Crane. In the original text, Jefferson speaks this part, at a level of optimism not altogether consonant with his new-found realism, though perhaps credible as the residue of his earlier idealism now transposed into a new key. In the revision, however, Warren gives the opening lines of this hymn to Meriwether whose bitter death under pathetic circumstances—the cause of his recriminations against Jefferson in this poem—could hardly have been forgotten by the reader. Warren does affirm good in this poem, with special qualifications, but in Meriwether Lewis' mouth the sentiment sounds downright giddy. Whether we found Meriwether to be problematic in the original, Warren's revisions have weakened his part in the poem.

We turn now to the third and final category under which we are analyzing Warren's revisions, that is, the reshaping of individual lines on the one hand and of the poem as a whole on the other. The basic structure of the line of verse in the original poem was disturbed in the process of carrying out the alterations described above. The momentum gathered by the unbroken sequence, over tens of pages at a time, of Warren's five- and six- and seven-beat lines simply does not occur in the revision. While Warren used lines of irregular length in the first

6. Leslie A. Fiedler, review of Robert Penn Warren's *Brother to Dragons*, in *Partisan Review*, XXI (March–April, 1954), 208–12.

version, the second employs so many more short lines than before that we lose the dominant impression of the long, epic-like poem executed in leisurely, long lines. The pattern made by the original lines disappears; the lines themselves are broken up. Even where Warren does not remove or add words to a passage, he will sometimes reapportion the words to create shorter lines. These three lines, for instance, become four in the revision:

> That fastidiousness was, I suppose, the ictus of horror,
> And my natural tremor of fatigue converted to the metaphysical chill
> And my soul sat in my hand and could not move.
>
> (1953, p. 34)

And,

> That fastidiousness was, I suppose, the ictus of horror,
> And my natural tremor of fatigue
> Was converted into the metaphysical chill, and my soul
> Sat in my hand and could not move.
>
> (1979, p. 24)

Warren will also cut a line in two, returning the remaining part to the lefthand margin below.

> Left on the sea-lapped shore, and the sea was Time.
>
> (1953, p. 21)

> Left on the sea-tongued shore,
> And the sea was Time.
>
> (1979, p. 17)

Much more often, final lines of stanzas ending at mid-line that used to be continued from that point in the first line of the next stanza now resume at the left-hand margin.

> . . . man
> Can't live without some glory after all,
> Even a poor kind.
>
> And Smithland too,
> Though it never came to much. . . .
>
> (1953, p. 20)

becomes

> . . . man
> Can't live without some glory after all,
> Even a poor kind.

> And Smithland too,
> Though it never came to much. . . .

(1979, p. 16)

This kind of change occurs almost every time a new stanza marks the beginning of a speech by another character. Whether such changes were done for typographical reasons alone we cannot know; but this small decision in effect chops up the lines and roughens the rhythm.

Also upsetting the rhythm of the poetry in this way, is the division of the long stanzas into three or four or five parts and sometimes into single lines. These divisions succeed in focusing greater attention upon the immediate content although, again, at some cost to the flow of lines. A stanza revised this way now reads:

> Lilburne would defend civilization, define
> The human mission, bring light to the dark place.
> But what does he defend?
>
> Only a pitcher, poor symbol.
>
> Does Lilburne know all this?
> He does not know.

(1979, p. 95)

But the original read thus:

> Lilburn would defend civilization and define
> The human mission, bring light to the dark place.
> But what does he defend? Only a pitcher,
> As some poor symbol, not the truth itself.
> He defends the letter while the spirit flees.
> And how define the human? By love of Mother,
> And in affirming love lifts high the meat-axe.
> How bring the light? He does not bring the light.
> He plunges his heart into the unredeemed dark of the wild land.
> Does Lilburn know all this? He does not know.

(1953, pp. 151–52)

The alteration of lines in this way is fundamentally a metrical issue. At the same time, because changes in rhythm impinge upon our sense of the poem as a whole, metrical differences have implications for structure. The impression left by the new text in this regard is of a decidedly less unified poem.

Adding to this impression of fragmentation, the revision divided the whole poem into seven parts. Warren has introduced breaks, headed by Roman numerals, that bring the events in the tragedy into greater relief than was the cause in the first text. Formerly the poem approximated being a seamless whole in which the reader's attention focused equally upon two kinds of "action," that is, Lilburn's story and the reflections Warren summons forth from all the characters involved in it, including the narrator. But the new divisions upset that balance slightly. They cause the dramatic action to be highlighted at the expense of the psychological action. Because the "plot" is revealed in the foreword, there can be no suspense surrounding the dramatic action; in this poem, any suspense there may be arises from the psychological "action." But the new organization of the poem diverts us intermittently from the fuller conception at work in it. So without altering the original order of events or speeches, Warren has altered the structure of the poem.

With these extensive changes, Warren effects "an important difference in the total feel" of the poem, just as he claims in the foreword (1979, p. xiv). Nevertheless, the basic themes remain intact. The thematic organization of the poem around pastoral and gothic motifs still stands, though now with somewhat less dramatic impact. If some lines disappear along with pastoral images like Jefferson's "green mountain," springtime's "new delicacy of green," and the "desperate innocence" of a cold, winter sky, just as many lines with images like them go untouched. Similarly, elements of the gothic techniques used by Warren undergo moderating changes. The terror's original high pitch has been subdued, it is true; but the fearful, ominous references to threats of evil from both nature and humanity still abound. It is on this account that one ventures to ask—for all that Warren's revision has conferred upon it an appreciably different "feel"—whether the text reemerges as a substantially different poem. Yet, while the paring and pruning have, far from improving the poem, only disrupted its former coherence, Warren's fundamental poetic task in *Brother to Dragons* of framing a "new definition of joy" in the light of new definitions of humanity has nevertheless survived the editing.

My assessment of the aesthetic losses incurred as a result of Warren's editorial decisions will have to await corroboration—or refutation—when the new edition has been available as long as the first one has at this point. In the meantime, however, there can be little doubt that Warren has, in this revision, at the very least contradicted his own sense of the poem. He warns in a prefatory note to both editions that *Brother to Dragons* is "definitely not a play, and must not be taken as such" (1979, p. xv). At the same time, we know Warren devoted considerable effort over a period of many years, as he himself declared in the new foreword, to adapting *Brother to Dragons* for stage performance and television screen. In the process some "dissatisfaction with several features of the poem grew" and he undertook to make changes by which "a number of dramatic effects" would be "sharpened" (1979, p. xiv). So the poem's workability as a play did concern him and, in practice, a consciousness of the poem precisely as a play seems to have influenced the revision. For the changes we have just documented could be said to "dramatize" the poem. The poem's rhythm and diction are certainly more "speakable" if not more readable; the characterizations conform a little better to conventional norms of dramatic realism; the action has been rendered into "acts"; and the narrative has been adapted for assimilation as a spoken medium. Altogether these changes argue for a view of the revision as a dramatization of the original, something which is foreign to Warren's explicit and abiding conception of the poem.

Versions of History and *Brother to Dragons*

Margaret Mills Harper

* I Tale *

On Sunday, December 15, 1811, a horrific series of incidents began in the frontier county of Livingston in western Kentucky: the murder, dismemberment, and cremation of an adolescent slave by two nephews of Thomas Jefferson; the coincidental timing of the first shocks of the New Madrid earthquake (whose epicenter was only seventy-five miles away); and later the bizarre misfiring of a mutual suicide pact between the two brothers who committed the crime. These events became sensational news throughout the region and beyond. Even in the wilds of Kentucky, at the very least "not a community / Famous for indirect action,"[1] the incident quickly captured the popular imagination: various versions of it were recorded in print, and folktales in the area still keep the legend of Lilburne and Isham Lewis alive. As might be expected, of course, many "facts" in these accounts and tales differ from one source to another, and even though some tempting historical records are available, the truth of the affair remains teasingly nebulous.

On August 21, 1953, Random House published *Brother to Dragons: A Tale in Verse and Voices* by Robert Penn Warren. In an interview conducted by Floyd Watkins in early 1979, Warren has recalled that he began entertaining the idea for the poem "back in the forties." He had been reading, he says, "a great deal of subhistorical material, like let-

---

This article appears in print for the first time in this collection.

1. Robert Penn Warren, *Brother to Dragons: A Tale in Verse and Voices* (New York: Random House, 1953), 65. Hereafter all references to this version of the poem will be indicated in the text by page number and date of publication. References to the 1979 version will be similarly indicated. For all historical data relating to the incident, see Boynton Merrill, Jr., *Jefferson's Nephews: A Frontier Tragedy* (Princeton: Princeton University Press, 1976).

ters and journals and things like that. . : . I was soaking myself in the period, and Lilburn [*sic*] Lewis and his story were practically unknown. I had known the folk-tale, garbled version in childhood. Then I began serious investigations of the court records and found that specialists know little about him."[2] Fascinated by the fact that "the philosopher of our liberties and the architect of our country and the prophet of human perfectibility had this in the family blood," Warren began serious work on the theme and form of the poem.[3] The theme defined itself quickly, but

> . . . the form didn't get settled. First I thought of a novel. But this wouldn't do—the historical material doesn't have the structure of a novel, it doesn't fulfill itself circumstantially, it spreads out and doesn't pull in at the end. A novel, too, couldn't bear the burden of comment probably necessary to interpret the material.
>
> Next I started a collaboration for a play in which Jefferson would serve as a commentator, a chorus, brooding over the affair. But again, the plot problem appeared. And also we discovered that the role of Jefferson would be disproportionate for a play. So we abandoned that.[4]

An early title, "Ballad of the Brothers," reminiscent of "The Ballad of Billie Potts," indicates another form tried and abandoned. The fragment of a ballad which remains in *Brother to Dragons* illustrates what the poem might have looked like, and the voice of R. P. W. explains there the dissatisfaction with that form: "the facile imitation / Of folk simplicity would scarcely serve, / . . . / No, the form was not adequate to the material" (1953, pp. 42–44; 1979, p. 31).

As it was finally settled in 1952, *Brother to Dragons* is "a kind of hybrid,"[5] a poem in the form of "a dialogue spoken by characters, but . . . not a play" (1953, p. xiii). It is an unusual form to suit the temperament both of the material and the maker, whose work in each genre—poetry, drama, prose fiction—betrays consistently his interest

2. Floyd C. Watkins, "A Dialogue with Robert Penn Warren on *Brother to Dragons,*" *Southern Review*, n.s., XVI (Winter, 1980), 4.
3. Robert Penn Warren, "The Way It Was Written," *New York Times Review of Books*, August 23, 1953, p. 6.
4. *Ibid.*
5. Robert Penn Warren, "A Self Interview," *New York Herald Tribune Book Review*, October 11, 1953; rpt. in Floyd C. Watkins and John T. Hiers (eds.), *Robert Penn Warren Talking* (New York: Random House, 1980), 4.

in and proficiency at the others. Through long narrative or specula-
tive speeches in smoothly flowing blank verse, the *dramatis personae*
relive in "no time" and "no space" their tragedy, arguing over and
discussing its meanings at length. Along with them, the reader gradually comes to understand what the poet intends the incident to sig-
nify; and at the climactic conclusion reader, Lucy and Thomas Jefferson, R. P. W., and Meriwether Lewis arrive together at the state
where "All is redeemed, / In Knowledge" (1953, p. 195).

Warren is careful to state in the preface to the 1953 version that he
is "trying to write a poem and not a history, and therefore [has] no
compunction about tampering with facts" (p. xii). Nonetheless, his
assertion that he has "stayed within the outlines of [the] record, but
[has] modified details in two respects" (p. x) certainly seems to indicate a knowledge of and respect for historical accuracy. Fourteen pages
of documented notes in the back of the book contribute to this effect,
as do the statements about "historical sense" at the conclusion of the
preface, that "Historical sense and poetic sense should not, in the
end, be contradictory, for if poetry is the little myth we make, history
is the big myth we live, and in our living, constantly remake" (p. xii).
Most critics of the poem assumed, "myth" notwithstanding, that
Brother to Dragons was faithful to actual incidents. Robert Lowell, in
fact, thought the poem was *too* historical: "Warren's tale is fact, but it
is too good melodramatically to be true," he noted in an early review.[6]

Brother to Dragons was something of a sensation. Despite a few
charges of melodrama and criticisms of its somewhat unflattering portrayal of Jefferson, it captured the imaginations of many both by its
powerful subject and theme and its unusual form, which combined
dramatic intensity with poetic introspection and narrative movement.
Randall Jarrell declared it "Robert Penn Warren's best book"; Lowell
ended his sensitive review calling "startling" Warren's "prose genius
in verse"; ending as it did a period of ten years during which Warren
published no poetry (and "didn't finish a single short poem, not one,"
as he tells it), and ushering in a major change in verse style, *Brother
to Dragons* understandably has consistently commanded much
attention.[7]

6. Robert Lowell, "Prose Genius in Verse," *Kenyon Review*, XV (Autumn, 1953), 621
[q.v., p. 164].
7. Randall Jarrell, "On the Underside of the Stone," *New York Times Review of Books*,
August 23, 1953, p. 6 [q.v., p. 160]; Lowell, "Prose Genius in Verse," 625; Richard B.

According to Warren, the poem did not satisfy its author, even when it first appeared. His wife was expecting their first child during the last rush of revising *Brother to Dragons* for the press, and he "wasn't as critical of what I had done as I might have been." In addition, in a last-minute flurry, he and his editor, Albert Erskine, confused manuscripts and briefcases, and some of the changes he *had* made "didn't get in." The changes that should have been made were poetic: "I had wandered into a trap—too often caught in the trap of blank verse—and that had meant some padding. And I published it without enough of the cooling off process—the last hard look."[8] There would have been, in Warren's words, "Quite some severe differences" in the poem if the right text had been printed.[9]

This tale, however, is not the first chapter in the quarter-century-long history of revisions and versions of *Brother to Dragons*. By sometime in 1952 Warren had finished the actual writing of the poem. Before it was published in its entirety, though, excerpts—slightly different from what would later be their respective sections in the book version—appeared in *Poetry* and the *Partisan Review*; and the first half was preprinted in the *Kenyon Review*.[10] Several editorial changes for the *Kenyon Review* version had been suggested by Allen Tate, to whom Warren had given a typescript of the poem.[11] Some of Tate's advice, which seems to have been concerned primarily with elevation of diction and clarification of images, was heeded at the time, and the result appears in the *Kenyon Review*; other suggestions, which Warren declined to follow in the *Kenyon Review* (perhaps because the publica-

---

Sale, "An Interview in New Haven with Robert Penn Warren," *Studies in the Novel*, II (Fall, 1970), 340–41.

8. Watkins, "A Dialogue," 1.

9. *Ibid.*, 2.

10. "The Death of Isham" appears in *Partisan Review*, XX (July–August, 1953), 393–96; "The Lie" (an altercation between Meriwether and Jefferson) in *Poetry*, LXXXII (June, 1953), 125–33; and *Brother to Dragons: A Tale in Verse and Voices* in *Kenyon Review*, XV (Winter, 1953), 1–103, with this note attached: "*Here appears the first half of a long poem. By permission of Random House, Inc., who will publish the entire poem in book form.*—The Editors."

11. This typescript, with Tate's suggestions written in the margins, is located in the Warren manuscripts at the Beinecke Manuscript and Rare Book Library at Yale. Its contents are not in the public domain, and I have not seen it. For what little knowledge of unpublished material I possess, I am indebted to Mr. Victor Strandberg, whose article appears beginning on p. 200 herein.

tion process for the journal was too far along), were adopted later for the book. With three portions from *Brother to Dragons* and the book itself being issued in one year, it hardly seems possible that *any* "cooling off" could have taken place.

After the (certainly) embarrassing episode with the briefcases, Erskine offered to publish another version of the poem; but other projects were in the wind, and for Mr. Warren the question of work on *Brother to Dragons* "became a matter of trying to make a play."[12] The play itself has a complicated history which includes a 1955 dramatic reading for the BBC (which Warren had no part in), a staging at Harvard, a Broadway production canceled on opening day, reworkings in Seattle and at the American Place Theatre in New York, and two productions directed by Adrian Hall in Providence in 1968 and 1973. In 1974, after seeing Hall's slightly modified road production at the Wilbur Theatre in Boston "stunningly, imaginatively done," Warren rewrote the play, and the new version appeared in the *Georgia Review* in 1976. (A recent version for television, which the poet "saw, but had no hand in," was, he felt, "a failure in conception.")[13]

The work on the play, says Warren, "changed my notion of the poem," and although there had been minor changes ("bit by bit, mind you") all along its history, "when it got on the stage, it changed my sense of the versification and led to a tremendous lot of rewriting and reorganization."[14] Warren took an axe to both verse and voices of *Brother to Dragons*, and in the autumn of 1979 "A New Version" of the poem appeared. It is with the New Version, and with the differences between it and the 1953 book-length version, that I am primarily concerned.

One more event of note in the history of *Brother to Dragons* concerns the publication in 1976 of *Jefferson's Nephews: A Frontier Tragedy* by Boynton Merrill, Jr., a thoroughly researched (and well written) "reconstruction of the crime, its consequences, and the circumstances that led to its commission."[15] Merrill mentions *Brother to Dragons* in

12. Watkins, "A Dialogue," 2.
13. See Warren's preface to "Brother to Dragons: A Play in Two Acts," *Georgia Review*, XXX (Spring, 1976), 65–138, for a history of the play. The comments on the television version are from Warren in a letter to me, January 7, 1981. *Editor's note*: In the PBS viewing, adapted by Adrian Hall and Ken Campbell for television, Warren, in fact, has a cameo role as R. P. W.'s father.
14. Watkins, "A Dialogue," 2.
15. Merrill, *Jefferson's Nephews*, ix.

his "Discussion of Sources," noting the poem's "unique literary and artistic quality" but, too, its historical inaccuracy:

> In regard to the historicity of *Brother to Dragons*, Warren states in the preface: "I am trying to write a poem and not a history, and therefore have no compunction about tampering with facts." Warren succeeded admirably, both in his poem and in tampering with the facts. However, it might be ventured that facts usually do stand in the way of poetic expression and artistic triumph, such as Warren has achieved.[16]

The data that Merrill has documented do indeed show *Brother to Dragons* to be much less historically accurate than it seemed. Warren has mentioned this several times, emphasizing in a slightly defensive tone that the new information is not consequential for the work. In the preface to the play in the *Georgia Review*, acknowledging "the several discrepancies between the poem (and play) and the record established by Mr. Merrill," he notes of the placing of Lucy's grave on the wrong estate that "This discrepancy no more than the others affects the meaning of the play."[17] In the New Version of the poem, he declares that Merrill's book, "fascinating and reliable as it is, does not change the basic thematic or dramatic outline of my tale." And in the Watkins interview he quickly and positively asserts that Merrill's work could have had no influence on his revision:

> WATKINS: You know there is a relatively new book out by the Princeton University Press. . . .
> WARREN: I've read it.
> WATKINS: I was going to ask you . . .
> WARREN: I know the man—Boynton Merrill, a delightful man—and a fascinating book.
> WATKINS: Did that affect your second version?
> WARREN: No. I had finished mine.
> WATKINS: You had finished it?
> WARREN: Before it came out. It wouldn't have affected me anyway. . . .[18]

The New Version, Warren says in the same interview, is "no different philosophically" from the 1953 version. "But it is very different

16. *Ibid.*, 426–27.
17. Warren, Preface to play version in *Georgia Review*, 67.
18. Watkins, "A Dialogue," 4–5.

technically—in rhythm (the important thing) and in organization."
There has been "a lot of cutting" of "repetitious and wordy" sections,
"there's less commentary," resulting in "a much more fluid and natural verse movement." "I didn't feel right about it," he concludes. "Put
it that way. It's as simple as that. I can get more out of it than I got out
of it."[19]

Warren has been temptingly explicit about his reasons for revising *Brother to Dragons*, and the results of his changes. The meshing of
certain details in his story with certain differences between the two
poems, though, remains teasingly nebulous. These details deal with
"history"—more specifically, the history of that Sunday in mid-
December, 1811. They are significant because in their light the themes
of the poem become more distinct. What the poet means by "the
spirit of his history" or that "Historical sense and poetic sense should
not . . . be contradictory" (1953, p. xii; 1979, p. xiii), two phrases in
the prefaces which do not change from one book-length version to
the other, may be made clear by exploring what *is* contradictory in the
history and poetry of *Brother to Dragons*.

* II Verse *

The most obvious differences between the 1953 and 1979 versions of
Brother to Dragons are in length: length of the poems themselves
(4,387 lines in 215 pages compared with 3,699 lines in 132 pages[20]),
length of speeches by the characters (who tend to discuss more and
speechify less in the 1979 version), length of the lines themselves. The
transformed prosody of the later version is especially noticeable: like
Warren's recent poetic style it has been made simpler and more direct,
and is much more rhythmically engaging.

The relaxed blank verse of the 1953 version has been broken and
syncopated through deletions and divisions, as in this passage describing the Mississippi catfish:

> And the year drove on. Winter. And from the Dakotas
> The wind veers, gathers itself in ice-glitter
> And star-gleam of dark, and finds the long sweep of the valley.

19.   *Ibid.*, 2.
20.   The calculations were done by "Simplicio," a character in the dialogue "Three Italians Visit Monticello," a discussion of the revised version of *Brother to Dragons* (among
other things) by William Harmon with Carol Eaton and Jeanne Heilakka in the *Southern
Literary Journal*, XII (Fall, 1980), 109–25 [q.v., p. 272].

A thousand miles and the fabulous river is ice in the starlight.
The ice is a foot thick, and beneath, the water slides black like a
    dream,
And in the interior of that unpulsing blackness and thrilled zero
The big channel-cat sleeps with eye lidless, and the brute face
Is the face of the last torturer, and the white belly
Brushes the delicious and icy blackness of mud.

(1953, p. 94)

In the 1979 version the passage becomes:

Winter: and from the Dakotas
Winter veers, gathers itself in ice-glitter
And star-gleam of dark, and finds
The long sweep of the valley.
A thousand miles and
The fabulous river is ice in the starlight.
The ice is a foot thick, and beneath,
In the interior of that unpulsing blackness
And thrilled zero, the big channel-cat, eye lidless, hangs
With white belly brushing
The delicious and icy blackness of mud.

(1979, p. 61)

The shorter, broken verses in the newer version seem to sweep down the vista of the "thousand miles" of river and valley, then contrast with the lengthened lines of "unpulsing blackness," in which the movement nearly stops. The finite verbs "slides," "sleeps," and "brushes" disappear, their active quality diminishing to reflect more closely the idea of stasis, "perfect adjustment," in the passage ("The catfish is in the Mississippi and / The Mississippi is in the catfish and / Under the ice both are at one / With God"). The subject and verb of the final sentence are placed together as they would be in everyday speech, and the last line is left pure description. The alliteration of "white belly brushing" is created, while the somewhat confusing image of "the face of the last torturer" is omitted entirely.

Now and then a line of blank verse is created or improved upon in the 1979 version, as where, for example, the meter of "The green leaf the lethal mantis at his prayer" becomes pure iambic pentameter while assonance is lessened in "The leaf the lethal mantis at his prayer" (1953, p. 30; 1979, p. 22). In general, though, the rather regular and sonorous verse of the 1953 version has been transformed into a chaster, more elliptical style. Most of the obvious rhetorical flourishes, which were for Randall Jarrell in 1953 "sometimes too noticeable to bear,"[21] have been deleted. Jefferson's declaration that

> Therefore all followed: the fat was in the fire.
> Therefore all followed: and I who once had said
> All liberty is bought with blood, now must say
> All truth is bought with blood, and the blood is ours. . . .
>
> (1953, p. 10)

loses much of its Senecan echo:

> The fat was in the fire.
> And I who once said, all liberty
> Is bought with blood, must now say,
> All truth is bought with blood, and the blood is ours. . . .
>
> (1979, p. 8)

Even the parallelism of "All liberty—All truth" is broken by the new line divisions. On the other hand, though, an interesting editorial decision is relevant here: in the new volume, each speech is printed so that it begins flush with the left margin, rather than indented to reflect its position in the blank verse line. This makes the verse *look* free, although in sound and stress it is in one respect at least more regular than it seems.

Conjunctions and articles are regularly left by the wayside in the hatchet-work of Warren's revisionary process, as are repetitions of pronouns, verbs, or exclamations. Repetitions or slight variations in descriptive adjectives or verbs also disappear: "the unleashed and unhouseled force of Nature" (1953, p. 95) loses the less vivid word "unleashed" by 1979 (62), and Bates, "whose hell-heart is a sink and bog" according to Meriwether in 1953 (182), has only the bog in the later version (113). Verbs become more vivid and personal (the modification of "He tries to stop it" [1953, p. 108] to "By God, he'll stop it!" [1979, p. 69] is typical), and philosophical passages are brought into present tense.

* **III Voices** *

Other glaring differences between the 1953 and 1979 versions of *Brother to Dragons* have to do with form: the shape of the poem as a whole, the placement of speeches and dialogues, the relegation of those

21. Jarrell, "On the Underside of the Stone," 6.

speeches to the various characters, their internal structure. Warren plays with who says what—and when—and certain aspects of characterization are subtly altered in the more theatrical newer volume.

To begin with, the 1979 text is no longer in one unbroken piece, but in seven numbered sections; these divisions, along with the many more stanza breaks than were in the 1953 text, make the work seem less a discursive "tale," more obviously a "poem," a structured artistic creation. Blocks of tightly written verse now stand alone, with pauses between them, and the logic of their progression seems more the associative logic of the mind, removed from the illusions of chronological and causative sequence, than it had in 1953.

Many structural elements reflect a greater emphasis on organization according to theme rather than story. Meriwether Lewis, who was brought in only on page 175 in the 1953 version to help Lucy Lewis as "provocation for Jefferson's redemption from mere shock and mere repudiation of his old dream"[22] appears near the beginning of the 1979 version; this earlier appearance not only stresses his thematic importance but also gives a sense of completion, having come full circle, when he reappears near the end. In an added passage Meriwether recalls the moment of epiphany when Jefferson kissed him and called him his son:

> And under mountain stars remembered your handgrip
> On each of my two shoulders,
> Old and bony the grip,
> But burned like fire—and then—
> Ah, then—the only, first and last, unique
> Kiss. You from your towering greatness leaned
> To place it on my cheek.
>
> (1979, p. 9)

The action described in this passage is repeated when Lilburne bestows his vision of depravity on Letitia:

> And sudden rose up from my side,
> And stood up tall like he would fill the room
> . . . .
> And way above, Lil's face, it swung,
> And his voice said: "—but now I see when angels
> Come down to earth, they step in dung, like us.
> And like it."
>
> (1979, p. 52)

22. Warren, "The Way It Was Written," 6.

The fragments of the song R. P. W. introduces in the 1953 version when he describes Smithland (17), "*All the way from Shawneetown, / Long time ago*," are heard again by Isham in the 1979 version as he and his brother sit in the darkness at "Rocky Hill" and Lilburne plans their suicide: "*Sliding down the river, / Lean on the beechen oar, / All the way to Shawneetown, / Long time ago*" (101).

That the poem is less strictly narrative does not mean, however, that it is less dramatic. In fact, the opposite is true. Robert Lowell lamented in 1953, "As for the characters, nothing limits the length of their speeches except the not very importunate necessity of eventually ending the story."[23] Warren's experiences with the play version of *Brother to Dragons* stood him in good stead as far as this aspect of the poem's texture is concerned. The dialogues and speeches do not read like portions of a play (the form is, of course, highly artificial, and strict drama would be inappropriate), but sections such as the one in which Letitia relives the night of the murder grow considerably in intensity from the theatrical elements introduced. In 1953, this passage read:

> [R. P. W.]: Night after night thus, until that night
> The scream came. Came once. Came twice. And came
> Again, and filled the vault of the December dark, and—
>
> LAETITIA: Yes, yes, that's right, it just filled the room,
> And the dark outside the room, and the whole world,
> Or seemed to. Yet it wasn't loud, far off,
> Being so far off, down there in the meat-house. (50)

In 1979 the same passage, with its quick interplay of thoughts and voices, is far more dramatic:

> [R. P. W.]: Night after night, until—
> JEFFERSON: In the December dark—
> R. P. W.: The scream—
> JEFFERSON: It came and filled the room.
> LETITIA: And the whole world so dark!
> Yet wasn't loud, being
> Far off—down in the meat-house, they say—(35–36)

All through the New Version speeches are broken and redistributed among the characters (with Meriwether getting a bigger share of the

23. Lowell, "Prose Genius in Verse," 621.

reapportioned lines). Attempts are made to characterize language more definitely: Lilburne's speech is altered to display his genteel background with great irony, Isham's is made more colloquial (his is a pliable and unpretentious personality, and he soon forgets his Virginian upbringing and takes on the qualities of the backwoodsman). Some other characterizing details are also added, such as the change in Lilburne's taste for liquor—gentleman's Madeira giving way to corn whiskey from a jug by the time of the murder. Lilburne's speech may be aristocratic, but he too is transformed by the West he came to civilize; his fondness for the jug graphically reminds us of this transformation.

Although, as Warren says, "the basic action and theme remain the same" (p. xiv) in the New Version, deletions and redistribution of speeches or parts of speeches do affect to some extent the portrayals of the characters, especially R. P. W., Jefferson, and Meriwether. The alterations are not major ones, and they represent shifts in emphasis rather than changes in basic meaning; but they are interesting nonetheless.

Many critics of the poem as it appeared in 1953 were distressed by R. P. W.'s apparent rhetorical advantage over Jefferson: the poet seemed to have second-guessed the President at every turn, giving quick answers to Jefferson's painful recognitions, often interrupting and correcting the great man with twentieth-century smugness (1953, pp. 49, 35–36, and 110–11). Although Warren was careful to make Lucy and Meriwether, not R. P. W., catalysts for Jefferson's revelation at the end, and although R. P. W. himself learned something from the tale ("You finished what you climbed up there for, Son?" asks his father in the final lines; "And I said: 'Yes, I've finished . . .'" [216]), the poet of *Brother to Dragons* was not, apparently, careful enough, given the almost mythic stature Americans have created for Thomas Jefferson. Most of these errors in judgment have been corrected, though. R. P. W. no longer "speaks . . . with greater imagination, power and intelligence" than any of the other characters.[24] Like the character "Writer" in the play, who speaks his crucial lines "with an air of discovery," R. P. W. in the 1979 version more clearly parallels, rather than leads, Jefferson in his search for knowledge. Jefferson, correspondingly, speaks with more authority and greater perception in the 1979

24. *Ibid.*, 623.

version, as he moves through its pages from innocence to cynicism to knowledge.

That Meriwether's role in the 1979 version is expanded from the earlier edition has already been mentioned; Lowell's assertion that he "seems altogether out of place in the work" is clearly no longer valid. In 1953 Meriwether appears near the end of the poem, tells his story and accuses Jefferson of his murder, then disappears. Lucy, realizing that "Yes, Meriwether's right. I begin to see" (186), takes over the final task of convincing her brother of his complicity in Lilburne's crime. In the 1979 version, in a stunningly dramatic interplay of dialogue, Lucy and Meriwether insist that Jefferson take Lilburne's hand, despite Jefferson's impassioned refusal. More lines are transposed, redistributed, and cut at this point than at any other in the poem; in the final reworking Meriwether, Lucy, and Jefferson all participate in the final revelation. One of Jefferson's monologues in the 1953 version shows the transformation well. He says:

> I think I begin to see the forging of the future.
> It will be forged beneath the hammer of truth
> On the anvil of our anguish. We shall be forged
> Beneath the hammer of truth on the anvil of anguish.
> It would be terrible to think that truth is lost.
> It would be worse to think that anguish is lost, ever.
>
> (1953, p. 194)

This section is given in the revised text to all three characters:

> MERIWETHER: I think I glimpse
> The forging of the future—
> JEFFERSON: Forged beneath the hammer of truth
> On the anvil of our anguish!
> LUCY: How terrible to think that truth may be lost.
> But worse to think that anguish is lost, ever.
>
> (1979, p. 118)

The climax of the New Version, the "touching" of Lilburne, is brought on by one final change in a "voice," that of John (George in the 1953 version), the murdered slave. In 1953 he speaks three lines only:

> I was lost in the world, and the trees were tall.
> I was lost in the world, and the dark swale heaved.
> I was lost in my anguish, and I did not know the reason.
>
> (1953, p. 194)

These three lines, the first composed of any in the poem,[25] are repeated verbatim in the 1979 version; but John, no longer purely victim, joins the others in urging Jefferson to touch Lilburne:

> LUCY: No, Brother, touch him. Touch Lilburne.
> JOHN: Yes—now is the time!—That's all I,
> In my ignorance, know.

(1979, p. 119)

*   **IV   New Version**   *

As far as content, the meat on the block, is concerned, Warren's lop-
pings seem to work to two ends: first (and with far greater frequency)
to explain less—trusting his readers in 1979 for the most part to fill in
details and interpret meanings on our own,[26] and second, to realign
certain particulars either to lie squarely with or flatly contrary to the
historical facts of the Lewis incident. Many of the half-truths and little
inaccuracies of the 1953 version are replaced in the New Version by
certainties, either of fact or fiction.

Charles L. Lewis, Lilburne Lewis's father, for example, mistak-
enly believed by many to have been a physician, was shown by Merrill to deserve no other title than that of his rank in the American Revolutionary Army.[27] In *Brother to Dragons*, Lucy's husband "Dr. Lewis"
becomes "Colonel Lewis" in the revised version, and loses "Potions
and pills, picked-lint, and scalpel, all" (1953, p. 12). The spelling of
Lilburne's and Letitia's names are corrected, as is Meriwether's familial relation (not first cousin) to the two brothers. And other facts uncovered by Merrill are taken into account. A brief mention of Lilburne
as Colonel Lewis's "first-born son" (1953, p. 98) is corrected to "son"
in the New Version; Warren mentions the eldest son Randolph (who
came to Kentucky with the family in 1807) in the 1979 preface as con-
fidently as he had neglected to mention him in 1953. The value of
George/John, too, has been corrected from $300 to $500 (1953, p. 150;
1979, p. 93); in 1953 an incorrect figure for Lilburne's bond was given;
in 1979 it is omitted entirely (1953, p. 160; 1979, p. 99). Although the

25. Watkins and Hiers, *Robert Penn Warren Talking*, 45.
26. Good examples of this kind of revision are too numerous to list, but a few may be
found in the center paragraph of 1953, p. 60 (1979, p. 41), at the top of 1953, pp. 111–12
(1979, p. 71), or in the explanation of "percoon" on 1953, pp. 204–205 (1979, p. 127).
27. Merrill, *Jefferson's Nephews*, 341–42.

fact that Letitia was pregnant at the time of the murder is not in the
poem proper (just the preface, p. xi), the time between Lilburne's sexual abuse of her and her flight away from "Rocky Hill" after the crime,
"a year" (1953, p. 80) in the first version, has become "nigh a durn
year" (1979, p. 52). Readers of the New Version who read either the
preface or Merrill's book will not be bothered by any discrepancies between these and the poem.[28]

Among the many historical inaccuracies of *Brother to Dragons* (such
as the placement of the murder in the meat-house, not the kitchen,
and Lilburne's murder by Isham instead of his accidental suicide), a
few, like the placing of Lucy's grave at "Rocky Hill" "for thematic reasons" (1979, p. xii), the omission of Lilburne's first wife and children,
and the changed name of the murdered slave, are explained in the
preface. The placement of Lucy's grave is noteworthy, since Warren
and others had, apparently (and quite naturally), assumed it was at
"Rocky Hill" until Merrill discovered that the marker there, erected in
1927 by a local historian named Mrs. Martha Grassham Purcell, is almost certainly in the wrong place.[29] The "thematic reasons" governing the choice of Lucy's grave site in 1979 were surely also thought to
be historically accurate in 1953, not that Warren's point is damaged either way.

"Thematic reasons" and historical accuracy—fact and fiction—in-
tertwine elusively all through the New Version of *Brother to Dragons*,
more so by far than in the 1953 edition. The question of how important Merrill's book was to the revising process is certainly worth asking, therefore. Warren has stated absolutely that he had not read
Jefferson's Nephews until his work on the poem was complete, yet textual evidence both in the poem and in the play seems to belie this
assertion. In the play several nondramatic sections which were altered by 1979 are unchanged from the 1953 version. These would
seem to indicate that the revising was not yet completed, for if Warren had finished the poem by this time, why would he not alter the
affected passages in the play to reflect his poetic preferences?[30]

---

28. As evidenced by the estate appraisals Merrill includes in his book, a young adult
male slave would probably have been worth at least $400 to $450 (pp. 241, 368). For the
account of the bond set for Lilburne and Isham, see Merrill, pp. 288–89.
29. *Ibid.*, 425–26.
30. Note passages on pp. 81 and 110 of the *Georgia Review* play. George's name had

Warren's interest in and use of history in his fiction and poetry are well known. He is one of the few twentieth-century writers who have created historical art with great sophistication and brilliance; the relationships between fact and imagination are themes that run throughout his entire corpus. Again in the case of the revised version of *Brother to Dragons*, Warren's philosophies of history and poetry become essential issues: the question is not whether he used Merrill's findings, but taking into account his repeated denial of their importance to the New Version, *why* he used them and what kind of sense his use of them makes.

When it appeared in 1953, *Brother to Dragons* represented perhaps Warren's most complex achievement with regard to the uses of history. The "voices" of *Brother to Dragons* had not learned the necessity of shouldering the responsibilities of time and admitting the complicities of their roles in time while they were alive. The main characters of Warren's earlier novels had been faced with this necessity, and to a degree their successes or failures in life hinged on their timely recognition of it. Percy Munn, the central figure of *Night Rider*, dies ignorant of the meanings of the movements of history he is trapped in, or the reasons for his ruined life and ignominious death; Jeremiah Beaumont of *World Enough and Time* learns it too late; in *All the King's Men* the learning of this lesson is what saves Jack Burden, while the failure to learn it destroys both Adam Stanton and Willie Stark. In *Brother to Dragons*, the characters, though "long dead," are given a second chance. Although still trapped by their memories, they are nonetheless free from the "space and time" of history and can therefore discuss the meanings of that history unimpeded. Striking on such a form as a "dialogue of verse and voices" was a masterstroke for Warren: For the first time he could combine history and the philosophy of history (as he could also combine poetic and prosaic elements) and explore the possibilities of both with almost complete freedom. As he says in the 1953 preface, "This is but a whimsical way of saying that the issue that the characters here discuss is, in my view at least, a human constant" (p. xiii). (In the 1979 preface, the sentence remains, but the mitigating word "whimsical" has disappeared.) Both charac-

---

already been changed, but "Lilburn" and "Laetitia" are still spelled as they were in the 1953 version; from the fact that some changes have occurred and some have not, I infer that the revision was underway, but unfinished.

ters and readers are forced to ponder the permanent values and significances of history, rather than the specific events.

But the myth must be grounded in fact; philosophy must be inductive, beginning with an examination of actual events, or it is invalid. Poetry, too, "is more than fantasy and is committed to the obligation of trying to say something about the human condition" (p. xii), and "historical sense and poetic sense should not, in the end, be contradictory."

Just how historical *sense* and historical *fact* relate is never quite clear, however. And when the fragile, somewhat nebulous "spirit of . . . history" and the factual basis for that spirit collide, as they did for *Brother to Dragons* with the publication of *Jefferson's Nephews*, a sensitive artist with an abiding interest in the truth of "the human condition" is going to be put in the position of doing some serious reflection on what he has created.

According to C. Vann Woodward, one of Warren's "major professional problems has been to define the relationship between history and poetry, to defend his use of both and to reconcile the sorts of truth they seek and the kinds of sense they make."[31] In the instance of *Brother to Dragons*, Warren's problem, it seems to me, was to redefine that relationship.

He did, and he reworked the poem in many ways; but Merrill's findings did not finally change his vision. From his "protracted and concentrated reliving of the whole process" (1979, p. xiv) of writing *Brother to Dragons*, a New Version, which is truly "no different philosophically" from the first version, emerged. Both historically and poetically related differences between the 1953 and 1979 versions exist— the one poem clearer in narrative and philosophical explanation and more regular in verse, the other more engaging in rhythm and more tightly organized with respect to theme. Artistic knowledge, or what Warren in his essay "Knowledge and the Image of Man" calls "knowledge of form," not knowledge of facts but intimately related to that kind of knowledge, has been refined in *Brother to Dragons*.[32] In poetry, Warren says in this essay, there must be an "organic relation among all the elements of the work, including, *most emphatically*, those ele-

31. C. Vann Woodward, "Reflections on a Centennial: The American Civil War," *Yale Review*, L (Autumn, 1961), 483–84.
32. Robert Penn Warren, "Knowledge and the Image of Man," in John Lewis Longley, Jr. (ed.), *Robert Penn Warren: A Collection of Critical Essays* (New York: New York University Press, 1965), 244–46.

ments drawn from the actual world and charged with all the urgencies of actuality."

It is the relation between the events of December 1811 and the poetry of Robert Penn Warren in 1979 which has been altered in the rewriting of this work. For those of us familiar with multiple versions of *Brother to Dragons*, it is difficult to guess how clearly readers not already acquainted with them will see the details of the Lewis story and the philosophical substance of the poem as they encounter the New Version alone. Whatever new readers may find, though, one thing is certain: Warren went back to *Brother to Dragons*, as R. P. W. went back to the site of the Lewis murder, to make sense of what he found there. That the truths in *Brother to Dragons* were strong enough to bear that second visit is a tribute to Warren's poetic genius. As R. P. W. says, "It is strange how that shift of scale may excite the heart" (1979, p. 131).

The Concept of the Historical Self in
Brother to Dragons

Lewis P. Simpson

Of the many changes Robert Penn Warren has made in the new version of *Brother to Dragons*, I think the substantial change in the introductory speech by Jefferson at the very beginning may be the most significant. This new-version speech is in two "sections" (Warren's term). In the first Jefferson speaks in the first person:

> My name is Thomas Jefferson. Thomas. I
> Lived. Died. But
> Dead, cannot lie down in the
> Dark. Cannot, though dead, set
> My mouth to the dark stream that I may unknow
> All my knowing. Cannot, for if,
> Kneeling in that final thirst, I thrust
> Down my face, I see come glimmering upward,
> White, white out of the absolute dark of depth,
> My face. And it is only human.[1]

In the second section of his initial speech, Jefferson speaks in the second person, presumably to the reader:

> Have you ever tried to kiss that face in the mirror?
> Or—ha, ha—has it ever tried to kiss you? Well,
> You are only human. Is that a boast?

(1979, p. 5)

In the old version of *Brother to Dragons*, Jefferson says simply:

A modified version of this paper was presented at the MLA convention's special session, "Robert Penn Warren's *Brother to Dragons* (New Version): A Discussion and a Tribute on the Occasion of His 75th Birthday," December 29, 1979, San Francisco, Calif.
1. Robert Penn Warren, *Brother to Dragons: A Tale in Verse and Voices, A New Version* (New York: Random House, 1979), 5. Hereafter, quotations from this edition are cited parenthetically with date in my text.

244

> My name is Thomas Jefferson. I am he
> Whose body is yet under the triple boast,
> On my green mountain—[2]

He gets no further before R. P. W. interrupts:

> Yes, I've read your boast
> Cut in the stone where your body still waits
> On your green mountain, off in Virginia, awaiting
> I suppose, whatever fulfillment of the boast
> May yet be.

(1953, p. 5)

In the new version R. P. W.'s response after the rather long and uninterrupted first speech by Jefferson is more succinct:

> Well, I've read your boast
> Cut in stone, on the mountain, off in Virginia.

(1979, p. 5)

The abbreviated response is, I take it, decreed by the rather dire implications of the beginning for the tone and movement of the whole poem. By leaving out "whatever fulfillment of the boast / May yet be," the poet foreshadows a subtle reduction (as contrasted with the old version) in his allowance for (perhaps we say in his tolerance of) "hope"—hope, that is, for its amelioration as, if one may put it so, a valid response to the human condition. This severe attitude toward such a fundamental spiritual trait of human kind—a trait that has often been considered to be the very essence of human kind in America—evidently results from Warren's intensified attention in the new poem to his lifelong search for the meaning of the self. Basically, I think, in the new-version *Brother to Dragons* Warren's search culminates in the compelling realization that the meaning of the self is to be discovered in the self's isolation in history; or, to put it in a contrary yet complementary way, in the isolation of history in the self.

Of course, there is nothing startling in the revelation that the central motive of *Brother to Dragons* is the definition of the self. Warren's subject throughout his novels and poems, this subject is, to be sure, the American literary subject: indeed all American poems and stories

---

2. Robert Penn Warren, *Brother to Dragons: A Tale in Verse and Voices* (New York: Random House, 1953), 5. Quotations from this edition will also be cited parenthetically with date in my text.

are attempted definitions of the self, being metaphors of the self's relation to history. The 1979 *Brother to Dragons* is Warren's most cogent formulation of the metaphor.

The protagonist in this drama is Thomas Jefferson, the author of the great central definition of the self in America, the Declaration of Independence, and of a major corollary document, the Virginia statute for religious freedom. In addition, the protagonist of Warren's poem was the father of the University of Virginia, an institution that he dedicated to the development of the American self as the major entity of secular (modern) history and through which he sought to institutionalize the self's drive toward its historical fulfillment. Essentially in the "boast / Cut in stone," his self-composed epitaph, Jefferson proclaimed himself to be his own father, the father (or the author-father) of the American self. To confront the irony of this boast, in its glory and in its grievous error, Warren's Jefferson, a self-reflective "spook," is brought together in the poet's imagination with other self-reflective spooks somehow involved in Lilburne Lewis's act of butchering a slave in Kentucky in 1811, and with one actual person, one person living in time, the poet (R. P. W.) himself. The "tale in verse and voices" that develops out of the confrontation between the ghosts and the living poet—in my opinion a major achievement in American letters—is predicated on the spooky (not the documentary) Jefferson's recognition that at the time of the American Revolution "every man-jack of us" was "lost" in "some blind alley" of "Time" or "Self"; and there encountered "hock-deep in ordure" the Minotaur. This man-beast, born of a queen's desire for the Cretan god-bull and then hidden from the world in a labyrinth of utterly confounding intricacy designed by the artificer Daedalus, is integral with time or self, or time-self. The Minotaur is the historical self; he is that deformation of being resulting, not from the original differentiation of human consciousness from cosmic unity or cosmological creaturehood, but from the defiance of this separation. When Minos, the king, and Daedalus contrive to secrete and contain the Minotaur in the labyrinth, they drastically compound the evil consequent upon the queen's wantonness by asserting the historical self's power to control its own psyche. The legend of Daedalus recognizes the error of the human will but nonetheless allows him to triumph. Imprisoned in the labyrinth of his own devising, he calls on his great inventive resources and makes wax wings as a means of escape. Although his son, Icarus, who has been imprisoned with his father, flies too near the sun and is killed when his wings melt, Daedalus is prudently cautious and has a successful flight. In his capacity to make existence conform to the increasing ingenuity—the cleverness, the rationality, the reason—of the historical self in its will to survive and to dominate history, he aspires to be godlike. But he is not foolish and does not attempt to be a god. He knows his identity with the deformed man-beast in the labyrinth.

Although in the Christian centuries the powerful admonitory legend of Faust emerges as its counter, the assertion of the historical self becomes a revolutionary force in the Renaissance. As an Enlightenment—a post-Christian, or fully modern—phenomenon, the self assumes that it not only can control its own psyche but can improve its powers; not only improve them but perfect them. Thus the self assumes that it is in effect its own maker. The Minotaur encountered by Jefferson in "some dark corner of Time and Self" is the self transfigured; "angelic, arrogant, abstract, / Greaved in glory, thewed with light, the bright / Brow tall as dawn" (1979, p. 8), the man-beast is the boastful definition of man as historical self. In the grip of the overwhelming Enlightenment illusion about the rational capacity of the self to perfect the self—an illusion generated by the dynamic secularization of the Christian vision of the Millennium—Jefferson, on that night after he meets the Minotaur transfigured, "seized the pen, and in the upper room . . . / Rectified, annealed, my past annulled / and Fate confirmed, wrote" (1979, p. 8). Wrote, that is, an unparalleled vision of hope for the individual man possessed of the unalienable right to "life, liberty, and the pursuit of happiness."

Underlying the conception of *Brother to Dragons*, it appears to me, is a movement toward a reconciliation of the vision of America as the land of hope (so graphically associated with the vision of the West in the poem) and the recognition of hope's illusory nature. To be fulfilled through the "intrinsic mediation" of the heart's ineffable knowledge of the self's origin and agonies, in both versions of *Brother to Dragons* this movement toward the reconciliation of hope and reality reaches a climax in the invocation to the Ghost Dance that follows the scene when Jefferson confronts Lilburne. In the first version Jefferson appeals, and the second version all the spooks appeal, to "the heart by which we must live and die." But in both versions this scene is subject to the interpretation of the story in the final meditation by R. P. W. In both instances the resolving line, as the poet passes through the gate of the forsaken domain of the Lewis family, speaks of entering a world "Sweeter than hope in the confirmation of that late light." Warren, however, has made a number of changes in the concluding portion of the poem. I would point especially to a difference effected in the new version—in tone and in explicit meaning—by the omission of the last three lines from one section.

> We have yearned in the heart for some identification
> With the glory of the human effort, and have yearned
> For an adequate definition of that glory.
> To make that definition would be, in itself,
> Of the nature of glory. This is not paradox.
> It is not paradox, but the best hope.
>
> (1953, pp. 213–14)

What is lost by dropping out the last three lines is the significance of hope as a part of the heart's "intrinsic mediation." Hope has been assigned completely to the illusion of the self's power to make its own history. Hope, the second version of *Brother to Dragons* implies, is far less sweet than the knowledge that it is an illusion.

What accounts for the more austere treatment of hope in the new *Brother to Dragons*? I would suggest that it is an increased awareness by the poet of what Jefferson—I mean Jefferson the spook—says about the human heart and its capacity to love.

> I've long since come to the considered conclusion
> That love, all kinds, is but a mask
> To hide the brute face of fact,
> And that fact is the un-uprootable ferocity of self. Even
> The face of love beneath your face at the first
> Definitive delight—even that—
> Is but a mirror
> For your own ferocity—a mirror blurred with breath,
> And slicked and slimed with love—
> And even then, through the interstices and gouts
> Of the hypocritical moisture, cold eyes spy out
> From the mirror's cold heart, and thus,
> Self spies on self
> In that unsummerable arctic of the human lot.
>
> (1979, p. 33)

The passage is not substantially altered from its first version, but one crucial change is to be noted. In the first version Jefferson refers to the "unsummerable arctic of the human alienation," whereas in the second he speaks of this condition as the undeviating state of humanity. Mirroring not another self but the same self, the self directs a ferocity against its own being; and this ferocity is necessary to, and integral with, its identity. The solipsistic aggressiveness of the historical self— the self that not only experiences the isolation of the self in history but experiences the isolation of history in the self—derives, we may suppose, from the self's immitigable need to possess its own identity, its own being. Compelled by its will to autonomy to rebel against its fate as the creature of history, the self cannot achieve freedom from its source of being in history. While superficially *Brother to Dragons* may suggest certain dualities of self—among these, a rational self and a primitive self, and a self of the head and a self of the heart—the poem fundamentally suggests, particularly in the new version, the terrifying integrality of the secular, historical self.

Although *Brother to Dragons* does not present a resolution of the meaning of the self in America—and is indeed primarily a struggle for the meaning of the American self, in which the polarities of thought and action, dream and reality are pronounced—the tendency of the argument is toward a revelation of the self as an entity. A complex of warring forces, the self is yet an entity in that it will do anything to survive. There is a glory in the definition of the American self in Warren's vision, but it is not a comfortable glory.

"Doom Is Always Domestic":
Familial Betrayal in *Brother to Dragons*

Richard G. Law

> A father, mother, child (a daughter or a son),
> That's how all natural or supernatural stories run.
>
> —W. B. Yeats

The famous Kentucky tragedy involving Jefferson's nephews and a slave owned by the family is presented in Warren's version of the events as a *domestic* tragedy. Jefferson's admonition to Lucy Lewis is practically a summation of the action: "Sister, / We are betrayed—and always / In the house!"[1] The reconstructed chain of events which leads to the axe-murder is cast in a pattern of double betrayal—most often a betrayal of child by parent and parent by child. Lilburne Lewis betrays and is betrayed by his mother, father, and "mammy," as well as his wife and brother. The victim is the murderer's body servant and therefore, in the mythology of the slaveholders, at least, one of the family. Meriwether Lewis, whose tragic death Warren connects to the story of his Kentucky cousins, dies a "victim" of his surrogate father, Jefferson. Even the town drunk of modern Smithland rounds out his briefly imagined existence by seeing himself betrayed by his "Baby Girl." As the character Jefferson insists, and the action reiterates: "We must always be betrayed by the most dear" (34). At the core of the action of *Brother to Dragons* lies this harsh paradigm of double betrayal.

Because of this pattern of action, the large intellectual concerns of the work—America's attempt to create itself in the image of Jefferson's elegant prose; the nature of history itself, both as life process and

A modified version of this paper was presented at the MLA convention's special session, "Robert Penn Warren's *Brother to Dragons* (New Version): A Discussion and a Tribute on the Occasion of His 75th Birthday," December 29, 1979, San Francisco, Calif.
1. Robert Penn Warren, *Brother to Dragons: A Tale in Verse and Voices, A New Version* (New York: Random House, 1979), 19. Other references to the new version are indicated by page number in the body of the text.

myth; the aesthetic and epistemological questions implicit in the artist's choice of form; and, finally, the problematical nature of self,
mind, identity—are dramatized in an action which tends downward
toward the child's nightmare of abandonment and rejection and the
parent's ultimate disappointment and extinction of hope. As a result,
the other issues in the work are forced down into the subterranean
murk of a single remorseless struggle:

> A struggle, dark, ferocious, in the dark
> For power—for power empty and abstract,
> But still, in the last analysis, the only
> Thing worth the struggle. (59)

This familial clawing is one of the traits that Warren knows best,
dramatizes best; and the emotions generated by this struggle in darkness appear to tap the artist's deepest sources of creative energy. Beyond any of Warren's other works, *Brother to Dragons* is charged with
a peculiar power to disturb. In the fitful glare of these primordial conflicts, issues such as our national identity or the nature of history take
on strange and unfamiliar shapes—and perhaps not altogether pre-
dictable ones.

Warren has recently drawn attention to the familial motifs of his
version of the Kentucky tragedy by suggesting in an interview given
in 1977 that the figure of "R. P. W.'s" father, a character who appears
only fleetingly in the work and who speaks only a handful of lines, is
one of the most important figures in the poem, representing one end,
one "pole," of human possibility, the other end of which is, of course,
Lilburne Lewis. Referring in general to characters in his work whose
nature is morally ambiguous, those "carriers of light" who become
unexpectedly "the emissaries of darkness," Warren went on to describe a remarkable polarization of moral attributes in the characters
in *Brother to Dragons*:

> There is man as monster; that's one pole. On one hand there is
> the world of monstrosity, sadism; on the other hand, there is a man
> [referring to his father] who had a hard life and who made a con-
> quest of it. Now these are the poles, you see. They're both there;
> man is both monster and angel.[2]

If these are indeed the extremes of behavior posited in the work, the
other characters, including (presumably) "R. P. W." himself, must oc-

2. Gerald Cooper, "A Talk with Robert Penn Warren," *Subject to Change* [Washington
University, St. Louis], III (April 28, 1977), 13.

cupy intermediate positions on the scale and represent that ambiguous moral doubleness mentioned by Warren earlier in the interview, in his remark that the "carriers of light become the emissaries of darkness." If the writer's father, rather than Jefferson, is seen as the antithesis of those potentials represented by Lilburne Lewis, then our view of all the characters is subtly altered. Moreover, the dialectic in the action is transformed. To oppose the quite palpable acts committed by Lilburne Lewis against the partly discredited ideals (or illusions) espoused by Jefferson would oppose apples to oranges, a concrete fact against an abstract (an apparently forlorn) hope, thereby giving away the case to the side of senseless evil. But if Warren's father is taken as the opposing pole, many of these difficulties disappear; and the mystery of the old man's achieved decency may somehow balance the mystery of Lilburne's iniquity.

In the original version, *Brother to Dragons* ends with a scene set in December, 1946, in which the writer of the poem descends from his "mountain," the ruins of the Lewis place at Rocky Hill, and returns, with whatever he has learned there, to his father:

> I walked down to the car where my father had been waiting.
> He woke from his cold drowse, and yawned, and said,
> "You finished what you climbed up there for, Son?"
> And I said: "Yes, I've finished. Let's go home."[3]

This exchange between son and father recalls the earlier visit, in summer, 1946, and implies, through the imagery of the descent from the mountain, that "R. P. W.'s" confrontation with the Lewis family tragedy had been a revelatory one, a "Pentecostal intuition," for the writer. It further suggests, simply in the fact of the father's presence on both visits, that the father had been an important part of this experience, that the experience had, in a sense, involved the son's coming to terms with his father's life, as well as with Lilburne's crime. While the four lines quoted above have been deleted from the new version, it does not appear that the father's role is thereby diminished.

One clue to the nature of that role as the artist originally envisioned it has come out of studies of early drafts of *Brother to Dragons*. The evidence suggests that Warren had the example of Virgil's *Aeneid* prominently in mind during the early stages of composition, and that

---

3.   Robert Penn Warren, *Brother to Dragons: A Tale in Verse and Voices* (New York: Random House, 1953), 216.

he found special significance in the image of Aeneas, founder of a new world, fleeing the death of the old but carrying his father on his back, symbol of the burden of piety necessary to the new enterprise.[4] In the language of the new version, the father represents something like the "fact of the past," without which a vision of the future is impossible. In a late speech by Jefferson, the Virginia patriarch recalls an argument over that issue with his old opponent, John Adams:

> I wrote and said
> That the dream of the future is better than
> The dream of the past.
>
> How could I hope to find courage to say
> That without the *fact of the past*, no matter
> How terrible, we cannot dream the future?[5]

(118, italics added)

The writer's father, however, does not function simply as an inert repository of values; his presence impinges upon and helps define the consciousness of "R. P. W.", one of the most intriguing of Warren's characters, and that impact is dramatic rather than merely iconographic.

Perhaps we can see something of the role of the writer's father and his relationship to "R. P. W." through another seemingly minor character, Meriwether Lewis. In the original version Meriwether had

---

4. I am indebted for this information to Victor Strandberg, who delivered a paper on the manuscript versions of *Brother to Dragons* at the MLA conference in San Francisco, December 29, 1979 [q.v., p. 200].

5. This passage summarizes a point which Warren discussed at greater length at one of the conversations during the Fugitives Reunion at Vanderbilt in 1956:

> [a] simpler world is something I think is always necessary—not a golden age, but the past imaginatively conceived and historically conceived in the strictest readings of the researchers. The past is always a rebuke to the present; it's bound to be, one way or another: it's [the] great rebuke. It's a better rebuke than any dream of the future . . . because you can see what some of the costs were, what frail virtues were achieved in the past by frail men. . . . And that is a much better rebuke than any dream of a golden age to come, because historians will correct, and imagination will correct, any notion of a simplistic and—well—childish notion of a golden age. The drama of the past that corrects us is the drama of our struggles to be human, or our struggles to define the values of our forebears in the face of their difficulties.

—in Rob Roy Purdy (ed.), *Fugitives' Reunion: Conversations at Vanderbilt* (Nashville: Vanderbilt University Press, 1959), 210.

been lugged in, so to speak, toward the end in order to shatter Jefferson's complacence in his own innocence. In the new version, as the author explains in the introduction, Meriwether "is given a more significant role."[6] His presence—and his status as Jefferson's "near-son"—is felt from the beginning. Dramatically speaking, Meriwether is the blood on Jefferson's own hands, and his presence thereby complicates Jefferson's character, implicates him in the universal guilt, and makes him a spiritual brother of Lilburne Lewis, as well as saintly Founding Father. Jefferson is thus made to resemble the other characters, who are betrayers as well as victims, slayers as well as slain. Through Meriwether, then, the double moral nature of man, imaged throughout the work in the combat of angel and dragon, is internalized in Jefferson's character.

Each character in the work wears two masks: the mask of victim and the mask of betrayer. And partly because of the presence of "R. P. W.'s" father, this moral doubleness finds expression through another set of antinomies prominent in the action: the several parent/child relationships, some of which are real, some surrogate. Protector and dependent, dominant and subordinate, the giver of love and the recipient of love—these pairings of characters in the action are another way of imaging potentials within the self, roles to be played out in experience. And these archetypal relationships, like the symbolic situations of fairy tales, provide stark images of essential human realities—love and the deprivation of love, the internecine warfare which is family life and, ultimately, the interior life as well. Indeed, the conflict of child and parent, like the combat of saint and dragon, seems intended as an externalization of an essentially inner reality, so that betrayal by the "most dear" means finally a betrayal of *self*. Jefferson implies as much in a remark early in the work: ". . . doom is always domestic, it purrs like a cat, / And the absolute traitor lurks in some sweet corner of the blood" (8).

The father's presence on the two visits to Rocky Hill implies, then, a good deal more than that a fundamental reassessment of self and world is going on in the mind of the writer. His presence is symbolically a rebuke to "R. P. W." in the same way that Meriwether Lewis is

6. See Warren's "Foreword" to the New Version, pp. xiii–xiv; and Floyd C. Watkins, "A Dialogue with Robert Penn Warren on *Brother to Dragons*," *Southern Review*, n.s., XVI (January, 1980), 3.

a reproach to his spiritual father, Jefferson. The father's presence complicates and partly undercuts the son's moral stance; he represents the standard by which the son must measure his own ambitions and test his own achievements. While this standard is obviously a positive one, its very presence appears to be a source of pain—and the source, perhaps, of the writer's scathing self-judgment: "A fellow of forty, a stranger, and a fool" (20). But affection is also part of the deeply mixed emotions which the father's presence evokes in the writer during the first visit to Rocky Hill:

> . . . I parked the car
> And left my father drowsing there,
> For he was old, already pushing eighty.
> No truth on mountains any more for him,
> Nor marvel in the bush that burns and yet is not consumed.
> Yes, he had climbed his mountain long ago,
> And met what face—ah, who can tell?
> He will not, who has filled the tract of Time
> With rectitude and natural sympathy, ·
> Past hope, ambition, and despair's delectable anodyne.
> What face he had met I do not know, but know
> That once, in a café in Paris, when an old friend said,
> "Tell me about your father," my heart suddenly
> Choked on my words, and in that throttlement
> Of inwardness and coil, light fell
> Like one great ray that gilds the deepest glade,
> And thus I saw his life a story told,
> Its glory and reproach domesticated. (20–21)

"Domesticated" is a slippery word here. Perhaps because the father has lived past all the things the son needs to live by, he becomes the fit guide, like Dante's Virgil, to lead the son in his descent into the implications of Lilburne Lewis's crime. "Who has seen man in his naked absoluteness?" the poet asks; "It was remembering my father that flushed these thoughts" (22). At the same time, whether the father's "story" is a paradigm of failure or success, its essential meaning for the son lies in its being a "story told," a completed pattern—its glory "domesticated." The nature of the father's "reproach" to the ambitions of the son—a son who yearns after "glory," desperately needs to "make communication," and entertains hopes for a redemptive or revelatory experience from his struggle to understand Lilburne Lewis's crime—derives from this perception of finality: a father who has lived *past* ambition, hope, and even despair, calls into question the value of the son's deepest needs. What the son wants is a means of reconciling himself to a world (or a self) which contains Lilburne Lewis, but a reconciliation which is not merely the "fatigue of the relaxed nerve." Even if the father's resignation is wisdom, however (and it may be *only* resignation), it offers the son nothing he can live by. As the passage continues, the effort to worry the complex emotions roused by his father into some rational category leads the poet into a bitter paradox:

> The failures of our fathers are failures we shall make,
> Their triumphs the triumphs we shall never have.
> But remembering even their failures, we are compelled to praise,
> And for their virtues hate them while we praise. . . . (21)

This is the child's quandary: to hate the parent for his virtues. The positive standard of achievement in the father's life thus has strangely ambiguous effects on the son; the father's light becomes the son's darkness. Significantly, the fable of the good parent whose very goodness destroys the son is the oldest story in Warren's fiction, dating back to the Hardin family of "Prime Leaf" (1930). There are several versions of that tale in *Brother to Dragons*, notably Lucy Lewis's love which had "infected" her son, and Jefferson's vision of man's nobility which had put out the sight of his near-son, Meriwether. The extent to which this is also the story of "R. P. W." is a question which the text raises but does not answer.

If, however, it is the parent's nature to "betray," the betrayal of love is not even the worst betrayal. The ground floor, the "bottom line" of individual experience, is apparently the terror of "separateness."[7] In *Brother to Dragons*, the most searching of Warren's depictions of the lonely ferocity of self, separateness is a fundamental premise. Abandonment at birth into a world which requires one's death is the first as well as the ultimate betrayal. Paradoxically, separateness implies a relationship, treacherous but real, with another: the parent and precursor. The relationship is treacherous because the parent's gift of life brings with it, like the ambiguous gifts of fairy

---

7.   See Warren's special use of the term in "Knowledge and the Image of Man," in John Lewis Longley, Jr. (ed.), *Robert Penn Warren: A Collection of Critical Essays* (New York: New York University Press, 1965), 241–42.

tales, decidedly mixed blessings; it carries, like a primeval curse—or a tasteless practical joke—the seed of one's own annihilation. In the parent's decline, in the completed arc of his life cycle, the child may trace, all too clearly, the trajectory of his own mortality. The death of the parent therefore threatens the dissolution of one's own hopes, the wearing out—or "domestication"—of the meanings one has struggled for:

> We wonder, even as we consider their virtue:
> What is wisdom and what the dimming of faculty?
> What kindliness, and what the guttering of desire?
> What philosophic wisdom, and what the fatigue of the relaxed nerve? (21)

Thus, while the parent's virtues are a reproach to the child, the *mortality* of the parent calls into question *all* virtue, even the very nature of virtue. This specter, once raised, is not easily exorcized, and *Brother to Dragons* in all its versions, is haunted by this shadow of total nihilism, of estrangement not only from love, but from all redeeming and meaning-giving values. While "R. P. W.'s" struggle with disillusionment represents only a faint exhalation from the pit into which Lilburne Lewis has descended, the terms of that struggle are more familiar and thereby help to authenticate the more radical estrangement of Lilburne. At the same time the lesser struggle involves the writer in his crime, for it is equally the child's nature to betray the parent: in his "separateness" the child fails as an extension of the parent's will; he provides the parent neither vindication nor redemption. And whatever knowledge he brings down from the mountain, he keeps to himself, thereby acquiescing in the parent's death.

Timor mortis conturbat me is the theme of much of Warren's best poetry, where fear of death is often combined with a revulsion at physicality, at the stable-floor conditions of existence—or a revulsion perhaps at the Freudian nightmare into which one is plunged by the conditions of mortality. *Brother to Dragons* is steeped in images of such fear and loathing: the chick in the sow's jaws, the images of birth as ejection or excretion, parcels squeezed out, the self as excrement, "stercorry," the linking of love-making with expectoration, the child Lilburne imagined as thrown to the hogs or brained on the hearthstone, and Pasiphaë, "mother of all," caught in the "infatuate machine" of her own invention. The judgment—perhaps even the *self-*

judgment—implicit in such pervasive imagery lends an atmosphere of near-hysteria to large sections of the work. Lilburne's assault on Letitia, who is a surrogate for his mother, may be seen as an unconscious revenge for his mother's betrayal of him—if giving birth is a kind of abandonment. The brutal symbolism of his assault is suggestive, and the act confirms him in nearly perfect "separateness" and isolation.

Lilburne Lewis does not have the last word, however, and few readers now regard the work as a testament of horror or confirmed nihilism. Those horrific aspects of the work, though of nearly overwhelming power and persuasiveness, are subsumed finally into a larger affirmation. But the difficulties of defining the *nature* of that affirmation are immense. Even in the streamlined, partly clarified new version, the dramatic resolution of the issues raised by Lilburne's bloody hands remains baffling. The ending may be partly clarified by examining the role played by the writer's father in the working out of that resolution. That the original version of *Brother to Dragons* marked a break with the poet's previous work has long been understood; the self-contained, craftsmanlike poem, beloved of New Critics, was abandoned—and not just abandoned, but *mocked*. *Brother to Dragons* spills over its own boundaries, points outside itself, alluding to large areas of the writer's private experience, while separate aspects of the work seem wildly incommensurate with their function—or *presumed* function—in any scheme of relationships yet offered in the criticism. Other parts (such as the axe-murder and the poet's apostrophe to the Ohio River) seem incompatible with one another or as strangely disparate as the objects visible in a magnified drop of swamp water. In short, the work practically abolishes traditional notions of artistic form based on an ideal of a "universe of discourse" complete unto itself. The poem reaches beyond "its own terms" not only in the matter of the poet's "new relationship" and "new acquaintance / With the nature of joy," images of which form a crucial part of the denouement,[8] but also—and preeminently—in the sections on the writer's father.

No aspect of the work is more puzzling on its own terms, or more requires illumination from the writer's other work or private life, than

8. The significance of this passage both to the resolution of the work and the larger question of artistic form is discussed in my essay, "*Brother to Dragons*: The Fact of Violence vs. the Possibility of Love," *American Literature*, XLIX (January, 1978), 578–79.

those sections in which the father appears. Those passages, in fact, may be better understood as the beginning notes of a decades-long, elegiac meditation than as complete or self-evident entities within the original work. Those images, like the first views of Sutpen in *Absalom, Absalom!*,[9] tease the reader by offering fragments of a puzzle and tantalizing hints, the significance of which exfoliates only later—in this case, in later works. Some of Warren's best poems, from "Mortmain" in *Promises* (1956) to his most recent work, are expansions and further explorations of the significance of a few lines or images from *Brother to Dragons*. On the first visit to Rocky Hill, for instance, the poet's meditation on "virtue" is interrupted (or concluded?) by a memory of his father:

> I recall one Sunday afternoon,
> How, after the chicken dinner and ice cream,
> Amid the comics and word of the world's disaster,
> I saw him sit and with grave patience teach
> Some small last Latin to a little child,
> My brother's child, aged five, and she would say
> The crazy words, and laugh, they were so crazy.
> There's worse, I guess, than in the end to offer
> Your last bright keepsake, some fragment of the vase
> That held your hopes, to offer it to a child.
> And the child took the crazy toy, and laughed.
> I wish you could tell me why I find this scene so sweet.[10]

The poet is unable here to fathom the significance of the memory; the same kind of memory, however—the human legacy from generation to generation, parent to child—frequently recurs as a preoccupation in Warren's later poems. "Reading Late at Night, Thermometer Falling" and "Sunset Walk in Thaw-Time in Vermont," poems written a quarter of a century later, appear to have grown out of the original meditation. There, however, the son, having lived to that time of life his father had reached in *Brother to Dragons*, can observe his father's success and failure from a double perspective—can forgive him for all of his virtues, even his "valor."[11] Made conscious by that double per-

9.   Floyd C. Watkins has also noted affinities between Warren's work and *Absalom, Absalom!*—"A Dialogue with Robert Penn Warren," 16.
10.   Warren, 1953 version, 30–31.
11.   Robert Penn Warren, "Reading Late at Night, Thermometer Falling," *Selected Poems: 1923–1975* (New York: Random House, 1976), 71.

spective of his place in a succession of lives in time, the poet gropes toward a benediction reaching forward in time to his own son, and to his son's sons, but at the same time (it seems to me), reaching backward to the memory of his father offering a memento of his own early ambitions to an uncomprehending grandchild:

> When my son is an old man, and I have not,
> For some fifty years, seen his face, and, if seeing it,
> Would not even be able to guess what name it wore, what
> Blessing should I ask for him?
>
> That some time, in thaw-season, at dusk, standing
> At woodside and staring
> Red-westward, with the sound of moving water
> In his ears, he
> Should thus, in that future moment, bless,
> Forward into that future's future,
> An old man who, as he is mine, had once
> Been his small son.
>
> For what blessing may a man hope for but
> An immortality in
> The loving vigilance of death?[12]

In the scene of the second visit to Rocky Hill, the cluster of anecdotes and images which constitute the elusive denouement of the work contains a recollection of the past by the writer's father. While the episode appears insignificant—a set of casual observations and reminiscences as writer and father motor to the scene of the Lewis tragedy—it represents one of the most important elements in the process of the writer's recovery of balance, hope, and a sense of joy. By a nice coincidence, the route of their journey takes them past the landscape of the father's early life:

> We pass the land where stood the house of his first light.
> No remnant remains of stone gone fire-black. The plow-point
> Has passed where the sill lay.

In a sense, then, the journey through space is also a journey backward in time—or rather in memory; the scene is a memory of a memory. The images evoked by those memories are eloquent of mutability,

12. Warren, "Sunset Walk in Thaw-Time in Vermont," *Selected Poems*, 77–78.

of motion, of a vulnerability beyond remedy to the destructive forces
of time:

> The old house, square, set on limestone, by cedars
> That I, in my mind, see,
> Is not a house I have seen. It is
> A fiction of human possibility past.
> We whirl past the spot it held, now woods.
> The grave of my father's father is lost in the woods.
> The oak-root has heaved down the headstone. (126)

Immediately following this testament to obliterating time—or perhaps
implicit in those preserved memories—is another thread of meaning,
a hint of continuity, a glimmer of something salvaged, something
gained: that same sense of human continuity through love and memory which the poet celebrated over two decades later in his blessing
for his son. In the scene before us, the writer's father recalls a custom
of his own father, a home remedy for evil, given to him and his brothers each spring of their childhood:

> . . . "About this time, December,
> I recollect my father, how he'd take
> Some yellow percoon, the root, and mash it
> And bark of prickly ash, and do the same,
> And cram it in a gallon jug, with whiskey."
> . . . .
> "My father said how winter thicked boys' blood
> And made 'em fit for devilment, and mean.
> But he'd sure fix that. Percoon would wry your tongue."
>
> "But what's percoon?" And he: "Why, Son,
> I just don't recollect. But it's percoon." (126–27)

Naïve folk remedy or magical elixir, the dose was somehow efficacious. The writer's father's life had embodied "rectitude and natural
sympathy," not malevolence. While such a life may appear at first a
mere feather to counterbalance the weight of Lilburne Lewis's evil—
or, to employ another set of images, a merely imagined "house" set
against the actual ruins at Rocky Hill, the father's life (and habitation)
is nonetheless offered as a valid counter-image of the human estate.
Its very presence—in memory, in the "loving vigilance of death"—
implies that the achievement of good is no less a mystery than the
committing of a crime. On the contrary, in a "naturalistic" world, such

as the world of the poem, it may represent an even greater mystery than iniquity.

The strange dramatic weight of the anecdote derives from the role played all along by the father, who is an emblem, not merely of the burden of piety which the son must carry to found the New Rome, but of the "*fact* of the past," the cornerstone of reality, the prime meridian, of any world the son may live in, or dream of. With this single, essential "fact," the son is armed for life. This image of his father as "a small boy, wide-eyed, stand[ing] on the hearthstone / And accept[ing] from his father's hand / The bitter dose of percoon" (131), provides a scale with which the son can measure any darkness, whether his own or the world's.

Three Italians Visit Monticello

William Harmon

Sagredo[1]— Journalist, based in Washington, known for hospitality to visiting countrymen. In his Alitalia shoulder bag, two books by Robert Penn Warren: *Brother to Dragons: A Tale in Verse and Voices* (New York: Random House, 1953) and *Brother to Dragons: A Tale in Verse and Voices, A New Version* (New York: Random House, 1979).

Simplicio— Critic and scholar; the Cristoforo Colombo Professor of American Studies, Bologna. In his Alitalia shoulder bag, a book by Boynton Merrill, Jr.: *Jefferson's Nephews: A Frontier Tragedy* (Princeton, N.J.: Princeton University Press, 1976).

Salviati— Their friend.

October, 1980.

Sagredo. Whoof!—out of breath! "Monti*cello*" indeed!

Simplicio. Some "little mount." I had pictured a small hill immediately overlooking picturesque Charlottesville.

Sagredo. I, too. Jefferson, or whoever named the place, ought to be retroactively indicted for fraud, or perjury, or—what would the word be?—*misdenomination*.

Salviati. We were all taken in. But here we are at last; and—behold—it is indeed a lovely place at this time of year. And now we may enjoy the tourist's most indulgent luxury.

"Three Italians Visit Monticello" by William Harmon. From *Southern Literary Journal*, XII (Fall, 1980), 109–25. Copyright © 1980 by the Department of English, University of North Carolina at Chapel Hill. Reprinted by permission. The author acknowledges with thanks the valuable contributions made to this article by his friends Carol Eaton and Jeanne Heilakka.

1. Instead of real names, those of the speakers in Galileo's dialogues on experimental physics have been used.

Sagredo.   And what might that be?

Salviati.   That of going home and telling our compatriots how stupid these foreigners are, pasting misnomers on every person, place, and thing, luring us into near-cardiac folly of walking for some hours this pleasant morning to get from scarcely picturesque Charlottesville to the large, steep mountain of "Monticello" with—behold!—a rather small mansion bearing the same name.

Simplicio.   America is misnomers. Rhode Island is not an island. Nevada is hardly *nevada*, snowy. And this house is smaller, the mount bigger, than we expected.

Sagredo.   Well, the *monte* is *cello* compared, say, to our Monte Viso.

Simplicio.   Which, in the picturesque idiom of the atlas, amounts to 3,842 meters of Latin earth.

Sagredo.   Let us sit on this old stone bench, where—who knows?—the great Jefferson himself may have rested. Perhaps we were deluded by our knowledge of our own Monticelli d'Ongina.

Simplicio.   Angina?

Sagredo.   No, no: Monticelli d'Ongina—Ongina.

Simplicio.   What is that? Or, what are they?

Sagredo.   It's a place between Piacenza and my native Cremona, on the Po.

Salviati.   A good place.

Simplicio.   Hilly?

Sagredo.   In a small way, but nothing like this—this—*alp!*

Salviati.   Look around. Poe saw some of this.

Simplicio.   We were referring, I thought, to the River Po, not the poet Poe.

Salviati.   The poet Poe wrote a poem to the River Po.

Sagredo.   I did not know that. What's it called?

Salviati.   "To the River ———."

Simplicio.   "———"?

Salviati.   Precisely. He knew in his Orphic bones that names—all words, but nouns especially and proper names *most* especially—mean both everything and nothing at the same time.

Simplicio.   That last item is valuable knowledge for scholars.

Salviati.	No!
Sagredo.	Explain that, please.
Simplicio.	I second the motion.
Salviati.	To begin with, I doubt that anyone can directly explain anything. The Po, let us say, in Poe's poem, like the putative Rivanna in Eliot's, is what it is, in its poem, *independently* of any actual river. As far as poetry *per se* is concerned, any river is the River ———. Furthermore, the poem's river is what *it* is independently of any river the writer may have had "in mind." Within the clearly marked limits of the poem—
Sagredo.	I think I anticipate another of your excursions into Franciscan metaphysics.
Simplicio.	Be precise, Sagredo: *ex*-Franciscan.
Salviati.	Alas. Both of you are right, as usual. And I beg your pardon. How keen you are to remember my adolescence among the Franciscans, and to make the connection between that excursion and the metaphysics of those notable Franciscan doctors, Duns Scotus and William of Ockham. Let me change the subject to something wholly remote from the utterly superseded philosophy of ——— and ———, whose names I shall not call, lest I invoke their terrible Orphic spirits, so alien to the setting of our discourse.
Sagredo.	How peaceful it seems suddenly!
Simplicio.	I was about to say the same thing myself. . . .
Salviati.	"Oronymy."
Simplicio.	What?
Sagredo.	Yes: what?
Salviati.	Nothing.
Sagredo.	No: what was that that you said?
Simplicio.	"O-ro-ro-ro-ny"?
Salviati.	Just my *ororotundity*, if I may. I was merely returning to our previous discussion of the naming of mountains, and my poor mind meandered. I found myself thinking of coining a word—if, indeed, one can truly think-of-coining without truly coining—
Sagredo.	Enough!
Simplicio.	Please!

Salviati.   Both of you are quite right, again, and I beg the pardon of both, again. I have coined a word: *oronymy*; it means "the naming of mountains." It has a bearing on Jefferson, obviously, and also on our reading of yet another enigmatic red-haired American polymath, Ezra Pound.

Sagredo.   The Fascist?

Simplicio. The maniac?

Salviati.   The Fascist; the maniac; the mountain-namer.

Simplicio. Wait! I think of Pound's *Jefferson and/or Mussolini*, and I wonder if the quintessentially American Jefferson might not have been a devotee of ironic *oronymy*.

Sagredo.   Now it's your turn to explain.

Salviati.   I concur.

Simplicio. Jefferson called this big mountain "Monticello," and he designed his Latinate tombstone—down there—to say, understatedly, that he had done three things in his life, without mentioning *any* of his service to the nation-state after 1776.

Sagredo.   Is that irony or arrogance?

Simplicio. Whichever, it has a really Roman ring to it—the Caesarian litotes. But Jefferson was no Caesar. He lacked the military dimension. He was more generally Roman, Roman in the sense of the Imperium that embraced France and Spain as well as Italy—

Salviati.   And most of the British Isles for most of their recorded history.

Sagredo.   That sounds odd.

Simplicio. It does indeed! With the exception of Ireland, which has remained heroically and steadfastly in the Roman fold, the British Isles are clearly Northern, an amalgam of Angles and Saxons and Jutes.

Salviati.   You may be right. I was simply replaying an idea I read somewhere in the prose of T. S. Eliot. England's Reformation was the *least Lutheran* of the Protestant apostasies, after all; and, among the Germanic languages, English remains the *least Germanic*, bearing the greatest proportion of elements from the Romance languages. In our age, England has repeatedly fought against Germany and on the side of France.

Sagredo.   But not on the side of Spain or Italy!

Simplicio.   But Salviati may be right. The interests of Roman Catholic Italy may have been betrayed by Lombard and other northern elements. The fact remains that what is European in America is now chiefly English (except for peripheral Spanish and French influences among its nearest neighbors); and what is European in England is chiefly Latin. So that we see all around us here, in this sacred American place, clear and abundant evidence of the continuity of the Roman spirit from antiquity to the present.

Salviati.   I couldn't have said it better. We can look around us here and understand the virtually automatic ease with which Jefferson felt at home in his world of Roman architecture, wine, politics, agriculture—rather a modern Cincinnatus, as was Washington and even as President Carter hints at being, now and then.

Sagredo.   And yet, for all that—well, my journalist's nose for irony tells me that any true travelogue is subtitled "Land of Contrasts," and any true political biography will have "Enigma" or "Irony" somewhere in its title. Jefferson, insofar as he was a person with a self and not merely the extension or incarnation of the Roman imperial spirit, remains the most baffling figure among the ten or twelve great Presidents.

Simplicio.   I have noticed something along those lines. Has it ever bothered you that Jefferson, a great writer, could not spell?

Sagredo.   That's not exactly what I had in mind, but you are right. I was thinking, rather, that he was a democrat almost to the point of anarchism, as when he remarked that governing best is "governing" least; and yet he was also a snobbish and class-conscious agrarian aristocrat. And he was a polymath in the finest sense and yet, at the same time, a dilettante in the worst (or American) sense. A monumentally great man, perhaps possessed of the loftiest intellect and widest learning of any of those among the American Presidents—

Simplicio.   And yet at the same time the uncle of one murderer, and possibly two.

Salviati.   There was something in this morning's paper about Wil-

liam Carter Spann, by the way: he is the current age's
felon who is also a President's nephew. You two, com-
bining your talents in American studies and popular
journalism, could produce a book on all of the criminals
who had uncles who were President. It would be what
an old American friend of mine used to call a "hum-
dinger."

Sagredo.   Another of your sure-fire ex-Franciscan ideas?

Salviati.   With one other condition: that the felons be nephews in
the true Roman sense.

Simplicio.   What   sense   is   that?

Salviati.   The sense in which Jefferson's nephews and Carter's
nephew all qualify: they are sons of the man's sister, in
each case.

Sagredo.   With Jefferson, we have yet another kinsman who was
ultimately a felon at least in the sense of a *felo-de-se*, a
felon concerning himself.

Simplicio.   Suicide?

Sagredo.   Yes: Meriwether Lewis, whose failure and suicide may
even have been caused, indirectly but potently, by the
actions of Jefferson, who was his "father" in something
like the old Roman sense.

Salviati.   As both of you know from the materials of your dignified callings, all of those matters constitute the inspiration of Robert Penn Warren's *Brother to Dragons*.

Sagredo.   Which one? The version of 1953, or that of 1979?

Simplicio.   As you might say, *Brother to Dragons* or *Son of Brother to
Dragons*?

Sagredo.   *Nephew to Dragons!*

Salviati.   Please, please. I cannot laugh while sitting down, so let
us walk around these pleasant grounds while we con-
tinue our conversation.

Sagredo.   All right, but I feel as though I've already walked enough
this day to satisfy a whole month's quota.

Simplicio.   I prefer the new version.

Sagredo.   I prefer the old version.

Simplicio.   The new version is more spacious. The "tale for verse
and voices" is broken up into seven parts whose dis-
tinctness clarifies the shapely dramatic structure of the

	whole. This sense of spaciousness, airiness, ventilation, even extends to the lines: old turgid blank-verse units are reduced or else broken into sharp pieces.
Sagredo.	The old version is more of a piece, a whole. And the blank verse, even in long, uninterrupted speeches, preserves the tale's kinship with other such studies, like Longfellow's *New England Tragedies* or Frost's dramatic poems.
Simplicio.	Luckily, I have brought both versions along, and we can compare them point for point. Sagredo, you hold the 1953 version—thank you—and you, Salviati, could help by holding the 1979 version.
Salviati.	Good heavens!
Simplicio.	What is it? What's wrong?
Salviati.	I was just admiring your text. It is like what Lamb said about books that Coleridge had been at. You have taken Warren's capital and increased it with compound interest a hundred per cent or more.
Simplicio.	That's just my notes.
Salviati.	Look, Sagredo. Exegeses, hermeneutic commentaries, color-coded glosses, diagrams, maps, marginalia, oblongs, arrows, eddying currents, abbreviations—even what I take to be ham radio operators' slang.
Simplicio.	Wait—hams' slang?
Salviati.	An old hobby of mine. See here: "4Q."
Simplicio.	That means *Four Quartets*!
Salviati.	Oh. How stupid of me.
Sagredo.	I forget the exact wording, but a very sharp critic said of the 1953 version that parts of it read like what would have happened if Robinson Jeffers had tried to write *Murder in the Cathedral*.
Salviati.	Who said that?
Sagredo.	Kenner.
Salviati.	The famous toy-maker?
Simplicio.	Good heavens, no. *Hugh* Kenner, the great critic.[2]
Salviati.	Alas. Again I say, "How stupid of me." I have been watching too much television on Saturday morning.

---

2. *Editor's note*: Hugh Kenner, *Hudson Review*, VI (Winter, 1954), 605–10.

Sagredo.   The *cartoons?*

Salviati.   I confess.

Simplicio.   But why?

Salviati.   Maybe it is like what Housman once almost said: Walt does more than *Walden* can to tell us what's American.

Sagredo.   Walt Whitman?

Salviati.   Walt Disney.

Sagredo.   Incredible.

Salviati.   I apologize once more. But look: a recurring trigram all along the margin: B V B. Sounds like underwear, almost.

Simplicio.   Salviati, you have a wicked streak. That's my abbreviation for "blank verse broken."

Salviati.   I see, I see.

Simplicio.   Sagredo, look in the 1953 version for this speech *here.* . . . This will be a good example. Would you read it?

Sagredo.   Gladly. Let me figure out the context here. . . . All right. Lucy—Jefferson's sister, the mother of Lilburne and Isham—has died, and we are approaching the time of the worst earthquake to hit this continent. (The decade from 1810 to 1820 was the worst for sunspots in many centuries, and there were floods, comets, earthquakes, and volcanic activity, years with no summer. All of that seems to be practically a character in Warren's tale.) All right: we are between events, and R. P. W., the author's own voice, speaks of what has come and what is to come:

> But not yet, and life proceeds at Rocky Hill.
> All spring you can look from the bluff-head, and see far,
> Far off, how the waters stand on the flat land.
> The waters subside too late for corn. But grass,
> Sparse and tentative, sprigs the raw earth
> Of Lucy's grave, and Lilburn comes from the house
> To stand and stare at the spot. He comes softly,
> And though it is in the broad light of day,
> Comes like a thief, or lecher, and setting the foot down
> With secrecy ominous on the unsounding earth.
> He does not understand what is big in his heart,

> Nor why something like guilt oppresses his breathing,
> Nor why there should be a nagging pain in the left groin.
> It has nagged him for days. He must have strained himself.
> He has been with a slut at the settlement and wonders
> If somehow he strained himself. He was drunk and cannot
> Recall clearly. But as for the guilt he feels,
> If it is guilt, it is not guilt for that.
> Laetitia has refused him. Well, that's that.

Simplicio.   Thank you very much indeed, Sagredo. You have furnished a good reading of a passage that well illustrates Warren's blank verse and the general idiom prevailing in the poem. That passage comes from pages 101–102 of the 1953 version, and my chart—here—shows that the corresponding passage in the 1979 version is on page 66. Salviati, if you please.

Salviati.   Page 66. . . . Oh, good: I have much less to read than did Sagredo. I note that in this new version this speech comes at the beginning of the fourth, the central section of seven. As before, it is R. P. W. who is speaking:

> But not yet, and life proceeds at Rocky Hill.
> All spring you can look from the bluff-head, and see
> Waters subside too late for corn. But grass,
> Sparse and tentative, sprigs the raw earth
> Of Lucy's grave, and Lilburne comes from the house.
> He comes, in broad daylight, softly.
> Like lecher or thief, foot on unsounding earth.
> Why should there be a nagging pain in the left groin?
> He must have strained himself with a slut at the settlement.
> He was drunk, and cannot
> Recall clearly.
> Letitia had refused him. Well, that's that.

Your notes indicate "B V B" twice here, a speech of nineteen lines reduced to twelve, elimination of some repetition, and some gain in drama by changing the line about the pain in the groin from a statement to a question. That's very tidy.

Simplicio.   According to my computation, the 1953 version contains 4,387 lines in 215 pages, with an average of 20.4 lines per page; the 1979 version contains 3,699 lines in 132 pages, with 28.0 lines per page. The later lines tend to be shorter. Note, as well, that the new version corrects certain errors of fact and spelling: "Lilburne" and "Letitia" in place of "Lilburn" and "Laetitia." And it changes the murdered slave's name from George—the real name of the poor Negro boy—to "John," so as to convert him into a pure symbol of the "victor-victim" (to use the noble coinage in James Shirley's magnificent poem, "The Glories of Our Blood and State," which is quoted in Brother to Dragons).

Sagredo.   Your argument is not consistent, my friend.

Simplicio.   No?

Sagredo.   No: you admire the change of "Lilburn" to "Lilburne," for instance, because it improves the fidelity to historical fact.

Simplicio.   That is so.

Sagredo.   At the same time, you admire the change of "George" to "John" because it creates a symbol in which fidelity to historical fact is repudiated.

Simplicio.   And that too is so.

Sagredo.   Well, as the Americans are fond of saying, you can't have it both ways.

Simplicio.   You, as the Americans are fond of saying, are all wet. A literary artwork contains both history and symbol—as Ezra Pound said of epic poetry—and both have dimensions of truth: accuracy and fidelity in history, consistency and radiance in symbol. The new version is better because it is both more accurate *and* more symbolic.

Sagredo.   But it preserves certain historical inaccuracies of the old version, particularly in the handling of the death of Lilburn-Lilburne. History says that Isham, the younger

	brother, more or less accidentally shot Lilburne with a rifle at the grave of Lilburne's first wife and later disappeared. *Brother to Dragons*, old and new, says that Isham, unwittingly implicated in Lilburne's scheme to kill himself or get himself killed, shot Lilburne with a pistol at the grave of their mother, and then went on to die heroically in the Battle of New Orleans in 1815.
Simplicio.	That is just poetic license. None of those elements is important. It's even possible that an artful distortion of gross historical facts can produce an eventual result the *spirit* of which is closer to the contour of history if not to the particular details. A few years ago, as part of my researches into Ernest Hemingway, I paid a visit to the Big-Two-Hearted River. I borrowed a lot of trout-fishing gear, in hopes of reliving the experience in Hemingway's fiction. My God, what a let-down! Nobody could ever have fished in that exiguous trickle! Hemingway had invented the whole thing, evidently with an entirely different river "in mind," as Salviati says. He just liked the poetical name of the Two-Hearted River. It is like a recent exchange I overheard between two Americans. One claimed, "Sherman never said, 'War is hell.'" His companion answered, "Well, if he never said it, he certainly *should* have."
Salviati.	I recall the famous case of The Soiled Fish—[3]
Sagredo.	Say no more! Soiled fish or coiled fish notwithstanding—and no one can call the White Whale a red herring—
Salviati.	*No* one?
Sagredo.	Well, no one but you, maybe—
Salviati.	Thanks.
Sagredo.	You're welcome. *But*—a small lapse between *soiled* and *coiled* aside—what Simplicio says of Americanists applies as well to us journalists. When we "get a story," we get more than brute facts; we look for the spirit behind

---

3.   *Editor's note:* See John W. Nichol, "Melville's 'Soiled' Fish of the Sea," *American Literature*, XXI (May, 1949), 338–39, which explains the embarrassing error made in textual criticism.

	the letter; we dig, we ferret, we investigate, we expose. Stop applauding, you two! That's better.
Salviati.	The problem at hand seems to be that neither of you seems particularly to care that there are two of these tales for verse and voices.
Simplicio.	I certainly do care. I am a scholar as well as a critic, after all. As a matter of fact, I have been doing some work on the evolution of certain American texts. We have been unusually fortunate in having a good deal of research material on such poets as Whitman and Dickinson. We can see, for example, how "Out of the rocked cradle" became "Out of the cradle endlessly rocking."
Salviati.	How did it, would you say?
Simplicio.	Why, clearly and obviously, by a process of evolution. We can see the creative process at work, improving the rhythm, dressing up the verb forms, moving from a rather static past participle to a more dynamic present participle. That's obvious.
Salviati.	Certainly. It makes you wonder why it was not so obvious to Whitman when he first wrote the line. Maybe he took a correspondence course in rhythms. It makes me wonder, moreover, whether later versions are invariably better.
Simplicio.	Clearly not.
Sagredo.	Clearly, clearly.
Salviati.	Would the bizarre Auden canon be an example of that?
Simplicio.	Yes, most of the time. Auden has a way of writing a fine poem and then, after it was published, having second, third, *fourth* thoughts that prompted him to alter, a little or a lot, and some of the time to chuck a whole poem out of his canon.
Salviati.	And Ransom?
Simplicio.	Ransom had a way of writing a fine poem and then ruining it later.
Salviati.	Marianne Moore?
Simplicio.	*Ditto.*
Sagredo.	We agreed to speak English.
Simplicio.	The said—I mean, the *same*. But I still insist, Salviati, that we have as many cases of evolution as of devolution. The editor must choose.

Salviati.   What should the editor choose in the case of Robert Lowell's late poems, those marvelous unrhymed fourteen-line verses that he kept modifying?

Simplicio.   Ah, yes: set pieces for American studies. I suppose the editor must rely on his tact and taste.

Salviati.   What about the poor author's tact and taste?

Simplicio.   I wonder. . . . The cases of Auden, Ransom, and Moore suggest that the author may be in no better a position to judge a work than any other reader. That applies especially to early and late versions of a single work.

Salviati.   Thank you for saying that: it helps me to clear up something in my own thinking. It occurs to me that we do not really have *versions* of real artworks. It is not as though you could array a series of exhibits—a fetus, an adult, a skeleton, a handful of dubious dust—and say that these are *versions* of some person. Nor could you say that the perfect adult specimen is but a *version* of some shimmering Platonic ideal that is never realized. It seems to me that we have some artworks that are whole and finished and perfect, and some artworks that—being incomplete—are not really artworks at all, but merely fetuses, torsos, thigh-bones. Consider a simple example. I write a one-line poem: "It rains in Madagascar." No one will dispute that those words could conceivably constitute a poem of some sort. Perhaps a title would point the way, something like *Paradise Lost* or *Vanity Fair* or (to choose something that Warren has used as a title more than once) "History." For some reason, the poem fails to satisfy me, so that I am prompted to review and revise it. Now, actually, I cannot do that. All I can do is write a new poem, wholly new. I am different, a changed man; the language is different. Accordingly, it makes no difference whether my new poem reads "It rains in Martinique" or "Danville was the last capital of the Confederacy": neither of those lines is any more or any less of a variation or version of my original line. In the former case, we have what *seems* to be a simple substitution—"Martinique" for "Madagascar"; in the latter, we have no words in common between the original and final forms. But both poems can legitimately claim to be

versions of the original, and neither poem can claim
such a status. It is somewhat like the situation in arithmetic: any natural number can be expressed as a function of any other natural number, including itself. Similarly, "she walked" has as much in common with "he
walked" as with "Rome burned," although the virtual or
ostensible relation seems different. Therefore, one cannot revise or rewrite an earlier work of art at all. One
can correct insignificant efforts, of course. In "The Dry
Salvages," for example, Eliot corrected "hermit crab" to
"horseshoe crab," which was what he meant all along.
But—if the work is genuine and whole to start with—
any substantial change at one point will require corresponding changes at every point. In effect, the author
would have to become a new person in order to approxi-
mate the whole manifold of authorship that produced
the work in the first place; as many writers have testi-
fied, that is impossible. In the case of Warren's tale, I
would say that we have two distinct works, each perfect
and complete enough to be called genuine art. But it is
confusing to say that the earlier is but a draft of the later,
or that the later is a variation or consummation or new
version of the earlier.

Sagredo.   I note on the title page that the 1979 *Brother to Dragons* is
called "A New Version."

Salviati.   I see, I see . . . .

Simplicio.   But we have agreed already that the author may not be
the best person to know what he has done.

Salviati.   Ah! Thank you, Simplicio. You have come to my rescue,
as usual. I would say that, most of the time, an author
published the canonical text in the first appearance of a
work in book form. In a later printing, he may correct
typographical errors and whatnot, but the canon is already there. So-called earlier versions—such as the
draft of Frost's "Design" that the poet included in a letter
long before the eventual poem appeared—do not really
count. Almost always, these embryonic sketches are unformed, incomplete. We can, as it were, see them go
into one end of a black box and come out the other in

much improved shape, but as for the creative process, that is, what may go on inside the black box, we can say nothing. Not even the author knows what goes on there. The Road to Xanadu is a treadmill.

Sagredo. But what of later versions of revisions?

Salviati. They qualify as new works. We ought not be forced to choose between two states of a finished work. I would be content to see both the 1953 and the 1979 *Brother to Dragons* published together in a single volume. It occurs to me that we, as readers, tend to read the same works over and over, loving them more each time, as we change, and the world changes, and the works themselves somehow change. It also occurs to me that writers tend to write the same works over and over. In a sense, Warren has created but one character: R. P. W. And in each of his writings—novels, stories, plays, poems, penetrating critical appraisals and appreciations of Conrad, Whittier, Dreiser—we can see R. P. W. challenging the same enemies, always trying out new weapons, new tactics, new attitudes—but, essentially and (I would add) heroically, engaged on one single quest.

Simplicio. Quest for what?

Salviati. A hard question. I suppose I would answer that R. P. W.'s quest is for the touchstone that will enable a man to tell the pure and the impure apart.

Sagredo. "Pure" and "impure" are not very precise terms, Salviati.

Simplicio. Indeed.

Salviati. Alas. You are right, both of you. I suppose that is why R. P. W.'s quest has gone on for so long; but that is also why the *precipitates* from his quest (if I may borrow a figure from Wittgenstein: the *Niederschlag*) are so genuine and touching. His works make up a prismatically tuned system of entities-in-progress. In such a system, all of the entities are cognate and concentric, as it were, so that any one work—early or late, prose or verse—is a variation of any other. The reader can admire the system as he can admire an orrery, say, but, as with an orrery, he can never see all of it at one time from an ideal perspective. Accordingly, he must not think he has to

	choose Saturn or Jupiter to admire—or the light or the dark side of our moon. He can have both.
Simplicio.	Then, Salviati, on the question of the 1953 version against the 1979 version, do you agree with Sagredo or me?
Salviati.	Oh, I agree; I always agree.
Sagredo.	With whom?
Salviati.	I think I would say that I agree with Eliot, who said, 'History is bunk.'
Simplicio.	That was Henry Ford. Henry Ford said, 'History is bunk.'
Sagredo.	No: I have read somewhere that Ford never really said that.
Salviati.	Well, if he never said it, somebody certainly *should* have. I was mixing that equation up with something in Eliot's poetry: 'History is now and England'; along with Robert Lowell's entry in the same sweepstakes: 'History is now and New England.' For us, here and now, history *is*, literally, now and Monticello.
Simplicio.	I thought history was 1492 and all that.
Salviati.	History is—*is*—1492 and all that, insofar as it *is* or *can be* anything. We make it up as we go along, and all of it is gone and forgotten, beyond retrieval or recording or recapturing, and certainly beyond imagination. History *qua* the history of causes and consequences is nothing but the anatomy of the present moment as it backs, so to speak, into the future; and the future is the only real stretch of time that is "at hand," available to us. The present is a zero. The past is an artifact.
Sagredo.	Come now. Leaving all of that mystic metaphysics aside, which version of *Brother to Dragons* do you prefer?
Simplicio.	Salviati: Sagredo has asked which version of *Brother to Dragons* you prefer.
Salviati.	Forgive me. Both! I prefer *both*.
Simplicio.	Now, my dear old friend, you must explain that paradox.
Sagredo.	Simplicio is quite right.
Salviati.	I love each book. I think it is a marvelous coincidence that a poet named Robert Penn Warren published a book called *Brother to Dragons* in 1953 and that a poet named Robert Penn Warren published a book called *Brother to Dragons* in 1979. They seem to have quite a lot in common.

Simplicio.   Seem?

Salviati.   Certainly. Po, Rivanna, Mississippi, Thames: you cannot step into the same river twice. In strict fact, one cannot step into the same river, or "————," even *once*, because the foot that comes out of the water is not the
same as the foot that went into the water, and the water
is universally notorious for mutability. If these Warrens
are one man, and if that is the same man who wrote so
many wonderfully varied novels, lyric poems, critical
essays, historical and ethical studies, textbooks—then
he must be yet another of those great American poly-
maths. I wonder what color his hair is.

Sagredo.   His *hair*?

Simplicio.   Hair? What difference could that make? What nonsense!

Salviati.   Of course, my friend, you are right, as usual.

Appendices

The Murder

Boynton Merrill, Jr.

Among Lilburne's slaves was one seventeen-year-old boy by the name of George. Unfortunately, almost no traces remain of his life except a few sketchy comments written in the legend sources, and a comment or two about him handed down verbally as part of the Rutter family tradition. These sources relate that George was an "ill-grown, ill-thrived" boy who served Lilburne as a house servant, errand boy, and general handy man. It was George who made the many trips to Dr. Campbell's house for medicine in 1809. George was, reportedly, rather ugly to look at, had a large scar over one of his eyes, and was of an independent nature. Occasionally George was insolent to Lilburne, but when Lilburne was drinking, George feared him and kept his distance.[1]

At the end of October all the patrollers in Livingston County were discharged "from any longer serving as patrollers,"[2] probably in preparation for the expected war. As a result of this step, there was no organized system to prevent slaves from sneaking away from their owners for short visits to other plantations, or, in fact, from running away entirely. Across the river from Rocky Hill in Illinois lay free territory, and in the Ohio River at that point was a shallow sand bar that stretched from shore to shore. In low water this bar was only three feet under the surface.[3] Escape should have been simple, but the dis-

From *Jefferson's Nephews: A Frontier Tragedy* by Boynton Merrill, Jr., copyright © 1976 by Princeton University Press, Princeton, N.J., pp. 256–65. Reprinted by permission of Princeton University Press.
1. Theodore D. Weld (comp.), *American Slavery As It Is: Testimony of a Thousand Witnesses* (New York: American Anti-Slavery Society, 1839), 93; interview with Grady Rutter, May 9, 1967.
2. Liv. Co. Order Book E, 1810–1816, October 28, 1811, p. 99. [Livingston County Court Clerk's Office, Smithland, Kentucky.]
3. Capt. H. Young, Capt. W. T. Poussin, and Lieut. S. Tuttle, "Reconnoissance of the

missal of the patrol indicates that, for the most part, the slaves in Livingston were orderly, if not contented.

At Rocky Hill, however, the family was apprehensive. Since Lilburne's marriage to Letitia, his business and community activities had all gone wrong, and his family had suffered tragedy and heartbreak. Lilburne was under fearful stress. Lilburne and Letitia, who was eight months pregnant with her first child, had not been especially happy together. Lilburne, whose pride and self-confidence were being undermined by his own flaws and by misfortune as well, began to show signs of character disintegration. It was said that earlier he had been a fair but firm master, but in 1811 he became oppressive and unreasonable with his slaves, and began to drink heavily.[4]

Driven by either resentment or fear of Lilburne, George took advantage of the absence of the patrol and ran off on a skulking spell. In a day or two George was either caught or returned voluntarily to Rocky Hill. On Sunday, December 15, shortly after his return, George was sent to fetch water from the spring at the foot of the steep north slope of Rocky Hill. He was given a pitcher in which to carry the water, and on this errand somehow or other he broke the pitcher, which supposedly had been Lucy's. In a transport of drunken rage, Lilburne, with Isham's help, dragged George into the kitchen cabin that stood near the residence, stretched him out on the floor and bound him securely. They next assembled the other slaves in the room and had them build up a roaring fire in the fireplace. It was late at night, and in the eerie light of the flames, Lilburne bolted the door and told the terrified slaves that he was going to teach them a lesson about disobeying his orders. He took up an axe and with a full two-handed swing sank it deep into George's neck. It was a mortal and nearly decapitating blow three inches deep and four inches wide.[5] If the spine

Mississippi & Ohio Rivers, 1821," map #16, U.S. Army Corps of Engineers, Louisville. The first engineers' survey of the Ohio was made ten years after the earthquake. It is possible that at this bar, number seventeen, the water was deeper before the earthquake. Or it may have been shallower. There is no way to tell now.

4. In one fictional account of the Lewis story, two slaves discuss Lilburne's change of character: "He ain't lak hisse'f, Jim. Ain't nuthin' lak hisse'f."

"I knows 'e ain't, Hanna. An' I'se wondehin' what's gwinter hap'n iffen 'e gits mo' lak what 'e ain't." Ruby D. Baugher, *The Wedgewood Pitcher* (Cynthiana, Ky.: Hobson Book Press, 1944), 301.

5. In one official document the wound was described as being four inches deep and four inches wide (first indictment, Liv. Cir. Ct. Bundles, March 1812).

was severed, and it probably was, then George's death was instanta-
neous. If it was not, and the carotid and jugular blood vessels were
cut, then George would have remained conscious from ten to forty
seconds, and it would have taken nearly a minute before George's
heart pumped out most of the four or five quarts of his blood onto the
cabin floor.

Lilburne and Isham then forced one of the negro men to take the
axe and dismember George's body. The pieces were cast on the fire so
there would be no evidence of the crime. It would have required several hours for a body to be consumed completely on a kitchen fireplace. While the grisly cremation was under way, it is said that Lilburne lectured his horror-stricken slaves, and warned them that if
they told anyone about George's death, they could expect the same
treatment. It was shortly after two o'clock on Monday morning when
the first mighty shock of the earthquake struck. The chimney immediately collapsed on top of the fire and George's sizzling remains,
smothered the flames, and brought the dreadful last rites to a halt.

Just after daylight came additional tremendous shocks from the
earthquake, and although the tremors moderated after eight o'clock,
there were not ten minutes during all of Monday when the earth was
still.[6] In this supernatural setting Lilburne supervised his slaves in re-
building the fireplace and the chimney. As the rocks were put in
place, most of the unburned pieces of bone and flesh were raked out
of the ashes and hidden in the masonry.

This account of George's murder may well be inaccurate. None of
the available sources are, at the same time, both detailed and of un-
questionable reliability. The four major sources of information about
the murder contradict each other on so many points that a true and
factual description of George's death will probably never be achieved.
This reconstruction of the crime is a combination of what appear to be
the most plausible parts of the four written statements that are quoted
and discussed below.

In order to examine the most credible source of information, it is
necessary to reveal prematurely that the crime of Lilburne and Isham
was eventually discovered and the brothers were indicted. The word-
ing of the indictment is illuminating.

6. Henry McMurtrie, *Sketches of Louisville and Its Environs* (1819; rpt. Louisville: G. R.
Clark Press, 1969), 234.

In the name and by the authority of the Commonwealth of Kentucky Livingston County set At the March term of the circuit Court held for said County in the year Eighteen hundred and twelve—The grand jury inpannelled and Sworn for the body of the county aforesaid upon their oath present Lilbourn Lewis senior, farmer late of said County and Isham Lewis yeoman late of said County not having the fear of God before their Eyes, But being moved & seduced by the Instigation of the Devil—on the fifteenth day of December Eighteen hundred and Eleven at the house of said Lilbourn Lewis senior in said County & within the Jurisdiction of the said Court with force and arms in & upon the body of a certain Negro Boy called George a slave the property of said Lilbourn Lewis senior of the county aforesaid in the peace of god & this commonwealth then and there living—feloniously wilfully violently and of their malice aforethought an assault did make—and that he the said Lilbourn Lewis senior with a certain ax there & then had & held in both his hands of the Value of two dollars did strike cut and penetrate in & upon the neck of him the said Negro Boy George giving to the said Negro Boy, George then & there with the ax aforesaid in and upon the neck of him the said Negro Boy George one Mortal wound of the Breadth of four inches and of the Depth of three inches of which said mortal wound he the said Negro Boy George Instantly did die in the County of Livingston aforesaid and that the said Isham Lewis then & there feloniously wilfully Violently and of his malice aforethought was present aiding helping abetting comforting assisting and maintaining the said Lilbourn Lewis senior the felony and murder aforesaid in manner and form aforesaid to do and Commit, and so the Jurors aforesaid upon their oath aforesaid do say that the said Lilbourn Lewis and Isham Lewis feloniously wilfully Volentarily out of their malice aforethought him the said Negro Boy George then & there in manner and form aforesaid did kill and Murder, contrary to the statute in such case made and provided and against the peace and Dignity of the said Commonwealth of Kentucky

John Gray atty, for
the Commonwealth[7]

The essence of attorney John Gray's indictment is that Lilburne himself swung the axe and cut a three-by-four-inch gash in George's neck, from which George "instantly did die." The meaning of the word "instantly" as used here may be misinterpreted. In this context,

7.   Liv. Cir. Ct. Bundles, March 1815. [Livingston Circuit Court Clerk's Office, Smithland, Kentucky.]

and at that time, the usual meaning of "instantly" was "consequently," or "as a result of." Miss Reba Smith, the present circuit clerk of Livingston, uncovered records of another murder case of that era in which the victim "did instantly die in a space of two hours." In any event, it seems fairly certain that George died quickly from an axe wound in the neck, and not slowly from a series of lesser wounds, as the next source claims.

Thirteen years after George was murdered, the Reverend William Dickey, the Lewis family pastor, wrote a letter describing the crime in lurid detail. Dickey was then the minister of the Presbyterian church in Bloomingburg, Ohio, and had become passionately interested in the abolition of slavery. It should be remembered that Dickey was a highly emotional preacher, and a person of impressive skill in working his audience into a religious "glow." It is clear that Dickey was using the same talent when he wrote this letter in behalf of abolition. The creative imagination that he used to describe the delights of heaven and the horrors of hell is obvious in this letter, which describes a thirteen-year-old crime he did not witness.

> In the county of Livingston, Ky. near the mouth of the Cumberland, lived Lilburn Lewis, a sister's son of the venerable Jefferson. He, who "suckled at fair Freedom's breast" was the wealthy owner of a considerable number of slaves, whom he drove constantly, fed sparingly and lashed severely. The consequence was, they would run away. This must have given to a man of spirit and a man of business great anxieties until he found them or until they had starved out and returned. Among the rest was an ill grown boy about seventeen, who having just returned from a skulking spell, was sent to the spring for water, and in returning let fall an elegant pitcher. It was dashed to shivers upon the rocks. This was the occasion. It was night, and the slaves all at home. The master had them collected into the most roomy negrohouse, and a rousing fire made. When the door was secured, that none might escape, either through fear of him or sympathy with George, he opened the design of the interview, namely, that they might be effectually taught to stay at home and obey his orders. All things being now in train, he called up George, who approached his master with the most unreserved submission. He bound him with cords, and by the assistance of his younger brother, laid him on the broad bench, or meat block. He now proceeded to WHANG off George by the ancles!! It was with the broad axe!—In vain did the unhappy victim SCREAM AND ROAR. He was completely in his master's power. Not a hand amongst so many

durst interfere. Casting the feet into the fire, he lectured them at some length. He WHACKED HIM OFF below the knees! George roaring out, and praying his master to BEGIN AT THE OTHER END! He admonished them again, throwing the legs into the fire! Then above the knees, tossing the joints into the fire! He again lectured them at leisure. The next stroke severed the thighs from the body. These were also committed to the flames. And so off the arms, head and trunk, until all was in the fire! Still protracting the intervals with lectures, and threatenings of like punishment, in case of disobedience, and running away, or disclosure of this tragedy. Nothing now remained but to consume the flesh and bones; and for this purpose the fire was briskly stirred, until two hours after midnight, when, as though the earth would cover out of sight the nefarious scene, and as though the great master in Heaven would put a mark of displeasure upon such monstrous cruelty, a sudden and surprising shock of earthquake overturned the coarse and heavy back wall, composed of rock and clay, which completely covered the fire, and the remains of George. This put an end to the amusement of the evening. The negroes were now permitted to disperse, with charges to keep this matter among themselves, and never to whisper it in the neighborhood, under the penalty of a like punishment. When he retired, the lady exclaimed, "O! Mr. Lewis, where have you been and what have you done!" She had heard a strange pounding, and dreadful screams, and had smelled something like fresh meat burning! He said that he had never enjoyed himself at a ball so well as he had enjoyed himself that evening. Next morning he ordered the negroes to rebuild the back wall, and he himself superintended the work, throwing the pieces of flesh that still remained with the bones, behind it as it went up, thus hoping to conceal the matter.[8]

Dickey's version states that Lilburne personally and leisurely cut George to bits, beginning with the feet, and pictures the boy's death as protracted. The next source, *Chronicles of a Kentucky Settlement*, agrees that George was murdered in this fashion, but says that one of the slave men was forced to wield the axe.

There were many strange and contradictory rumors about Lilburne and his second wife. There were those who said that, owing to his dissipation and cruelty to his slaves, his young and beautiful wife was not only thoroughly miserable, but was in constant apprehension lest her husband should do herself some personal vio-

---

8. John Rankin, *Letters on American Society* (2d ed.; Newburyport, Conn.: Charles Whipple, 1837), 62–64, quoting William Dickey to Thomas Rankin, October 8, 1824.

lence. On the other hand, there were those who said that Lilburne, during the lifetime of his first wife, was a temperate man, a kind husband, and a strict but not unkind master, and that his cold, proud, and scornful young wife—his "cruel Letitia," as he was known to have once called her—was the cause of most of the troubles into which he fell.

About a year after Lilburne Lewis's second marriage, and when his wife was confined to her bed—she having a few days before given birth to a child,—a negro boy named George, a kind of general house servant, suddenly disappeared, and, after remaining secreted for a few days, was arrested and bound with chains in one of the cabins near the residence. That night, horrible to relate, Lilburne Lewis and his younger brother, Isham, caused most of the slaves on the farm to assemble in the cabin where George was bound, flat upon the floor, with each limb extended, and, with drawn pistols, forced one of the negro men to literally chop the bound boy to pieces, and, as joint by joint and limb by limb were severed from the body, they were cast into a roaring fire prepared for the purpose of consuming every trace of the body. When the hellish work was done, the assembled slaves were given to understand that such a fate as George's awaited any of them who should ever whisper a word about George's fate; and, if questioned regarding his disappearance, they were to answer that he had run away and had never been heard from. The cowed slaves were further told that should any of them ever run away they would, when captured, be treated as George had been.

When the two drunken and fiendish brothers left the cabin and were returning to their house, a sudden and terrific rumbling noise was heard, and soon the surface of the earth seemed to rise and fall—rise and fall again like quick succeeding waves. To add to the horror of the phenomena, what appeared like a great blazing ball of fire darted hissing through the heavens, apparently close by, and by its brilliancy momentarily lighting up every object around, which but a moment before was shrouded in dense darkness. The drunken brothers were each prostrated upon the ground by the violence of the earthquake shock (for such it was), and one of them, Isham, in his horrible affright, cried out: "My God! my God!! what is this?" The reply of the beastly brother by his side was: "It's only the devil in h——l rejoicing over having got hold of George!"[9]

---

9. William C. Watts, *Chronicles of a Kentucky Settlement* (New York: G. P. Putnam's Sons, 1897), 194–95. The actual names of the characters have been substituted here for the pseudonyms used by Watts.

The author of this account, William Courtney Watts, was born in Salem, Kentucky, in 1830, nineteen years after George was murdered. In his later years Watts wrote *Chronicles of a Kentucky Settlement*. This 490-page book, his only literary work, was published in 1897. Discussing the historical accuracy of this book, Watts wrote in his preface: "The book, however, is not, as some may infer from its title, a Local History. I endeavored to make it of interest to general readers. . . . To make my work the more interesting, I wove it into the form of a continuous story. The incidents, however, are not arranged strictly in chronological order, but as suited the exigencies of the tales I had to tell." Respected historians have held this book in high regard, even though it contains many factual errors.[10]

Watts did not consult the court records in preparing his book. He relied entirely on local traditions, which were seventy years old when he began to write *Chronicles*. No doubt there is much truth in his account of George's death, but it is certain that some, and perhaps many, of the details are incorrect. For example, Letitia's baby was not born just before George was murdered, but rather forty-seven days afterward. In Watts' version of the murder, George died as a result of being chopped to pieces joint by joint. This agrees with Dickey's letter, but Watts says the axe was swung not by Lilburne, but by a slave man who was forced to do so at the point of Lilburne's gun.

Another element of the crime is the subject of conflicting reports in these three sources: was Lilburne drinking at the time of the murder? The indictment simply stated that the Lewis brothers were "moved and seduced by the instigation of the devil," a routine phrase in felony indictments. Dickey's account did not mention alcohol at all in connection with the crime. Watts, however, said that for some time Lilburne had not been "temperate," and further, that the brothers were drunk on the night of the murder. Later accounts of the murder, although based on the above sources, are so inaccurate that they are nearly useless as sources of historical fact. Nevertheless, some of these make the not unreasonable claim that Lilburne was drinking heavily on that night.[11]

William H. Townsend, a respected Kentucky historian and raconteur of national reputation, was known for his byword, "Never let

10.   Otto A. Rothert, "The Tragedy of the Lewis Brothers: Two Sons of Lucy Jefferson Lewis," *Filson Club History Quarterly*, XX (October, 1936), 232.
11.   *Author's Note*: See Merrill's Bibliography, *Jefferson's Nephews*, 425–27.

facts stand in the way of a good story!" It appears that this precept was being followed to some degree by both Dickey and Watts when they wrote their accounts of George's murder. In Dickey's case, the more depraved he could make Lilburne's crime appear, the better his crusade for abolition would be served. As for Watts's *Chronicles*, the more horribly dramatic the story, the greater would be his reader's interest. Both Dickey and Watts were inaccurate in some of the statements in their accounts. In addition, their versions of the crime did not agree in every respect. It is interesting that while Watts did not purport to tell the exact facts of the case, the Reverend William Dickey did present his version as factual. It was not completely so.

The fourth useful source of information contains very little information about the murder itself. It is a one-paragraph newspaper article that appeared in the *Kentucky Gazette* of May 12, 1812. Datelined, "Russellville, April 22," and under the headline, "Murder! Horrid Murder!" the article reported that "Capt. Lilburne and Isham Lewis" had been taken to court "for murdering a negro boy, (the property of the former) and burning him on a kitchen fire."[12]

This brief statement raises some question as to where the murder and cremation actually took place. Watts said it was in one of the cabins near the residence. Dickey said it was "in the most roomy negro-house." The indictment stated the crime occurred "at the house of said Lilburne Lewis," and the newspaper reported simply that the negro boy had been burned "on a kitchen fire." On many of the west Kentucky farms or plantations at that time the cooking was done in a cabin building near but separate from the main house. Three of the four sources quoted above admit the possibility that the scene of George's death was Lilburne's own kitchen cabin. If these three sources are combined, it appears George was murdered "at the house of said Lilburne Lewis," "in one of the cabins near the residence," and was burned "on a kitchen fire." Only Dickey's letter disagrees with this, claiming that George's death occurred "in the most roomy negro-house." The exact location of the crime is probably not important, except that if the deed was done in the kitchen cabin next to or near the residence, then it is unlikely that Letitia and the other occupants of the house slept through that fearful night undisturbed until two-o'clock, when the earthquake struck.

12. *Author's Note*: Other sections of this article may be found in Merrill, *Jefferson's Nephews*, Ch. 28, n. 17, and Ch. 29, n. 18.

If George was murdered in the nearby kitchen, and if Letitia and the others in the house were awakened by the sounds and odors of the scene, as seems likely, then they became witnesses to the crime, not eyewitnesses, but witnesses nonetheless. The point has some relevance. Although the murder room was crowded with Lilburne's slaves at the time George died, there were no legal witnesses to the murder in that room other than Lilburne and Isham. The laws of the Commonwealth of Kentucky prohibited negroes from testifying against whites in the court.[13]

In this nearly inconceivable episode, Lilburne approached the nadir of his life. Lawyer James McLaughlan's curse upon Lilburne, "God damn your soul," had come to pass.

The people of Rocky Hill were not alone in their anguish for long. A few weeks later, early in the dreadful spring of 1812, a final tragedy came to Randolph's family. Mary, Randolph's beloved widow, the last surviving adult in that home, died at the age of thirty-six. The cause of her death is unknown. The Reverend William Dickey, having been invited to preach at their home, was there on the day she died. Writing of this sad occasion, he noted that Mary had passed away shortly before he arrived, and added that she had been a widow about one year. She probably died sometime in February. The family was bereft. Dickey remembered the grief of the old slave, Frank, who "lamented the loss of his pious Massa & Missis. . . . Solemnity appeared in his face, and a few big tears tumbled down his sable & withered cheeks."[14]

Mary left eight orphans. Warner, the youngest, was not yet two years old. Five of the children were under twelve. The oldest, Charles Lilburne (also called Lilburne Lewis, Jr.) who was in his twentieth year, might have taken the full burden of the family on his shoulders. His two brothers, Howell and Tucker, could have been some help, but the prospect of these three boys raising five young children, and running a plantation as well, was not encouraging.[15] They could expect

13.   William Littell and Jacob Swigert, *A Digest of the Statute Law of Kentucky: Being a Collection of All the Acts of the General Assembly* (2 vols.; Frankfort: Kendall and Russell, 1822), 2:1150. "Sec. 2 No negro or mulatto shall be a witness, except in pleas of the commonwealth against negroes or mulattoes, or in civil pleas where negroes or mulattoes alone shall be parties."
14.   William Dickey to James Dickey, June 29, 1812, MS. 81008, Presbyterian Historical Society, Philadelphia.
15.   It appears that Randolph had some reservations about his son Charles. In his will Randolph left Charles a one-eighth part of his estate during Charles's natural life. At

absolutely no help from Lilburne and Letitia, for their life at Rocky Hill was in utter shambles, and the situation of Colonel Lewis and his three daughters was very little better. Nevertheless, the remnants of Randolph's family clustered around their grandfather and his three daughters during this time of emergency, and cared for each other as best they could. It was an unworkable expedient, but it had to suffice until the estate could be sold and other arrangements made. Perhaps, in February, they still hoped that Lilburne would survive his troubles and come to their aid in some way. For the moment they were a pathetic little flock without leadership or direction.

Charles's death that portion was to return to the estate, whether or not Charles had heirs. The other seven children could pass on their portions of Randolph's estate to their heirs. The reason for this distinction between Charles and the other children is unknown.

The Jefferson Family

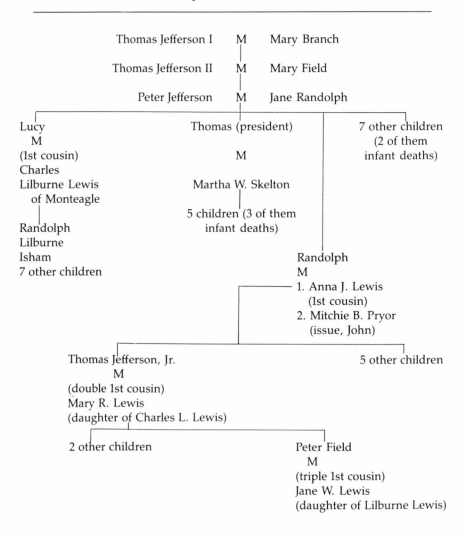

Thomas Jefferson I   M   Mary Branch

Thomas Jefferson II   M   Mary Field

Peter Jefferson   M   Jane Randolph

Lucy
M
(1st cousin)
Charles
Lilburne Lewis
  of Monteagle

Randolph
Lilburne
Isham
7 other children

Thomas (president)

M

Martha W. Skelton

5 children (3 of them
infant deaths)

7 other children
(2 of them
infant deaths)

Randolph
M
1. Anna J. Lewis
  (1st cousin)
2. Mitchie B. Pryor
  (issue, John)

Thomas Jefferson, Jr.
M
(double 1st cousin)
Mary R. Lewis
(daughter of Charles L. Lewis)

5 other children

2 other children

Peter Field
M
(triple 1st cousin)
Jane W. Lewis
(daughter of Lilburne Lewis)

Foreword to *Brother to Dragons: A Play in Two Acts*

Robert Penn Warren

This play is based on the narrative poem *Brother to Dragons: A Tale in Verse and Voices*, which deals with an appalling episode in American history, appalling in both literal and symbolic dimensions.

In the early nineteenth century Colonel Charles Lewis, of Albemarle County, Virginia, moved his household—his wife Lucy, who was the sister of Thomas Jefferson, his sons Lilburn and Randolph, and his slaves—to the frontier land of West Kentucky, in Livingston County. There, on a bluff above the confluence of the Ohio and Cumberland Rivers, he built his log house, Rocky Hill, an establishment somewhat grand for the place and time, with outbuildings and quarters for his "people." Lucy Lewis died shortly after the removal to Kentucky, and Charles Lewis spent less and less time there, making at least one protracted journey to Virginia.

The central event of the story of the Lewis family occurred on the night of December 15, 1811, the night when the New Madrid Earthquake struck its first blow at the Mississippi Valley, an earthquake that literally tore the country up, made the Mississippi run backward three days, left Reelsfoot Lake in Tennessee as a memento, and, had the region been well populated, would be remembered as one of the great natural disasters of modern times. It was on that night that Lilburn, with the assistance of his younger brother Isham, a sort of drifter who was there on a visit, and before the eyes of the assembled slaves, butchered with a meat-axe a boy named George (John here), who had broken the favorite pitcher of the dead Lucy. About this time, under circumstances that are not clear in the records, the wife of Lilburn, Letitia Rutter (Laetitia here), left Rocky Hill.

After some weeks the crime became known; the Lewis brothers, in spite of their high place in the world, were arrested, indicted for

"Foreword" to *Brother to Dragons: A Play in Two Acts* by Robert Penn Warren. From *Georgia Review*, XXX (Spring, 1976), 65–70. Copyright © 1976 by Robert Penn Warren. Reprinted by kind permission of the author.

murder, and released on bail. Back at Rocky Hill, they decided to shoot each other—according to one legend, across the grave of their mother, for whom, presumably, they had performed the butchery. But something went wrong, Isham fired first, and Lilburn, with his will in his pocket and Isham's lead in his body, fell dead.

Isham, who had panicked and fled to the woods, was captured, brought to trial, convicted, and sentenced to be hanged. He broke jail, however, and in spite of a heavy reward—five hundred dollars in gold—was not taken. Three years later, militiamen from West Kentucky, returning from the Battle of New Orleans, reported that they had seen and talked with Isham, and that he had been killed there by a British musket ball.

In both the poem and the play I have followed the outline of historical fact, making, however, certain simplifications and omissions, and introducing two new characters, Aunt Cat and Billy Rutter. Naturally, I had to interpret—it may be said, to "create"—all the characters. As for Jefferson, several eminent authorities had assured me, while I was working on the poem, that, as far as records show, he never alluded to the events in Kentucky and its blot on the family blood and his dream of humanity; and one authority even declared spontaneously that he believed it impossible for Jefferson to bring himself to face the truth. This fact of Jefferson's failure to allude to the event (a fact that may be "unfacted" by further research[1]) is convenient for the interpretation offered in my play, but is not essential to it; for what I am concerned with is the symbolic implication of the event for the Jeffersonian notion of the perfectibility of man and the good American notion of our inevitable righteousness in action and purity in motive.

The play involves, as does the poem, two levels of action, one of the present and one of the past, with the suggestion that an under-

---

1. Since this foreword was written I have been privileged to read the manuscript of a recently completed book by Boynton Merrill, Jr., who has scrupulously investigated the life and circumstances of the Lewis family, both in Virginia and after the removal to Kentucky (1807). Severe financial reverses had led to the removal, which included the oldest and most responsible brother Randolph and his family. Isham had not formed part of the original group, but appears later on in Kentucky, something of a feckless wanderer. The death of Randolph, as well as that of Lucy and of Lilburn's first wife, seems to have contributed to Lilburn's derangement. There was, too, the general failure

standing of their interpenetration is crucial. On one level, the character here called the Writer, haunted by the shocking episode and hoping to make sense of it, visits the spot where the Lewis house once stood and where the unmarked graves of Lucy and Lilburn are lost in a tangle of brush and briar. His presence, for the second level of action, summons up the spirits of the persons involved in the old tragedy, who, yet unassuaged and unreconciled, reenact the crisis of their earthly lives, seeking a resolution in understanding and forgiveness —and in, it may be added, a new sense of the historical role of Americans.

The play, in the form here offered, was developed from a number of different productions. The first, in which I had no hand, was a dramatic reading adapted from the poem and presented by the British Broadcasting Company in 1955. A little later I wrote a play which, after a production at Harvard and some adventures on Broadway, was revised and produced in Seattle, under the direction of Aaron Frankel. A reworked version, directed by Wynn Handman, was produced at the American Place Theater in New York in 1964. In 1968, at the suggestion of Adrian Hall, I again took up the play and worked on it for his first production at the Trinity Square Theater in Providence. In 1973, at the inauguration of the new theater of the Trinity Square Company, Mr. Hall produced and directed his second version. In the summer of 1974, on a little tour with several of his plays, Mr. Hall made further modifications leading to the form presented at the Wilbur Theater in Boston in September of that year. From this production I set myself to rewrite the text which is here printed. The notes on the stage and the production also follow the version at the Wilbur Theater.

The Set. From the raked-thrust stage of raw boards rises a wide semicircle of axe-hewn uprights, some with bits of bark or stubs of boughs yet showing, suggesting a primitive frontier world but also, in the lack of specificity, a quality of timelessness. A crude girder of beams extends across the stage from one upright to another, but the wings are left open. At right there is an open stair, with two levels, the higher serving as the second floor for interior scenes at Rocky

---

to improve his financial situation. Among the several discrepancies between the poem (and play) and the record established by Mr. Merrill is the fact that Lucy was buried, not on Lilburn's place, but on Randolph's. This discrepancy no more than the others affects the meaning of the play.

Hill. At left rises a sort of open scaffolding, some nine or ten feet
high, with several projecting beams, one extending over the playing
area, attached to it a large pulley with a rope capable of supporting a
man's body. A low platform, some four by six and a half feet, serves
various purposes: the base for the "live" family portrait, the level on
which Lucy's harpsichord is set for the minuet, and Laetitia's bed.

The stage presents three dominant images. A section of the stage
floor opens up in the shape of a coffin lid, with the traditional death's
head painted on the exposed inner surface. A meat block made from
the cross section of a very large tree is always visible at stage left, but is
brought forward for the butchery of John. A short-handled, double-
bitted meat axe is stuck into the block at a convenient angle. At the
opening of the play, however, the most immediately striking image
appears center stage, a roughly hung curtain painted with the nearly
life-size bound figure of a stark-eyed "nigger" dangling from a hook
attached at the back below the shoulder blades. The curtain pulls to
stage left.

It should be emphasized that there is a fundamental contrast between the raw wood and crude carpentering of the set and the ele-
gance of the eighteenth-century furniture, silver, portraits, and general accoutrements of the Lewis household.

Production Values. There are two basic ideas in the production.
The first is the general involvement of the cast, the second, the pervasive sense of contrast, with tension and vibrance.

The stage is open, and after a scene in which an actor is directly
concerned, he does not make an exit. He may go to the back wall, for
instance, or to one side, to sit on a beam, to crouch, or stand, in light
or shadow. There is sometimes an impression of figures wandering in
shadow. A line may be spoken from the shadows at, say, the back of
the stage, and replied to by a person in full light; or a line may be
begun by a character in light and completed by one in shadow. There
should be constantly the impression of watchfulness, awareness, concern on the part of all: all are caught in a nightmare they must repeat
endlessly until some way is found to stop it and allow them to sleep.

On various occasions actors are used to represent an event itself, or
to merge with an event, as in the earthquake (when actors mounted on
the shoulders of others swing the big slit-sided lanterns to make
shadows leap and sway, while others do somersaults and cartwheels);
the scene of Laetitia's flight (when the actors make the horse that gal-
lops around the stage with her clinging to their backs); or the forest

scene with Lilburn and Laetitia (when actors become trees). Actors are seen cranking wind-machines, or imitating natural sounds, such as bird calls or the barking of a dog in the distance.

The production should establish a rhythm of contrasts. Various kinds of contrast are involved. There is that of light and dark, a fully lighted stage as against a shadily focused area, and associated with this the sense of space against constriction. Pacing may provide another basis of contrast. Certain scenes invite almost unnatural speed, urgency, violence of motion, and others, for instance the scene of the moth in Act II, depend on quietness for their effect. Another type of contrast runs throughout, that of realistic elements against fantastic, symbolic, and poetic elements. For instance, a scene in the immediate action would be treated at a realistic level, but the chorus would obviously intrude other elements (and in this connection it should be observed that the choruses are stylized in various degrees, ritualized, and that in general, in such cases, the idiom is markedly not that of the frontier people in their literal life).

As for the characters, these brief comments: Jefferson should maintain his distance and dignity, but this dignity is slashed across by despairing anger and irony. Lilburn is very much the self-conscious aristocrat, lithe and graceful but strongly built, with elegant dress and manner under all circumstances and with natural charm, but often under a tense and brittle control, edged with irony, and self-irony. This brittle surface is occasionally broken by a burst of human warmth or suffering. Isham, much younger, is less firmly rooted in the tradition of a great Virginia family, and in the course of the play it is indicated, by costume and other details, that he is moving into the life of the frontier, not by joining in the local life, but by becoming the solitary hunter and man of the wilderness. The hunting shirt, the coonskin cap, and the long rifle mark him more and more. Laetitia is a simple, warm-hearted daughter of the frontier, overwhelmed by her love for Lilburn and by grateful wonder that he has chosen her.

Lucy stands in contrast to her husband on the one hand and to Aunt Cat on the other. Her power of will, her capacity for affection, and her selfless concern for others are set against the spiritual weakness and inward-turning sense of defeat of Charles Lewis. Lucy, though quite unself-conscious in the role, is the aristocrat and great lady, and her love for her sons, though deep and sincere, lacks the warm physicality and sensual dimension suggested by Aunt Cat.

Costume should be of the period, and should clearly indicate the three classes represented here—the gentry, the frontier people, and the black slaves. It should be noticed here that Aunt Cat, the head-man, John, and two of the black women (including the young girl) are house servants and do not wear the rough garb of those who are field hands.

Selected Bibliography

*   **Warren's Poetry**   *

Thirty-Six Poems. New York: Alcestis Press, 1935.
Eleven Poems on the Same Theme. Norfolk, Conn.: New Directions, 1942.
Selected Poems, 1923–1943. New York: Harcourt, Brace, 1944.
Brother to Dragons: A Tale in Verse and Voices. New York: Random House, 1953.
Promises, Poems 1954–1956. New York: Random House, 1957.
You, Emperors, and Others: Poems 1957–1960. New York: Random House, 1960.
Selected Poems: New and Old, 1923–1966. New York: Random House, 1966.
Incarnations: Poems 1966–1968. New York: Random House, 1968.
Audubon: A Vision. New York: Random House, 1969.
Or Else—Poem/Poems 1968–1974. New York: Random House, 1974.
Selected Poems, 1923–1975. New York: Random House, 1976.
Now and Then: Poems 1976–1978. New York: Random House, 1978.
Brother to Dragons: A Tale in Verse and Voices, A New Version. New York: Random House, 1979.
Two Poems. Winston-Salem, N.C.: Palaemon Press Limited, 1979.
Being Here: Poetry 1977–1980. New York: Random House, 1980.
Rumor Verified: Poems 1979–1980. New York: Random House, 1981.
Love: Four Versions. Winston-Salem, N.C.: Palaemon Press Limited [1981].

From James A. Grimshaw, Jr., *Robert Penn Warren: A Descriptive Bibliography, 1922–1979* (Charlottesville: University Press of Virginia, 1981). Reprinted by permission of the Rector and Visitors of the University of Virginia.

*   **Criticisms on** *Brother to Dragons*   *

Books

Bohner, Charles H. *Robert Penn Warren*. New York: Twayne Publishers, Inc., 1964.

Casper, Leonard. *Robert Penn Warren: The Dark and Bloody Ground*. Seattle: University of Washington Press, 1960.

Holman, C. Hugh. *The Immoderate Past: The Southern Writer and History*. Wesleyan College Lamar Memorial Lecture. Athens: University of Georgia Press, 1977.

Justus, James H. *The Achievement of Robert Penn Warren*. Baton Rouge: Louisiana State University Press, 1981.

Merrill, Boynton, Jr. *Jefferson's Nephews: A Frontier Tragedy*. Princeton, N.J.: Princeton University Press, 1976.

Moore, L. Hugh, Jr. *Robert Penn Warren and History*. The Hague: Mouton, 1970.

Rubin, Louis D., Jr. *The Wary Fugitives: Four Poets and the South*. Baton Rouge: Louisiana State University Press, 1978.

Simpson, Lewis P. *The Brazen Face of History: Studies in the Literary Consciousness in America*. Baton Rouge: Louisiana State University Press, 1980.

Stewart, John L. *The Burden of Time: The Fugitives and Agrarians*. Princeton, N.J.: Princeton University Press, 1965.

Strandberg, Victor H. *A Colder Fire: The Poetry of Robert Penn Warren*. Lexington: University of Kentucky Press, 1965.

———. *The Poetic Vision of Robert Penn Warren*. Lexington: University of Kentucky Press, 1977.

Walker, Marshall. *Robert Penn Warren: A Vision Earned*. Edinburgh: Paul Harris Publishing, 1979.

Watkins, Floyd C., and John T. Hiers, eds. *Robert Penn Warren Talking: Interviews 1950–1978*. New York: Random House, 1980.

Periodicals

Buffington, Robert. "The Poetry of the Master's Old Age." *Georgia Review*, XXV (Spring, 1971), 5–16.

Clark, William Bedford. "A Meditation on Folk-History: The Dramatic Structure of Robert Penn Warren's 'The Ballad of Billie Potts.'" *American Literature*, XLIX (January, 1978), 635–45.

Clements, A. L. "Sacramental Vision: The Poetry of Robert Penn Warren." *South Atlantic Bulletin*, XLIII, no. 4 (1978), 47–65.

Core, George. "In the Heart's Ambiguity: Robert Penn Warren as Poet." *Mississippi Quarterly*, XXII (Fall, 1969), 313–26.

Dwyer, William F. "Light Religiously Dim: The Poetry of Robert Penn Warren." *Fresco*, n.s. I (1960), 43–55.

Link, Franz H. "Über das Geschichtsbewusstsein einiger amerikanischer Dichter des 20. Jahrhunderts: Hart Crane's 'The Bridge,' Stephen Vincent Benét's 'Western Star,' and Robert Penn Warren's *Brother to Dragons*." *Jahrbuch für Amerikastudien*, IV (1959), 143–60.

Plumley, Stanley. "Warren Selected: An American Poetry, 1923–1975." *Ohio Review*, XVIII (Winter, 1977), 37–48.

Rosenthal, M. L. "Robert Penn Warren's Poetry." *South Atlantic Quarterly*, LXII (Autumn, 1963), 499–507.

Spears, M. K. "The Latest Poetry of Robert Penn Warren." *Sewanee Review*, LXXVIII (Spring, 1970), 348–58.

Stitt, Peter. "Robert Penn Warren, the Poet." *Southern Review*, n.s. XII (Spring, 1976), 261–76.

Tjenos, William. "The Poetry of Robert Penn Warren: The Art to Transfigure." *Southern Literary Journal*, IX (Fall, 1976), 3–12.

Reviews

(1953 edition)

Ames, Alfred C. *Chicago Sunday Tribune of Books*, August 23, 1953, p. 3.

Bogan, Louise. *New Yorker*, October 24, 1953, pp. 157–59.

Booklist, September 15, 1953, p. 31.

Bookmark (New York State Library), XIII (October, 1953), 9.

Bulletin from Virginia Kirkus' Bookshop Service, August 1, 1953, p. 510.

Deutsch, Babette. *Yale Review*, XLIII (Winter, 1954), 277–81.

Edwards, John. *San Francisco Chronicle*, September 6, 1953, p. 18.

Fiedler, Leslie A. *Partisan Review*, XXI (March–April, 1954), 208–12.

Flint, F. Cudworth. *Virginia Quarterly Review*, XXX (Winter, 1954), 143–48.

Honig, Edwin. *Voices*, no. 154 (May–August, 1954), pp. 41–44.

Joost, Nicholas. *Commonweal*, December 4, 1953, pp. 231–32.

Kenner, Hugh. *Hudson Review*, VI (Winter, 1954), 605–10.

Kristol, Irving. *Encounter*, III (July, 1954), 73–75.

McCormick, John. *Western Review*, XVIII (Winter, 1954), 163–67.

McDonald, G. D. *Library Journal*, LXXVIII (December, 1953), 2221.

Nation, November 7, 1953, p. 376.

Prescott, Orville. New York *Times*, August 21, 1953, p. 15.

Schwartz, Delmore. *New Republic*, September 14, 1953, pp. 17–18.
Swallow, Alan. *Talisman*, no. 4 (Winter, 1953), pp. 38–42.
Time, August 24, 1953, p. 82.
Times Literary Supplement, June 11, 1954, p. 378.
Webster, Harvey C. *Saturday Review*, August 22, 1953, pp. 11–12.
Wilder, Amos N. *Christianity and Crisis*, July 20, 1953, pp. 97–98.

(1979 edition)
Booklist, September 1, 1979, p. 20.
Dickerson, James. Jackson, Miss. *Clarion-Leader*, September 16, 1979, p. 4.
Hall, Wade. Louisville, Ky. *Courier-Journal*, October 28, 1979, p. D-5.
Henigan, Robert. Springfield, Mo. *Leader & Press*, September 8, 1979, p. 6-A.
Holladay, Robert. Nashville *Banner*, September 15, 1979, p. 5.
Kirkus Review, July 15, 1979, p. 850.
Marten, Harry. Washington *Post Book World*, September 30, 1979, p. 10.
Vest, Quentin. *Library Journal*, September 1, 1979, p. 1703.
Virginia Quarterly Review, LVI (Spring, 1980), 62–63.

Unpublished Material

Burnes, Ann P. "Mannerist Mythopoesis: A Reading of Warren's *Brother to Dragons*." Ph.D. dissertation, St. Louis University, 1978.
Englebrecht, Donald H. "*Brother to Dragons*: The Many Voices of Robert Penn Warren." M.A. thesis, Arizona State University, 1959.
Lubarsky, Richard J. "The Instructive Fact of History: A Study of Robert Penn Warren's *Brother to Dragons*." Ph.D. dissertation, University of Pennsylvania, 1976.
Orta, Marjorie P. H. "'Identity,' the 'Unconscious Self,' and the 'Journey to the West' as Themes in Robert Penn Warren's *Brother to Dragons*." M.A. thesis, University of Georgia, 1969.

Notes on Contributors

Harold BLOOM, poetry critic, author, DeVane Professor of the Humanities at Yale University, has written *Kabbalah and Criticism* (1974), *An American Gnosis* (1981), and *Agon: Towards a Theory of Revisionism* (1982). In 1971 he received the Melville Cane Award, Poetry Society of America, for his book *Yeats*.

John M. BRADBURY (1908–1969) received his Ph.D. from the University of Iowa in 1949. He was a Fulbright lecturer, University of Istanbul, 1964–65, and published *The Southern Renaissance* (1963) in addition to scholarly articles in *Sewanee Review, American Literature, Poetry*, and other leading journals.

Cleanth BROOKS, Gray Professor of Rhetoric Emeritus at Yale University, held, among many distinguished posts, an Oxford University Rhodes Scholarship 1929–32 and the post as cultural attaché, American Embassy, London, 1964–66. His work includes literary theory, practical criticism, textual editing, language and dialect study, literary history and biography, and journal editing. Among his works are *Understanding Poetry* (1938) with Robert Penn Warren, *The Well Wrought Urn* (1947), and *William Faulkner: Toward Yoknapatawpha and Beyond* (1978).

Richard N. CHRISMAN, minister of a Congregational church in Los Angeles, holds a B.A. in English from Princeton, an M.A. in theology and a Ph.D. in religion and literature from the University of Chicago Divinity School. He also teaches at Loyola Marymount University in Los Angeles and serves on the Board of Directors of the Society for Art, Religion, and Contemporary Culture.

William Bedford CLARK, an associate professor of English at Texas A&M University, is a native of Oklahoma. He completed his graduate study at Louisiana State University; during 1973–74, he was a post-doctoral fellow in Afro-American studies at Yale. The author of a wide range of articles on American literature and culture, he has also edited the volume on Robert Penn Warren for the G. K. Hall Critical Essays in American Literature series.

Babette DEUTSCH was lecturer in poetry at Columbia University from 1944 to 1971. She is a translator and author of poetry, novels, criticism, and children's books. Among her works are *Mask of Silenus* (novel, 1933), *Poetry in Our Time* (rev. ed., 1963), *The Poems of Samuel Taylor Coleridge* (1967), and *The Collected Poems of Babette Deutsch* (1969). She resides in New York City.

Dennis M. DOOLEY, a native of Baltimore, earned his Ph.D. in English from Vanderbilt University. He is an associate professor of English at Wofford College.

Irvin EHRENPREIS, Linden Kent Professor of English, University of Virginia, served as a Fulbright fellow at Oxford 1949–50 and received Guggenheim Fellowships in 1955–56 and 1962–63. Among his writings are *The Personality of Jonathan Swift* (1958) and *Literary Meaning and Augustan Values* (1974).

George Palmer GARRETT, a professional writer, has taught and been writer-in-residence at various universities, has worked for CBS television and in Hollywood, and has served as senior fellow of the Council of Humanities (1975–77). He received a Guggenheim Fellowship in 1974–75. Among his diverse writings are *For a Bitter Season: New and Selected Poems* (1967), *Death of the Fox* (novel, 1971), and *The Magic Striptease* (novel, 1973). He lists York Harbor, Maine, as his residence.

James A. GRIMSHAW, Jr., professor of English, United States Air Force Academy, has published *Cleanth Brooks at the USAF Academy* (1980), *The Flannery O'Connor Companion* (1981), and *Robert Penn Warren: A Descriptive Bibliography* (1981). He was the Flannery O'Connor Visiting Professor of English, Georgia College, in 1977 and visiting fellow in bibliography at the Beinecke Rare Book and Manuscript Library, Yale, in 1979–80.

William HARMON, professor of English, University of North Carolina at Chapel Hill, is author of four volumes of poetry, most recently *One Long Poem* (1982); a critical study of Ezra Pound; and *The Oxford Book of American Light Verse*. His articles have appeared in *PMLA*, *American Anthropologist*, *Sewanee Review*, *Parnassus*, and other journals.

Margaret Mills HARPER received her B.A. *summa cum laude* from Florida State University. She is currently at work on a Ph.D. in modern American literature at the University of North Carolina at Chapel Hill.

C. Hugh HOLMAN (1914–1981) had an active career as radio director, academic dean, provost, and Kenan Professor of English, University of North Carolina at Chapel Hill. In 1967–68, he received a Guggenheim Fellowship. Best known for his literary criticism, he also wrote detective novels such as *Another Man's Poison* (1947). Among his other titles are *A Handbook to Literature* (4th ed., 1980) and *Windows on the World: Essays on American Social Fiction* (1979).

Randall JARRELL (1914–1965) was writer, editor, professor of English, consultant in poetry at the Library of Congress, and chancellor of the Academy of American Poets. Among his awards were a Guggenheim Fellowship (1946), the Levinson Prize for Poetry (1948), and a National Book Award (1961). His *Complete Poems* appeared in 1968 and in 1980 another volume of his prose, *Kipling, Auden & Company: Essays and Reviews, 1935–1964*.

Richard G. LAW, associate professor of English, Washington State University, has published articles on Robert Penn Warren in *American Literature, Southern Literary Journal*, and *Studies in American Fiction*. He is also book review editor of *ESQ: A Journal of the American Renaissance*.

Robert LOWELL (1917–1977) was poet, lecturer, teacher, playwright, and translator. He received a Guggenheim Fellowship in 1947; was consultant in poetry at the Library of Congress, 1947–48; and received a Pulitzer Prize in 1947, a National Book Award in 1960, and an honorary degree from Columbia University in 1969. Among his writings are a revised edition of *Notebook* (1970), *Selected Poems* (1976), and his acclaimed translation of the *Orestia of Aeschylus* (1978).

Frederick P. W. McDOWELL received his Ph.D. from Harvard University in 1947. During his tenure as professor of English at the University of Iowa, he has published *Ellen Glasgow and the Ironic Art of Fiction* (1960), *Elizabeth Madox Roberts* (1963), and *Caroline Gordon* (1966).

Boynton MERRILL, Jr., a gentleman farmer who lives near Henderson, Kentucky, is a historian and the author of *A Bestiary* (poems, 1976), which is also available on recording.

Neil NAKADATE is associate professor of English at Iowa State University. He is the editor of *Robert Penn Warren: A Reference Guide* (1977) and *Robert Penn Warren: Critical Perspectives* (1981), as well as articles and reviews on ethnic American literature and on the teaching of writing.

William Van O'CONNOR (1915–1966) received his Ph.D. from Columbia University in 1947. His awards included a Rockefeller Foundation Humanities Fellowship (1946–47) and a Fulbright appointment as lecturer in England (1964–65). He wrote *Climates of Tragedy* (1943), *The Shaping Spirit: A Study of Wallace Stevens* (1950), *The Grotesque: An American Genre* (1962), *High Meadow* (poems, 1964), and *In the Cage* (play, 1967).

Sister M. Bernetta QUINN, O.S.F., is a professor of English at St. Andrews Presbyterian College, North Carolina, and a poetry critic whose works include *Metamorphic Tradition in Modern Poetry* (1955) and *Ezra Pound: An Introduction to the Poetry* (1972). In 1966, she received a National Foundation on the Arts and Humanities grant.

Lewis P. SIMPSON, Boyd Professor of English at Louisiana State University, is co-editor of the *Southern Review* and author of *The Man of Letters in New England and the South* (1973), *The Dispossessed Garden* (1975), *The Possibilities of Order: The Work of Cleanth Brooks* (edited, 1976), and *The Brazen Face of History* (1980). He received a Guggenheim Fellowship in 1954–55 and was an NEH fellow in 1977–78.

Victor STRANDBERG, professor of English, Duke University, is the author of numerous essays in English and American literature. He has twice held Fulbright professorships, as senior lecturer in American literature at the University of Uppsala in Sweden (1973) and at the University of Louvain in Belgium (1980). His recent books include *The Poetic Vision of Robert Penn Warren* (1977), *Religious Psychology in American Literature: A Study in the Relevance of William James* (1981), and *A Faulkner Overview* (1981).

Parker TYLER (1907–1974) was a lecturer, writer, and critic from New Orleans. In 1958, he received the Longview Award for Poetry and, in 1965, a Guggenheim Fellowship. Two of his works are *Florine Stettheimer: A Life in Art* (1963) and *Sex, Psyche, Etcetera in the Film* (1969).

Robert Penn WARREN, who has published over sixty books, has most recently been awarded the Presidential Medal of Freedom, the Common Wealth Award for Literature, the Hubbell Memorial Award (all in 1980) and a Prize Fellowship of the John D. and Catherine T. MacArthur Foundation (1981). His latest book is *Rumor Verified: Poems, 1979–1980*, and he has at press a long poem on Chief Joseph.